«Beyond the Bounds of Unknown» series
Larisa Seklitova
Ludmila Strelnikova

SECRETS
OF HIGHER WORLDS

Order this book online at www.trafford.com
or email orders@trafford.com

Most Trafford titles are also available at major online book retailers.

Printed in the United States of America.

ISBN: 978-1-4269-6508-1 (sc)
ISBN: 978-1-4269-6509-8 (e)

Trafford rev. 04/08/2011

 www.trafford.com

North America & international
toll-free: 1 888 232 4444 (USA & Canada)
phone: 250 383 6864 ♦ fax: 812 355 4082

CONTENTS

Larisa Seklitova
Ludmila Strelnikova
(«**Beyond the Bounds of Unknown**»)

Translated from Russian by Eugenia Yakovchenko

At the turn of the 21st century Higher Mind for the first time discloses to mankind the latest information about the organization of Higher worlds governed by God and Devil; about laws they live up to; about the role of civilizations in our planet development, reasons for their appearance and disappearance; about experiment of the Higher with the Earth and peculiarities of its future development.

A keen reader will discover a lot of extraordinary things about private lives of God and Devil, perceive the difference between minus and plus improvement, get to know peculiarities of human beings development in the next sixth race, the role stones and precious metals have in a man's life, and reasons for their use. Besides he / she will get acquainted with Medical and Material Systems of the Cosmos, find out the ways souls develop in Devil's System. This book will compel the reader to have a look at his life and life of people around in a different way.

The writers appreciate material assistance of all the readers in translation of this book.

«««« INTRODUCTION »»»»»

This book discloses to mankind new knowledge about a man's origin on the Earth, the goal of his creation and existence. The reader will get to know the reason of civilizations' origin and rotation from the point of view that is perfectly unknown to mankind; he will disclose to himself many secrets about the Earth itself and experiments conducted on it by Higher Creators.

The reader will be carried away with information concerning a new golden race following our fifth race. He will learn for what purpose ageing is given to a human being and for what reason children won't have childhood in the sixth race.

And the most important thing is that he will be struck by revelations of God and Devil, who talk about the worlds They live in. Moreover, God and Devil give some details of their past.

What does a man know about God's and Devil's private life, about the paths They followed in their development and how They managed to reach such a high-level position?

And it is for the fist time that God and Devil disclose secrets of their personal existence to envoys.

The envoys, or the present authors, were given the right to talk to God Himself and Prince of darkness Himself. And that were God and Devil who disclosed much new to people in their dialogues. Every word of Theirs is lifting a veil of some secrecy which is unknown to mankind.

The information was taken through the contacts with a Higher world. The channeler is Larisa A. Seklitova, through her the channelings with God were carried out. Ludmila L. Strelnikova questioned, made up topics (for discussion) and wrote books. Hence this book is presented in dialogues, the way the channelings were conducted. This allows explaining, in an intelligible way, those complicated truths our life is built upon and according to which the Universe exists to the contemporary development level of a human being.

Study the books of the channelers with Higher Mind, whose emblem is an eight pointed star as a symbol of the Higher Cosmic Commonwealth «UNION».

Chapter 1
Unfamiliar Earth

NEW ABOUT THE EARTH

The Earth as a heavenly body doesn't exist eternally, but appeared in the Cosmos from a particular moment of time after the Higher Cosmic Hierarchy needed to create such a high-powered object as our planet for its own purpose.

It was created together with the solar system at the request of the Higher Hierarchy by another Hierarchy which is lower in terms of its Level and which specializes directly in planetary design works.

This is what God tells us, answering our following question:

- "What caused the necessity to create our planet in the Cosmos for You: was it energy shortage experienced by Higher Cosmic Systems or the necessity for The Divine Hierarchy expansion?"

- «The creation of Earth didn't originate directly from Our need, but it was rather the Decree given to Us from the Above, where everything is completely different. The Earth is a component part of a big machine without which it wouldn't work. When the need for such a component part appeared in the course of evolution of the overall Cosmos body We created it.

The Earth was created concurrently by Our Divine System together with the Advanced Material System (as advanced as Ours) which reproduced, according to My plan, all the physiology on the planet, all the flora and fauna, and the humans themselves as material forms-bodies, and My spiritual System created subtle mechanisms for them, which set in motion rough forms necessary for different stages in development. In the course of creation and further functioning the Material System led the development of the planet's physiology and of everything that was created on it in its own fashion, while My Spiritual System led the spiritual development of the soul's subtle base in its own.

The man got used to treat the planet as if it were something inanimate, dead and unable to act on its own. And such a viewpoint separated him both from the nature and the Cosmos thus making people self-contained and of major importance in the Universe, they began to perceive themselves as the only living and rational beings. That is why now it is so hard for the humans adhering to the old rigid dogma to accept the new, to grasp the overall structure of the Universe and rightly identify their place in it.

But all the new knowledge, that seems to be incredible and wild to the old, obsolescent human psychology, is given not to the moribund fifth civilization but to the emerging sixth civilization. Therefore those who can step over their conventional notions and ideas about the world will take a step ahead in their development already in this life, while the rest will need new incarnations and new programs of development to accept the new».

So what unknown is God going to tell us about our planet? We ask Him another question:

- "Should the changes taking place on the Earth be regarded as evolutionary landmarks in her development?"

- "The Earth is a living body, – He answers, – the same as you, people, have; it is built of the same chemical substances as your material bodies. Therefore it doesn't remain the same and changes in the course of time. Its landscape, continents, vegetation, climate and living world change all the time. In the very beginning its surface was covered with water, but later one mainland appeared there which cleaved into a few continents and went apart in different directions. And everything didn't happen randomly, but followed the evolutionary program for the Earth's physical body. Similarly, a human appearance doesn't change at random with age but becomes different according to the development program for physical body."

- "If the Earth changes according to the program, who has written the program for her?" – We address God once again.

- «There is a specific Highly Advanced System, – He replies proudly. Dignity and greatness of Mind always sound in His intonation. – This System is engaged in planetary building. It includes programmers-calculationalists of the highest rank who write programs for planets in accordance with their level of development. Each planet must have its individual program. The System elaborates the kind of landscape that corresponds to a particular stage of the Earth's development, codes the consequence of forming vegetable and other worlds aligning with the energy they are to produce. The landscape is created not only for the sake of beauty but primarily for the sake of production of specific energy types and for global energy exchange. There is nothing on the Earth that evolves on its own and for its own sake. Everything is subject to the general scheme of energy generation and interrelation of different energy types».

Then our conversation continues as a series of questions and answers. We ask God, and He answers us.

- "If the natural world contributes to energy production, then what do deserts exist for?"

- "A desert is a place on the Earth that concentrates more energy than any other one, and powerful energy stream kills all the living, therefore its fauna is scanty. Energy concentration is implemented through deserts. Deserts are the planet's accumulators. The same can be said about hot countries, they possess great energy volumes as well."

- "How is the Earth's evolutionary program interconnected with programs of flora, fauna and humanity?"

- «First of all individual programs of each world are calculated together with all the particular subprograms, and then these separate programs are interlinked into one overall program for the Earth. Everything is based on precise calculations. Someone calculates the program of the whole system, someone calculates the program for society, another one deals with continents, and everything is done in mutual agreement between these programs and the Earth's energy demand satisfied by people. Demands of continents for animals, birds and plants are precisely estimated and sorted in descending order: where they shall be more or less, where in general they shall be absent, and where and what type of energy they are to produce. It is determined where water shall flow or sand shall continue to exist, where cold or heat shall be implemented together with the terms of their existence. The time frame is determined. And everything is created on the basis of precise estimation, and is interconnected by energy, physical, chemical and biological processes as well as by processes going on in the subtle worlds.

The man is connected both with nature and all natural worlds of the planet, with cities and even with particular spots on the Earth. There are some spots where general energies to and from people and other things on the Earth are united. Linking human energy to these spots is obligatory, as energy transmission is carried out through them from people to the planet and back. Thereby calculations are made where villages, towns, cities and other things shall be located. All of this is interconnected through the

5

Earth's general program, which is vast and omnibus compared to the human private program».

- "Consequently the landscape on the Earth is not random, is it?"

- "Landscape pictures develop over time in strict accordance with the input planet program and have particular goals. The landscape on every piece of the Earth was designed to evoke some feelings and emotions in people, because every work of their senses contributes to energy production, corresponding to a particular place on the Earth. Moreover the formation of every plant, animal, or anything else in a particular place is already designed to produce the demanded energy for this very place of the planet. That is why everything is interconnected."

- "The Earth's program covers a lasting period of time. Do any adjustments ever take place?"

- "Certainly, adjustments are carried out. We keep under observation the Earth all the time. Since the human race has appeared on the planet, We interfere into the program every two thousand years at this stage of evolution, mainly at the end of the period, just as now. To be more precise, We don't interfere into the program itself, but only into situations such as war for instance. Concerning the Earth itself and changes in her landscape, everything goes according to the input program of physical body development."

- "Why do the Earth and all the other planets of the solar system have to move? They could have stayed motionless in space, thus it would have been easier to produce the systems."

- "We set a goal to make them move like every other living body, because it helps many physical processes progress better and favorably effects constant renewal, not inside but in general direction of evolution."

- "What is the main cosmic task of the Earth?"

- "There is no task as such. There is a goal. It consists in energies processing as well as the planet's self-perfection as a living being. Everything should not stand still but evolve."

- "Is a planet perfection similar to a human perfection?"

- "Yes, everyone must ascend and get higher than one is. But the forms of perfection depend on the development Level which the soul has reached."

- "Does the Earth produce spiritual energy?"

- "It surely does."

- "In what way?"

- "With the help of mental activity of planetary character. Religion exists there, some kinds of art, particular reality situations; they are designed for the person to produce spiritual energy, so there are a number of ways. The Earth has its own ways of spiritual energy production through some processes which let it develop its subtle structures concurrently."

- "Is the spiritual energy type the highest one that can be produced by the planet?"

- "Yes, for the planet it is the absolute, as well as for the man. That means the planet is designed on the subtle plane so that it cannot produce higher energy frequencies. It is like you have a car that is structurally designed to accelerate one hundred twenty kilometers per hour and not more. To get higher speed you need to change the hardware. Here is the same thing. The Earth's planetary formation is meant for spiritual energy frequency as for the highest possible."

- "What effect does Earth have on the man?"

- "A human being is under its mesmerism."

- "We have heard that the Earth contributes to the degradation of man, focusing his/her attention on the benefits. Is it true?"

- "That is what its mesmerism consists in. But a person should pay more attention not to the material benefits but to his soul and its perfection. Still the Earth concentrates too much of your attention on itself, on the beauty of its landscapes, though the man should learn to love everything that exists even beyond the Earth. But mainly everything alien repulses people or is perceived with terror, and there is a share of her mesmerism in this as well. The Earth is merely a stage in human development, and each subsequent stage is much more interesting than the previous one, hence a human should know for sure that the Earth is not the best that a soul can have for its development. However it shouldn't make him disrespect his habitat. It is always necessary to pay homage to and have respect for the world you live in."

The Birth of the Planet

The process of a planet material formation is highly interesting. Scientists interpret this fact in their own way, but what will the Creator himself tell us about this issue? And we asked Him the question:

- "How did the planet's physical body appear?"

7

- "The material body was formed as a result of an explosion of some mass containing the initial elements, which served as building material for physical structures. The body evolves under the program set in the gene code of the planet. The powerful energy of the explosion is the trigger which breaks the seal off the lock and sets the program in motion. Then all the elements contained in the initial mass get involved into the reaction which starts building up the planned material structures in sequential binding. Everything is built under the program, which is unwound by time."

- "One of human theories says that the sun in turn gives rise to all the planets of its system, is that the case?"

- "No, this assumption is not correct. People have many erroneous theories."

- "And did the Earth's subtle bodies appear in the very beginning?"

- "Yes, the protective body appeared from the moment of its formation, the rest of them appeared in the course of evolution, to be more precise, subtle bodies existed from the very beginning, but they remained vacant, and it took time for the planet to develop them."

- "Does the development program also include development of subtle bodies?"

- "Every body has its separate program which is encoded in the corresponding envelope, i.e. the development program of an astral body is encoded in the astral envelope, the one of a mental body – in the mental envelope and so on. But together, they are joined in a common development program, which is located in the body close to the soul. Planets have different Levels of development too; therefore the number of their bodies differs. Naturally, the older the planet, the greater the number of its bodies."

- "Are all the programs written by the same programmers?"

- "Planetary programmers have their specialization, and every level of programmers works with its own type of energy and is in charge of its own Level. For example, programs for the astral body are written by programmers of one Level, programs for the mental body – by specialists of a higher Level, those for the spiritual one need to be written by programmers of even higher Level."

- "How is the planet soul incarnated into a physical body?"

-"This process is complicated and constructions are complex. Usually auxiliary devices are used to incarnate a soul. The process is maintained by a few specialists and a Determinant who will guide this planet farther on. The process of a planet soul incarnation is the same as a human soul incarnation, as their physiology is almost alike."

- "A human soul comes to the Earth due to demands of the Earth herself. And what is the necessity determining a planet soul to be sent into a physical body? Where does the demand stem from?"

- "The demand originates in a larger Volume where the Cosmos body exists."

- "Is it also a need for some type of energy?"

- "Yes, it is."

- "What kinds of difficulties can take place in the course of the planet soul incarnation into a material object?"

- "Everyone has his own difficulties."

- "Does the planet Determinant watch, if the planet's material body is formed correctly or is the whole process set automatically?"

- "Certainly he does. And he does not do it on his own, there are a few specialists involved in the process. Everyone shall control one's own sphere, as the planet comprises a variety of processes."

- "Does it happen so, that the planet's physical body is somehow being formed abnormally and then the formation is stopped?"

- "Yes, such things happen."

- "Does the soul incarnation into big and small bodies differ? There are big and small planets, aren't they?"

- "No, there is no particular difference, for example, when comparing very thick and skinny people. The only difference is in development programs."

SUBTLE FORMATION OF THE EARTH

Planet's Brain

If the planet is a living body, here emerges the question whether it possesses a cogitative apparatus. It provoked our interest.

- "Does the Earth possess mind?"
- "Sure, like all the other creatures alive, it has mind and memory. But this differs from what humans know about themselves. The Earth's mind surpasses a human's mind many thousand times, and each of them remains at their own level of thinking. Thinking through images is characteristic of the human, while the Earth's process of thinking runs on a different principle and is more intense in the private sphere of existence. The Earth possesses a planetary mind – peculiar and powerful. As fragmentary display of its activity one can survey some atmospheric phenomena, magnetic and electric processes, but the main mechanism of its thinking is harbored beyond people's perception and understanding."
- "What can be said about the Earth's thinking? How does it manifest itself in cataclysms of nature?"
- "Certain cataclysms, depending on its emotions, can take part in processes of thinking. But predominantly, all cataclysms are the planet's emotions. And thinking itself can only be traced on the energetic plane."
- "Where is the Earth's brain?"
- "The planet's cogitative mechanism is represented by a complex construction, which begins on the physical plane and ends up in her subtle bodies. The Earth's frame is not restricted only to physical body but together with subtle bodies represents a complex conglomeration that cannot be perceived by human vision sense."
- "Does the Earth have a pulse ring, as humans do?"
- "Yes. The pulse ring is placed beyond the physical body."
- "How many center-brains does the Earth have, compared to the five that people have?"

- "On the physical plane there is only one, but on the subtle plane each planet's body has a center-brain."

The Earth's bodies

In knowing new about the Earth we proceeded from the subtle human construction well-known to us. If the man possesses seven bodies (one physical and six subtle bodies), then a similar question arises:

- "How many bodies does the Earth have?"

- "There were seven of them in total, but now because of the transition onto a new stage of development, it gains three more."

- "Will the growing number of bodies be followed by the planet's gain of any new properties?"

- "Here the things happen just the other way round: first makings of properties should appear, and then new bodies will be added. Nothing is given from the Above for free without such preliminary makings. That means the Earth gains some properties in the first place through some kind of activity, which reflects the process of self-actualization of its wishes and self-defense. According to the accrued properties, or energies of a particular type, if their quality and quantity reach the set planetary limits, a planet is given a new body, which it continues to fill with new energies of a still higher rate than those filling its older bodies."

-"How are bodies filled up with new types of energy?"

- "According to this particular development stage, the Earth has already filled her volumes in existing bodies with energy. If all the volumes are filled, new volumes open up automatically to be filled further. And if these new volumes are engaged in the new work stage, the Determinant of the Earth places an additional body around it to protect. That means that this new body serves as a new volume for farther development of new properties and constitutes a protective shield which keeps all the reaped energies within the planet's field."

- "Was this method created long ago?"

- "Yes, of course. For the Earth it is accurate computation, however of a higher rate than for the man."

- "Is it necessary for a planet to go through the set number of Levels, like humans do, to ascend a step higher?"

- "Yes. Everything and everyone make a transfer onto a next stage only by means of going through the number of Levels set for their form. Your planet has its own Level system, its own Hierarchy."

- "There is a one-hundred-Level system for the man. And how many Levels are set for a planet to make transfer into a new life form?"

- "There are about fifty Levels for planets. But these Levels are more powerful than human's ones. And at the upper Levels they gradually become less powerful."

- "What is the reason for the recent (year 1998) one thousand times' surge in solar activity and consequently the corresponding increase in solar energy transmitted to the Earth?

- "It was done for the sake of mutations and changes of physical bodies for the sixth race. Certainly, not only humans but also animals and plants – everything that is on the Earth – are to mutate."

- "Is this very energy used for transformation of the Earth itself?"

- "Solar emission does not have any significant impact on the Earth. This is not enough for it. It is We who transmit the energy for the planet's transformation. This energy serves as an impulse for the Earth's transfer onto the new orbital* and simultaneously works as fuel for her."

- "Is the Earth thus recharged once in two thousand years?"

- "No. That is only for the human race. The Earth is recharged for a thousand years."

- "Does the Earth's transfer onto the new orbital happen only after Your energy is transmitted to it?"

- "Yes. Without this its transfer could not have taken place."

- "How does the term "orbital" differ from the term "orbit"?"

- "The difference between these words is the same as between matter and energy. An orbital is a higher form of evolution, that is the trajectory for evolution at the energetic Level, that is expressed in the planet's transfer onto a higher stage of perfection in the band of higher frequency energy. And an orbit is a form of a physical body's movement on the material plane."

- "What is the essence of transfer onto the new orbital?"

- "It takes place a step higher in its own development. Its energetics changes, what means its inner qualitative state changes."

- "What kind of changes in structure of atoms and molecules take place when a planet transfers onto a new orbital?"

- "Physically the atomic structure remains the same, but it is adjusted for another Level, that is the atomic structure remains as it was, but it becomes more advanced and elaborate. The new energy is admitted into the atoms and molecules through both chemical and physical processes and all the following processes proceed with the help of this energy. As a result, the recharge of all atoms, molecules and elementary particles of the world is performed. They also make the transfer onto the new energetic Level. Gradual spread of the new energy inside the matter and its components takes place. Thus, the inner subtle base of elementary particles, their inner contents is consequently renewed and reorganized over time, which will make it possible for the Earth to produce the energy of a more improved form on every subtle plane. We Ourselves will work at this modernization in future."

- "Will the planet's proper time change during the transfer onto the new orbital?"

- "No, it will remain the same."

- "Are the other solar system planets transferred onto the new orbital together with the Earth?"

- "No."

- "Why?"

- "The thing is that Our experiment with people here, on the Earth, was not a success, and therefore We continue it by refining it in many details. And on the other planets of your system everything goes normally. Everywhere else except the Earth it goes normally. Though this transfer is most likely to partially affect them. Minor amendments will be needed for the other solar system planets but there will not be such global alterations as here."

- "How will the connections between the planets change, if one of them transfers onto the new orbital and the others remain at their former Levels?"

- "The energy that other planets will receive from the Earth will be subtler. The quality of the transmitted energy will be higher. Now the other solar system planets receive coarse energy, therefore the energies produced by them are of lower frequency band than they are to deliver. If We improve the quality of the energy produced by the Earth, respectively the figures of the other planets, connected with the Earth, will be enhanced. Then everything in the solar system will be back to normal."

- "Energy transformation between Earth and the Cosmos is held through people, isn't it?"

- "Yes, indeed, such transformation is held."

- "But can the energy from the Earth be transmitted into the Cosmos directly?"

- "It is transmitted both from the Earth and through people. When the energy passes through people, the energy of different types, different qualities is produced, that is the difference. <u>People are needed to deliver energy of a different quality,</u> that is the Earth uses them for such energy quality alteration."

- "Consequently has the appearance of people on the Earth a particular aim?"

- "The appearance of people on the Earth caused by development demands of your planet, by features of its structure. Human beings as transformers were to take upon themselves the energy sent by the Cosmic System, to convert and transmit it to the Earth. Each spot on the planet requires a particular energy type. That is why people are born not at random but at the call of the planet that needs to be recharged in particular places. Therefore after We get the signal from the Earth that it needs such and such energy in this place, the Hierarchic System selects a human soul according to its quality properties, which is capable of producing a particular energy potential in due circumstances. And this potential will just correspond to the demands the planet has in this particular place. This implies that before a man is born in some place on the Earth this human is energetically built up in a proper way. And every person meets the place where he/she lives in terms of energy. If the quality of energy changes and there is discrepancy between the person's and the place's energetics, the person moves to a different place that suits them. This is the connection between human's and Earth's energetics.

In the course of evolution the needs of Earth changed and it required energies more complex in quality and considerably different from each other in their characteristics, therefore nations, races and peoples producing different energy bands were created. It means that all the people of the same nation produce the same energy band, while different nations themselves produce different energy bands. Everything fluctuates within some range".

- "But human beings have not existed on the Earth forever. Millions of years it did well without them."

- "At the initial stage the Earth produced single-type energy for the Cosmos which was scanty. But at the same time she was preparing to have animals and human beings in accordance with its unwinding program and was forming environmental conditions as habitat. The simpler the world, the more meager the energies produced. Therefore complication of life forms happens gradually in the physical world of the Earth."

- "How does the early stage of the Earth's development differ from the later one?"

- "When a planet is at its initial stage of development, the range of its energies is always meager, so it does not need intense energy exchange. At a low Level it can do without flora and living beings. But in the course of evolution the need for a more intense energy exchange appears and, depending on to what extent it evolved, flora, fauna and human race are introduced. This all is the gradual complication of its energy types. It was **the appearance of the first civilization that aided the Earth's first transfer into a new state, that is the transfer onto the first orbital.**"

- "Was it after the appearance of the first civilization that the Earth made her transfer onto the first orbital*?"

- "Earth got its first body as a protective envelope before the appearance of the first civilization. The need to fill bodies with a variety of energies was the driving force of its transfer onto the first orbital."

- "Consequently, our planet has already changed orbitals a few times, hasn't it? Is the appearance of the sixth race on the Earth connected with its transfer onto the new orbital?"

- "**Civilizations do not live and evolve for their own sake, they are <u>constructional</u> necessity on the bases of which the planet transfers to a higher stage in development.** Your Earth made transfer onto the new orbital after each civilization. Now (year 2000 AD) it is transferring onto the new orbital for the sixth time, so this means that **the sixth race requires the sixth orbital.**"

- "What is primary and what is secondary: the appearance of the sixth race triggers the Earth's transfer onto the new Orbital or vice versa – the Earth transfers and requires the new race to be formed?"

- "Both things happen at the same time. These two processes are interrelated and cannot exist without each other. For instance, on having transferred onto the sixth orbital, the people of the fifth race will die out, as they won't bear the new frequency of that energy which will correspond to the new state of the planet."

- "What is the energetic and physical essence of the planet's transfer onto the new orbital?"

- "The Earth remains on its orbit, but its energetics changes for one of a higher frequency band. Everything will change because of this: nature, animals, and people. The new race will appear that will be capable to forbear many adverse effects connected with restructuring of both land

and (water) reservoirs. After the transfer onto the new orbital the planet will start the new stage in its development. With every transfer the planet begins to fill the new body with necessary energy types. But it does it in unison with a human activity."

- "What is the principle of the Earth's transfer onto the new orbital? How will it be transferred?"

- "You are already transferring it (addressing us)*. All the psychics and mediums do help its transfer. And the essence of the transfer is that through them the new energy is sent to the Earth, thus changing its state to higher frequencies than those ones it used at the previous stage of evolution. Human beings serve as conductors, elements in the scheme for energy transmission, through people energy is transmitted from the Hierarchic System to some objects. The important thing is that the man does not simply transmit the energy he gets, but only having converted the quality of this energy, he sends it over to the planet. The same thing happens backwards: a human being gets energies of one quality from the Earth and converts them inside and relays them (already in a different quality) to the Hierarchic System."

- "What are the forms of energy transmission to the Earth?"

- "Some part of the converted energy is transmitted to the Earth through a man's feet, some part is sent over through his mental activity, as human thinking produces the frequencies of the type that is partially perceived by the Earth as well, and some part of the energy certainly returns to the Hierarchic System. This means that men relay new converted energy back to the System that sent it and to the Earth as well. But there are some other ways of energy transmission."

- "Now (the question was asked on 8th of August 1999)* a huge mass of energy, coming from the Cosmos, is approaching the Earth which will cause all kinds of earthquakes. What will this energy bring to the Earth? Is it some fuel for it?"

- "Yes, We can say it is a kind of fuel. This energy will be a driving force for the new stage of development. To transfer some body from a lower Level onto a higher one, an impulse from outside is needed to put the energy of a higher rank into it. It bounces like a ball from a blow into the air. The same thing happens to the man. To make a person ascend a Level higher one needs to put high energy into him, just like into you. So from time to time the Earth also gets energy in the form of open luminous volumes sent by the Hierarchic Systems just as now. But this energy will enter Earth's (water) reservoirs smoothly even though it will still cause some earthquakes in particular areas and some other negative effects though we try to smooth the moment of entering."

- "Consequently is appearance of a luminous object connected with the planet's transfer onto the new orbital?"

- "No doubt."

- "And what about the energy transmitted through us? You have said that energy is also sent down to the Earth through people maintaining contact with higher worlds."

- "Transmission is carried out both through you and from the outside. There are a number of ways. When energy is transmitted through people like you, this serves as run-up. If the new is mixed with the old without any preparation, it will all result in a great fault. And if the energy first is implemented in small doses during at least a few years, which is the term of your contacts, then We get the desirable effect. The new energy will be restrained by your energy, i.e. Our energy, that We sent through you in small doses. It will smooth the transmission and the destructive aftermath."

- "Will the transmission of the new Earth development program for the next two thousand years, along with the given energy, take place?"

- "Yes, it will."

- "Is it known where the new energy will be transmitted to: reservoirs of Russia, America or Africa?"

- "It will be transmitted onto the ocean, and We'll endeavor to do that far from residential areas. Water is intrinsic to strong attraction of subtle energies; therefore ocean is chosen for energy descent. But there won't be any splash as it takes place at a meteoritic fall, this is subtle energy indeed. However the water energy level will rise and there will be vibrations coming from the Earth's energy structure, followed by extending impact on the material body; a series of earthquakes and various calamities will occur. But We are trying to smooth all of it."

- "And how will this energy affect the system, which is inside the Earth?"

- "Restructuring is happening everywhere. Therefore, in the System you are interested in things will happen according to Our demands. Of course, it will face calamities and cataclysms, similar as yours. Currently, they are already taking place both among them and people. And there are victims, of course, here and there. There are casualties everywhere, with respect to the Earth."

- "Will the descending energy influence parallel worlds?"
- "Certainly, it will. Everything is being rebuilt at once. New energy passes through all subtle bodies of the Earth, thus changing them. But the energetics alone is not enough. The process of energy entering is not one-time-only. It started to come in the year of 89 (1989)* and will continue the gradual implementation till 2005. In addition, in order to be restructured each body requires certain energy types, so different types of energy will come to the Earth many times."
- "Will the energy be approaching the Earth in the form of luminous objects?"
- "Methods to deliver energy to the Earth are various. For people that will be manifested in various celestial phenomena. If the man could understand that this phenomenon is Our implementation, that would be good. If he cannot, then he will explore the incomprehensible phenomenon over the years to come, and this will contribute to the development of his intellect."
- "On the Earth, there are spots that require energy feed, and there are spots where surplus energy concentrates, thus, there are two opposite processes: energy intake and energy delivery. And if the man is involved in these processes, how do they affect him and his behavior in society?"
- "Both processes favor people's activity, followed by all kinds of their performances: riots, revolutions, wars, and so on. If some places experience lack of energy, or conversely, its excess, it affects primarily the mental state of the man. Therefore, to feel comfortable at some spot, there should be balance in the energy spots surrounding the man so that they won't have surplus of energy, or its losses."
- "And which process takes place at spots where there is war: lack of energy or its excess?"
- "The lack. The Earth takes from people something that it lacks for, so in such places it absorbs human energy."
- "And what happens in case of energy excess?"
- "With plenty of energy the planet distributes it to people. The man takes the energy and distributes it further. But the energy excess can also affect his psyche adversely, leading to intensified action in the form of any outbreaks in the community. Human feedback both to the lack of energy and its surplus is the same – intensified action."

Turn of the Earth by 90 degrees

It was interesting to ask God to verify the sensational theories of earth scientists, so we addressed Him:
- "Scientists assert that the Earth overturns poles. Is it possible?"
- "Relative to what do they allege this overturn happens?"
- "Relative to the rotation axis and to the equator. Scientists believe that in a few tens of thousands of years the Earth is expected to turn by ninety degrees."
- "Yes, these turns occur."
- "What makes the Earth rotate by ninety degrees: due to ice caps accumulated at the poles, which outweigh and create a moment to rotate?"
- "No, they do not outweigh. It is the other mechanism. On the physical plane, the reason is that the center of gravity changes inside the Earth."
- "Is it taken into account that such tumble is accompanied with total life destruction on the Earth?"
- "No, it is possible to overturn imperceptibly and keeping everything alive."
- "Keeping alive?"
- "Yes. Nothing has ever been destroyed on the Earth completely. Life certainly remained."
- "What purpose does our planet make this turn for?"
- "The Earth requires this in relation to other planets. Interaction between the planets of the solar system is necessary, only somewhat from the other side."

Earth's Time

We have learned a lot of interesting and complex things about time, but the knowledge of the topic began with simple questions.
- "On the Earth, all the living develops over time. Time is a special kind of matter, isn't it?"
- "No, it is not the matter, but a special unit of measure, which exists only for you. Everything is different in Our world. In other words, time exists because it is built into the development program of the Earth and of all living beings connected with it."

- "Why does the Earth's time consist of three components: past, present, and future?"
- "A human being does not need other forms of time at this Level of development. Such components allow a Unit* to better develop at the initial stage of development, allow it feeling the focus of the movement of development, correlate the results achieved, compare and direct his thoughts towards evolution. Three time components are the first three stages to the infinite evolution of a soul."
- "How does the present differ from the past or the future?"
- "There is frequency range discrepancy towards the one way, as well as towards the opposite way."

The Role of Water on the Earth

In each response God revealed something new and non-conventional to us.

- "What is there water on Earth for? What role unknown to man does it perform?"
- "Water is an energy carrier. It helps distribute energy to the surface of the planet. Somewhere on the Earth, for example, much energy is produced, and it is transferred by the river to another location, where it is not enough. Through seas and oceans energy is balanced. In addition, water is the Earth's physical organ of vision, though it sounds paradoxical for you. But as any living organism it has the organ of cosmic vision. A human eye also has a liquid composition. But as for the Earth, of course, it is much more complicated and hence it is difficult for human consciousness to perceive. But the human eye is also capable of conducting energy through itself, although the source of its radiation is outside the visual organs."
- "What is the increase or decrease in water reservoirs on the Earth connected with?"
- "With change of energy volume stored by water. Each civilization needed its own energy storages that water is deemed to be, that is, water absorbs the surplus energy produced by mankind and flora. It was energy reservoir. So, if a civilization produces more energy than the previous one, then its energy storages, i.e. water reservoirs extend. There is increase in the water cover of the Earth, and vice versa. For example, the new sixth race will produce energy several times as much compared to yours, and

water reserves available now are small. There will be no place to throw off surplus energy to, which would result in the fact that the surplus energy will be taken back to the bodies of the man, destroying them and killing the man himself. Therefore, restructuring of the entire surface of the Earth is required for the surplus energy not to cause harm to people.

Therefore, after the year of two thousand changes in its landscape will take place: flooding of margins and continents will occur; many islands will go under water. All margins and your northern areas will gradually hide under water. Continents shift will occur; initially it will be insignificant, and later – more noticeable. Some part of land, i.e. continents, will become larger, some part – less. The area of water reservoirs will increase significantly and will take all the surplus energy produced by a new race, it means that the planet's energy storages will increase. The structure of land and stones will change towards a greater density of energetics; energy intensity of solid substances will also rise.

And because of the fact that your planet will be rebuilt to create a new environment for the sixth race, it will long undergo various disasters as it is disasters that are a form of restructuring of the Earth's physical body. In the initial stage of development, the sixth race will have to stand a great deal of adverse environmental impacts due to this restructuring".

- "Will the only continent be left in view of the said changes?"
- "Yes, the total land area will decrease. And finally, in the distant future, the only mainland will remain."
- "Scientists have discovered that water has memory."
- "Each object has it. Water also has its own program, its time and, therefore, it must have memory to remember the past and the present, which lay the foundation of the future. Any future is built based on the past, so everything that develops over time and outside it needs memory."
- "Does water possess any blocks of memory in view of the said?"
- "All liquids are specifically built; they have elements recording information."
- "At the expense of what does water absorb different kinds of energy?"
- "Among all the substances on the Earth liquid is considered to be the most energy intensive. Speaking metaphorically, it is possible to say that water formation includes the presence of many energy magnets that pull excess energy to themselves. That is, it has the ability to absorb energy in places having its surpluses and give it to those places facing its shortage. For this purpose serve all rivers and undercurrents in seas and oceans. Therefore, when there is huge energy splash in any place of the Earth,

river water absorbs it and the latter is spread through the liquid across the surface of the planet. There is alignment of energy."

- "At present water in rivers is heavily polluted. Will its self-purification occur?"

- "Soil and underlying aquifers purify water of chemistry and all kinds of impurities. The Earth is changing the structure of water in such a way that, thanks to its new structure, self-purification of liquid occurs. And there is a program for such water purification and restructuring. Water as such cannot do anything for itself; it can only memorize and transmit energy."

- "Does ice at the poles of the Earth play any role in its energy intensity?"

- "Yes. Where there is ice mass, it can be said, frozen energy is stored because it cannot flow anywhere or move like water. But the energy is pure."

- "For what purpose are the storages of this pure energy set at opposite poles?"

- "For the balance of the Earth and to make it easier for it to cope with energy, easier to process it. Basically, already purified energy is transmitted though water, while the purest one is kept in ice. Ice is the frozen-up energy in its purest state."

- "Is energy located in seas and oceans used by Hierarchic Systems?"

- "Yes, interchange of energies takes place. They take some energy and give the other, already purified. The point is that for the Earth, the energies contained in water pools are considered to be pure, while for Hierarchic Systems they are dirty, because it is a lower plane for the Higher. That which is considered clean for people does not mean it remains clean to others. That is why there is such interchangeability of energies between the Upper and the Lower. Some energies the purest for the Earth are taken from it and the others, used but purified ones, are given back."

- "Does the Earth currently provide less energy than it would do in the subsequent cycle of development?"

- "At the new development stage given the advent of the sixth race the Earth's energy efficiency to the Cosmos will increase several times."

- "Does the Earth itself use energy contained in the seas and oceans for some purposes?"

- "It uses it constantly for all sorts of calamities, and for everything that happens on it. The energy contained in water feeds flora and fauna, not to mention the man. There is energy circulation on the surface of the planet."

- "Will people use this energy, for example, to their industry?"

- "This has already been invented, but not disclosed."

- "At the advent of a new race on the Earth it will produce more energy for the Cosmos. And how will the quality of this energy change?"

- "The energy type will be the same, but energy itself will be cleaner and better, that is, its spectrum will change towards high frequencies. The man of the fifth race produces a lot of dirty and rough energy, and Our cleaners just cannot resist the influx of rejects they have to cope with. But given the increased awareness of human beings, originating in the transitional period of rejection and decoding of low-level souls, it will be able to make changes in the quality of the population, making it higher and spiritual. We'll separate «grains of darnel» and it will help increase the number of higher individuals in relation to the total population number. This in turn will enable Us to improve the quality of available energy."

Weather

We had to look at weather from the new point of view, after a series of replies of God.

- "What are weather conditions created on the Earth for?"

- "The Weather or climate is a regulation form of different types of plants, animals, and nations within the particular borders of the planet. In addition, weather is a form of human upbringing."

- "Who controls the weather on the Earth?"

- "At present We, Our Center manages all the weather changes. Earth's Managers* and Determinants* observe it and regulate it by means of weather, using their computer*[1] . Previously, before the planet's restructuring, when everything was under the program, the weather was regulated by an automatic device."

- "Is this device located on the subtle plane?"

- "Yes, it is. For humanity all our machines keep being invisible."

- "Is the machine beyond the Earth?"

- "Yes, near the Earth."

- "On the Earth, vortex cavities are often observed in the atmosphere. What causes their formation?"

---

[1]   **computer*** – Of course, They have computers different to those which are available on the Earth, similar to them, or rather a specific subtle plane construction which resembles our earthly computer, hence their equipment is called an earthly term.

- "Vortex formation is caused through a special subtle structure of the Earth, using its subtle constructions that correspond to locations in a human formation, known as chakras. At these locations, energy release into the Cosmos occurs."

- "And does the Earth itself influence weather anyway?"

- "Sure, it does. It is known that based on temperature difference winds arise. Generally the Earth creates cyclones, intertwines vortices spiral-wise. All this originates from the Earth, from its functioning."

- "Does it contradict the weather, which the Earth's Determinant makes using his own computer?"

- "No, on the contrary, there is interrelation. All is done according to the program of the Earth. And fixed recurrence of weather cycles, due to which you create folk omens, is provided by the computer in conjunction with the work of the Earth's program. Now (1998) in connection with the overall restructuring of your planet, we are forced to intervene in the regulation of weather conditions in relation to their adaptation to a new civilization. That is, we are adjusting the climate for the new people of the Earth."

- "Does collective meditation impact weather or is it self-deception of the man?"

- "It does. The Earth hears a petition coming from a person.

Hearing is implemented through the Earth's body, and then it decides whether to comply with their request or not: if it would be useful to it, from its point of view, to comply with people's plea or not.

For example, if your hand aches, a signal for help comes through the nerves to the brain. And the man begins to take steps to remove painful sensations. Similarly, Earth takes the signal coming from people, and then decides what to do. She can facilitate the process, desired by people, or may oppose it if she does not need it."

The Higher's Experiment with the Earth

Everyone is interested in the mission our planet has in the universe. We have always considered it the most important and essential in the solar system because it has life on it. But what would God say about the mission of our planet, if you ask Him the following question:

- "Is the Earth the most important in the solar system?"

- "No, she is not the most important."

- "Our Planet is grain of sand in the universe, one of the millions of other planets. Why do you currently pay so much attention to it and spend so much energy on it?"

- "Because it is Our experiment. You are not alone. In addition to your Earth, there are two more Earths, the same as yours, but with a shift in time, that is, one can say that there is one Earth in your future and the other one– in the past."

- "What is this shift in time needed for?"

- "You'd like to say that all of them could be alike, would you?"– Clarifies God.

- "Yes", – we affirm.

- "The shift in time was needed to better adjust the program for the development of your Earth and its consciousness."

- "So, using the program of two other Earths, is it possible to correct the program of our planet in a certain way that is, using the future Earth's program to correct something in the present time?"

- "Here We're regulating the program through you."

- "How does the Earth which is now in the future develop?"

- "It does not exist anymore. It crashed."

- "Sorry? What happened to it?"

- "Nuclear explosion. Nuclear war this is the Earth of the future in two hundred years; the war will destroy all life on the planet and the planet itself. The civilization, similar to yours, perished completely, so We want to save your Earth and the planet, which is in terms of time left eighteen years behind you. That explains Our strong interest in your planet. We do not want it to explode, as it happened to the planet of the future."

- "Were there Earths which moved successfully into the future?"

- "No, that was the first. It died."

- "Do planets die only due to explosions? What reasons do they die for?"

- "Planets can die of disease because they also have their diseases like any other living being. Normal forms of death of the planet in your system include damping, cooling and compression. As a result, a dead lump is formed, which then begins to crumble."

- "Does a form of death have any meaning for the soul of the planet?"

- "Of course, any form of death is associated with the karma of the planet and necessarily affects the soul."

- "Then what awaits humanity in the next 100 years?"

- "Based on the Earth, which exploded?"– He repeats our question, trying to understand in what area we would like to hear a prediction: it can refer economy, politics, and social welfare, and so on.

- "Yes", – we confirmed. – "Does a similar death threaten humanity?"

- "At present such threat does exist. But everything depends on people: whether they are able to destroy nuclear weapons."

- "At present, are You working simultaneously with the Earth that is behind us in terms of time that is, with the Earth in the past?"

- "Naturally, the programs are being corrected."

- "Is there the principle of counterparts in other universes, like our Earth and the Earth in the past?"

- "No. This experiment is only yours, but in other universes other experiments are carried out."

- "One of these new given laws states that the principle of counterparts is used to control development. Are these counterparts created for the most responsible forms?"

- "Yes, for responsible constructions only not have a zero result. This is a kind of insurance."

- "Do Entities or Higher Entities have such counterparts?"

- "No, They don't. Any Entity exists always as a single copy, as They are individual."

- "And what other forms, besides planets, may have counterparts?"

- "Any responsible constructions can have counterparts. Besides them, any double conditions can be used, that is the same conditions of existence specially designed for certain purposes may be planned."

- "Had our Earth had a counterpart since her creation, or did it appear later?"

- "This counterpart was made at a certain stage of development of your planet. When there was the era of dinosaurs, it did not exist yet. A new phase began with the advent of humanity. It was it that caused the necessity to create counterparts. Monitoring the development of primary mankind, the very first race, led us to conclude that it could go to where We do not want, and We need some insurance. We saw that most of humanity, from its first steps, distorted and Our experiment with mankind could not survive, so an alternate was needed, and after the first race We decided to create a counterpart. So the counterpart appeared after the first race."

- "Was it the future of the Earth?"

- "Yes. It was decided to work out situations and make amendments to the development of your Earth on its base. To protect Our experiment later on the Earth with lag of time was created, in other words, that is you staying in the past."

- "Planet-counterparts pass through some stage of development together, and then their ways diverge, do they?"

- "Yes, everyone goes its own way."

- "To what extent are the souls chosen to planetary counterparts identical? They are supposed to be similar to each other; otherwise they will not be able to go one way, are they?"

- "Souls for counterparts are taken from the same Level, i.e. they have the same Levels. Souls themselves are different, but are at the same development Level. But prior to this stage, the Earth-to-backup existed in the other world, in other circumstances, and went its own way. Thus, for this experiment, it was taken from the corresponding to your Earth stage of development."

- "So, when our Earth completes successfully the required stage of development, will they depart?"

- "Of course, each will improve separately, having chosen an individual path."

- "In fact, counterparts pass through the programs of the same type. Does it mean they fill in their matrixes with energies of the same type?"

- "Yes, at this stage of gaining – the same. But, you see, the Earth-to-backup came having different energy type and composition in the matrix, and in the course of passing through the same program, it will fill the cells with negligible amount of energy compared to what it already has. The same composition will be too little for their volumes, their proportions. If, for instance, all the energies accumulated according to the program be combined each will make up only a small cell. And only those energies can be compared."

- "Does adjustment of one of the counterparts accelerate the progression of both or does it only protect from destruction?"

- "There is no doubt that the adjustment of one of the world will contribute to progress of the other planet. The overall progression increases in both, if the experiment is carried out successfully. But one can say that the souls of your contemporaries are less fortunate than theirs, because they are behind you in terms of time. Where you will make mistakes, they will make corrections; which will allow them accelerating their progression, so that in this respect souls on the planet of the past have benefits in development."

- "That is, we will be degrading while their souls will escape it?"
- "Yes, this is due to the shift in time. But We will not stop there, and then We will move earthly souls, using advanced programs, closer to the required Level."
- "Are the Determinants handling planet-counterparts different?"
- "Yes, they are."
- "Does it turn out that different Determinants handle two souls under two similar programs?"
- "Yes. But They are naturally linked, communicate with each other, consult each other on any issues, solve together general issues in relation of handling the planets."
- "As for the Earth of the future, which exploded; is its soul considered to be degrading?"
- "Of course, it has not complied with the program."
- "Do planets' souls work out karma?"
- "Yes, all forms of existence in your System have their karma."

- - -

- "Our Earth is being restructured at the moment. Do other planets of the solar system undergo simultaneous reconstruction?"
- "Yes, some adjustments occur in accordance with changes in Earth's functioning. It is experiencing a transition onto a new orbital, and the whole of your solar system should also transfer to a subsequent stage of development that is, the other orbital."
- "Will all other planets transfer to a higher stage too?"
- "Yes, you can say – higher."
- "Who works with other planets in the solar system and other star systems – You or Determinants?"
- "Planetary Determinants work with planets of the solar system, and They are subordinate to Us that is, We work and point out what to do."
- "Do You personally participate in other experiments or are You engaged to the Earth alone?"
- "We monitor everything that happens in your Universe that is, there is constant monitoring."
- "Then why is there so much evil and aggression on the Earth?"

- "Minus Cosmic Systems that are disposed against your Earth have made the introduction of alien energies on the planet, contrary to wishes of «Union»*[2]. Similarly, scouts from other countries penetrate your country contrary to your will."

- "Where are these minus Systems located in which constellation?"

- "To the west of you. We can say in the western celestial hemisphere."

- "Does the Earth have enemies? Who are they?"

- "The Enemy of the Earth is someone who wants to seize it for his purposes."

- "There are some in the Cosmos. This is the minus System, which specializes in using planets for its own purposes, pumping all the information out of them, all the energy and then throws them as not wanted."

- "And what then happens to the planets?"

- "The death of the soul. They devastate the soul. To prevent the threat with the Earth's soul, we have tried to make contact with it, although the hostile forces prevented this."

- "And You have established contact with the soul of the Earth, haven't You?"

- "Yes. To do this We needed a special approach to it."

- "Who is meant by the name Lucifer?"

- "On your earthly plane this is Devil's Assistant."

- "But is He a Manager of that minus System that wanted to conquer Earth?"

- "There are lots of minus Systems."

- "Hence, is He one of them?"

- "He belongs to one layer of your Earth. This Level is rather low to Us. And there are many of those like him in the Cosmos. They have different Managers, i.e. those who guide them."

- "And yet they say that inside of our planet, in its nucleus there is also some kind of civilization. What does it represent?"

- "Inside the Earth exists a civilization, which absorbs the energy of people, processes it and sends to the moon for further processing. For people this civilization remains invisible, but since it is very close to your matter, some of its manifestations can be seen by people sometimes."

- "What is the name of this civilization?"

- "For you its name doesn't mean anything."

---

[2]   **«Union»*** – The name of the cosmic association, which includes 9 Hierarchical Systems

- "Does it belong to a minus System of Mind?"
- "Yes, it does."
- "Why is it minus?"
- "Because it works in minus Cosmic Systems' favor, and among its functions there is work with minus energies of earth dwellers that is, it collects people's energy of aggression, evil, cruelty and other negative emotions."
- "Who manages this civilization inside the Earth? Devil himself?"
- "No, His subordinates. There are plenty of them."
- "Are many people connected from the Below with this civilization?"
- "Yes, there are such people. In their behavior, you can watch a lot of reprehensible. Basically, these are people who commit bad acts, behave aggressively in the community in relation to other people."
- "Are there people who are connected from the Above?"
- "Yes, some are linked to Us or our Determinants. These are plus persons. And you can determine yourselves by people's behavior those connected from the Below and those – from the Above. However, many individuals are sometimes so complex and secretive in their true intentions, that a human being can hardly discern them."
- "Are earthquakes associated with the minus System, which is inside the Earth?"
- "Yes, they are directly related to it, to its work."

Different Types of Earthly Energies

- "The strength of gravity combines all the physical forces on the Earth. But there are parallel universes, and some force also brings them together. What are the forces that unite both physical and subtle worlds?"
- "There is a sort of specific binding energies."
- "Love is a special sort of gravitational phenomena, relating to binding energies, isn't it?"
- "I may say so. But the man knows nothing of these forces and their properties as they relate to subtle matter."
- "Cosmic energy, too, belongs to the same kind of subtle energies. What can serve as a cosmic energy storage system on the physical plane? Are there any installations available for this?"
- "Cosmic energy as a separate type does not exist. People use this term in reference to all energies that come to the Earth from outside. Indeed, this

is an infinite range of energies, which comprises those that people get from other planets of the solar system and those – from stars, and those sent to the Earth by her watchers. As energy storage systems serve, for instance, churches, or triangular constructions such as pyramids – any pyramids that are not necessarily correct, or with a certain ratio of sides."

- "These are energy concentrates. Could they serve as energy storage systems, so that this energy could be used later?"

- "Energy in these figures is not only concentrated, but stored up inside. To use the stored up energy there's a special code – the code for the strategic use of energy. But possession of the code is not available for the man, as the level of his consciousness still is not high."

- "The Earth has no facilities for the use of cosmic energy, has it?"

- "At present there are only installations to generate energy, not to use it."

- "According to our history, the Earth had two strong explosions. What kind of explosions were they?"

- "One of them relates to the Tunguska meteorite, although any meteorite fall in any area could be perceived earlier as an explosion due to the fact that until the twentieth century, your civilization did not know anything more powerful than cannon shells."

- "But the legend states that after the explosion, darkness descended on the Earth for several million years. What do people mean by this? What event?"

- "This was the change of times, life was also changing. But there was no explosion as such. Within that period, the powerful energy was descending to the Earth, compared to what it had been before, and the appearance of that great energy was seen as a very bright light. Much energy being brought down in a relatively short period of time begins to glow. And if a human being looks at the bright glow, and then – aside, due to special formation of his eyes, he will always see the darkness after the bright light. As for large extension in time, which was attributed to the darkness seen, the human is intrinsic to exaggeration, especially it relates to something that is scaring or unknown to him. This should also be taken into account."

- "What else happened during that change of eras on the Earth?"

- "Just the same as you have in the given period that is, people who did not prove to be useful were being removed, and the Earth was being populated with a new race. The planet was also transferring onto a new energy level, higher than the previous one."

- "Our Earth, in addition to cosmic energy, gets energy from other planets of the solar system. What for?"
- "There is energy recycling and no extra quantity of energy can go aside that is, energy interchange is regarded as inner."
- "Is the sun involved in this process?"
- "Of course. All bodies and all the planets are involved."

Parallel Worlds of the Earth

- "We were told that besides mankind, there are two civilizations on the Earth. Are they of energy type?"
- "One of them is as material as you, and the other – of energy type."
- "Where is the material one? Why don't we see it?"
- "In Tibet. They have a strong defense; therefore people do not see them."
- "Is this the white brotherhood?"
- "Yes, it is."
- "We know something about them. And where is the energy-type civilization located? Do they have control over people?"
- "No, they don't. They live by themselves."
- "Are they humanoid too or are they other beings, standing above us in their development?"
- "They are not human. And they do not stand above you either. You are on the same development level."
- "What is their purpose on the Earth?"
- "The same as that of the humanity, only they do not have physical bodies."
- "Do they have a possibility to penetrate into our world?"
- "Yes, sometimes they penetrate."
- "Are they the creatures which cause poltergeist?"
- "No. Poltergeist is caused by people themselves, with their mental energy."
- "Are they able to materialize in the forms known to us?"
- "No, they can not materialize. You do not see and will not see them."
- "Can people penetrate into their world then?"
- "No."
- "Are programs for parallel worlds of the Earth drawn up separately from that of Earth itself?"

- "First the overall objective of the Earth's development is determined, and in accordance with this objective individual programs for each of the parallel worlds are developed, which are then joined to the overall program, thus creating a whole structure. Always changes in one program, directly or indirectly, affect all the other programs, requiring some corrections to be made in them."

Restructuring of the Earth
(Summarizing)

Summarizing the information given in the chapter «The New About the Earth», you can trace the chain of successive interactions between the energies of man, the planet and the Hierarchic Systems, their direct correlation to each other and find out that grand holistic process in which they work together for the common goal – ensuring the normal functioning of all living forms in the holistic organism of the Nature*.

For God and His Hierarchic Systems the Earth represents some physiological structure manufacturing some products for Them and improving itself.

Like all the living evolving over time it has no constant form, i.e. construction, but changes in its building configurations in accordance with the development program, which sets all forms of change that must occur over time in it. It is the development program of the Earth's material body that specifies when and at what time continents and oceans shall be formed, mountains – grow, when one mainland shall split into several parts and how far they shall move away from each other and so forth, i.e. the outer shape of the Earth changes in accordance with the operation of the program of the material body.

But what purposes are these changes needed for? Couldn't it be better to leave it stable for the entire period of existence?

Life is a form of change of processes within an organism, which entails as a consequence changes in appearance. As long as the processes are directed towards vital energy increase in the body, there is evolution of an organism. When the processes decay the program begins phasing out. So it implies that in a living organism certain reactions should constantly occur; otherwise it ceases to be a living form.

But for the processes to take place, they should constantly change something. In stable environments they do not develop but stop. Therefore, changes in shape are necessary condition of life of the Earth's material body and its subtle structures as well.

Changes are the form of life, the form of existence. All these changes are connected with some other cosmic processes, so we can say that the Earth needs changes as a form of life manifestation, which comprises proceeding of physical and other processes.

Hence, it can be concluded that the Earth cannot remain unchanged as long as she lives, as, indeed, she cannot remain unchanged after the death either. Therefore, the fact that its shape changes is a natural and legitimate process taking place in accordance with the program development. What do changes imply?

The Earth, like people, has some organs of its own too, but they are not as explicit as human ones. These areas are characterized by a particular formation, starting with the rocks of ground, soil layers, vegetation, a network of energy channels and numerous «subtle» constructions, which people are not capable of perceiving with an eye. Thus, the Earth's organs are formed in the material and «subtle» spheres in such a way that we'll never be able to see them as something isolated, functioning separately, because we are the small value for the Earth.

Places formed in different ways require different energy recharge.

When the Earth was underdeveloped, it had a structure, primitive and simple for planets and thus it was satisfied with only flora and fauna on it.

In the course of its development, as it grew older, more complex volumes began to be formed within it, which required recharge of other types of energy. Therefore an additional element was required, which through its functioning would provide the given place (organ) with the necessary type of energies. In addition, Cosmic Systems also needed to obtain new energy from the Earth. All this necessitated the creation of a unified mechanism that would combine the needs of the Earth and Cosmic Systems through its single technological process.

Our material world became such a mechanism in which the working elements such as plants, animals, and human beings started producing energy both for the Earth and the Cosmos.

Each of these elements is attached to the habitat area by means of certain climatic conditions, has the formation, appropriate for the place, and works for a particular part of the Earth. And it is the fact that Earth as well as Cosmic Systems required energies of different quality, that the Celestial designers invented nations, races, which began manufacturing various types of energy.

Cities, towns and any other settlements arise on the Earth not spontaneously and chaotically but, firstly, according to the general program of the Earth's evolution and, secondly, on the basis of energy needs for recharge, which places of the planet have. Thus, settlements are always built in places that require intensive energy interchange (roughly speaking, in organs that require power).

In these places of the Earth both energy intake and energy discharge occur, i.e. energy flows are moving, directed here and there and up and down, as there are appropriate energy channels of the Earth here.

As the Earth as a living organism is constantly changing, so external rough changes concurrently occur, which are already visible for the man himself: outlines of continents are changing, the landscape and river channels are changing, and so on.

Methods of restructuring the Earth are earthquakes, floods, Earth's crust faults, failures, changes in weather and climate in general.

On the subtle plane the emergence of increased radiation and increased energy coming from the Cosmos indicates the occurrence of changes in the subtle structure of the Earth.

The goal of any restructuring of the Earth is the correspondence of her formation and quality content to a new coming civilization.

As each civilization, i.e. the new man is built energetically in a new fashion in accordance with the needs required from the Above so it demands a corresponding environment to live in. For new people with their new energies to get acclimatized to the Earth and exist further on, the structure of the planet should have necessarily undergone changes.

Subtle structures of the Earth and material microstructures are saturated with new energy directly through channelers and psychics receiving a huge flow of energy from Hierarchic Systems.

Channelers and psychics built since their birth for maximum reception of the huge energy potential, having received the bulk of huge potential, then redistribute it in a mild form among ordinary people with a lower potential energy (this is the essence of the treatment by psychics, and so on), and the latter distribute it to other people they communicate with, having even smaller energy potential, etc. (The people who believe in the healing through psychics, always have larger energy potential compared to those who do not believe because faith is the extent to determine the maturity of the soul, that is, achievement of a certain energy level in its development.)

Those who are incapable of perceiving new energy die out in a natural way.

Through soil and solar radiation energy is transformed and transferred to plants, animals and so on, all of them being totally interrelated. Through interrelation all of them re-distribute the new to each other by a chain of successive links. Natural conditions are being prepared for the new man.

The Hierarchic System, dealing with nature, introduces new types of plants and animals, which correspond in their constructions to the new needs of the time. Here comes the new civilization and everything around is changing.

And the process of transfer of the planet into a new energy state is referred to as «the transition of the Earth onto a new orbital». With regard to the planet's subtle structures this means not only the new energy qualitative state of the world, but also the emergence of a new body, a certain subtle structure of a higher order than the existing ones. That is, each civilization has developed a framework for the emergence of a new subtle body of the Earth or more precisely – of its sub-bodies.

And the human being, through complex biochemical and physical reactions, developed qualitatively new energies for this body, processing the new energy sent to him by the Hierarchical System. That is, apart from the fact that the man drops low frequencies to the depths of the Earth, into her coarse matter, he supplies its subtle bodies with a higher frequency spectrum as well as with the energies that he develops for Hierarchic Systems.

So the scheme of circulation of energies associated with the man in global processes is as follows: (see Figure 1)

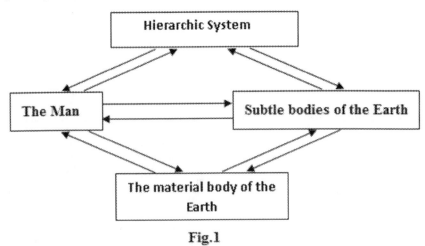

Fig.1

At present (2000)*, the Earth is being transferred onto a new orbital for the sixth time, that is, for the sixth body it will have to develop energy types of a higher order than it has.

All in all the Earth is planned to be transferred onto orbitals seven times. This is the life cycle of our planet at this Level, after that it shall move to a new qualitative state, and therefore disappear as the material body in the star system «Logos», moving to a higher range of existence.

The solar system should disappear along with the Earth and mankind as «the solar system is designed for the same period of its existence along with all its planets».

Transfer of the Earth onto the second, third ... fifth orbital occurred exactly the same way as it takes place concerning the sixth one, that is, They descended messengers, channelers to the planet into the human environment; through them They dropped energy to other people and the Earth.

But for all that, every time energy potential and volume rose from one orbital to another, for instance, during the transition onto the third orbital the potential of delivered energy was lower than during the transition onto the fourth one, and during the fourth it was correspondingly less than during the fifth, and so on.

At the same time, from one civilization to another there was increase in energy amount and its capacity, as the Earth's subsequent body required more pumping and more energy amount, which led in turn to gradual increase in energy capacity of the man, as he had to work under high voltage and process larger amounts of energy.

When the Earth transfers onto a new orbital for the seventh time and fills the corresponding body with the energy of required quality it will reach perfection at this material Level of development, followed by ceasing to exist on the material Level.

«That will be like a single Soul, which will take steps to improve itself on the energy plane i.e. at a new Level of development as well as in other worlds, in other bodies. And the path of its development is as endless as the human one, but in its own direction».

*   *   *

Chapter 2

The Role of Civilizations
for the Cosmos

REASON OF CIVILIZATIONS CHANGING

Introduction

Talking with God about the civilizations, we tried to learn not only the reasons according to which they were created and the ways they were created, but also without going into details to learn a little about their lifestyles, specify the basic conditions of their existence in order to understand the essence of the given processes. Without knowing the way of life it is difficult to reconstruct the true face of civilization and to understand its value.

A lifestyle is regarded as certain situations. Situations in their turn represent the development of specific energy. The situations may be similar, but if people vary in subtle energy formations and their internal structures they also have a qualitatively different chemical composition, then two different persons would produce different energies in identical situations.

The previous civilizations never represented just one ethnic group. At one and the same period of time there could be two, three or more civilizations varying in the development degree and lifestyle.

Some civilizations developed through the technical progress, while others – through the connection with nature, the third ones – through the telepathic communication with Hierarchic Systems. Thus, in such a way the experiments were conducted: which way to direct a person in the future for him to achieve certain results as soon as possible.

– – –

Everything in the world evolves, nothing stands still – this truth is old and it has been existing as long as a man has been aware of it. But sometimes the evolution is carried out in an absolutely different way compared to how people currently consider it to be.

For example, Engels regarded the evolution of man as the path that a species of animal passed from apes to man, improving under

41

the influence of labor. But the evolution of man followed the entirely different way. Even six thousand years ago the appearance of man was apparently the same as now: neither the forehead has grown nor hands have become more nimble because of systematic training. Sometimes we come across some people, whose skull surprisingly resembles a monkey skull and a hand looks so as if he has learned to hold a stone ax for the first time.

All those evidences found in excavations of ancient civilizations that lived a few dozen centuries before our era, can be successfully found in our society, in our villages and suburbs, where life is more primitive.

If one examines the skull of a prehistoric man and that of a contemporary one, but staying at a low development level, hanging around beer stalls, they appear to be identical: the same narrow forehead, large superciliary arches, an outstanding lower jaw, and even walk – on slightly half-bent lower extremities – is all the same. Such individuals may be found in the twentieth century and they are not in single copies.

Our society is mixed by representatives of the Stone Age, of the Iron Age, and by wonderful specimens of man of the future. This medley shows that the evolution follows a somewhat different path than materialists consider it to do.

The evolution of a species occurs only when our Heavenly Teachers from the Above more precisely those who manage and maintain the Earth along the path of progress want that. And a human appearance will change only in case if some efforts from the Above are made to implement it. Although, of course, some mutations happen, but a man will not be allowed to mutate in an arbitrary direction: if it happens, such a copy is destroyed because mutants, like weeds, produce energy of the wrong quality, which Hierarchic Systems do not require.

From the point of view of his appearance, the man of the fifth civilization has remained the same since his creation: he has remained the same as he was created a few thousand years ago. Within the limits of all Earthly civilizations the external form of a human body has remained constant though small deviations took place i.e. the basis was constant, while the parts were polished, replaced, and improved in the desired direction.

The Creators considered the original material embodiment in the form of the primitive man to be an unsuccessful model.

A primitive man existed as a species, but the program that he was given didn't contribute to progress of the soul, as the original wild human being

42

was oriented at eating beings like him. Therefore, the Hierarchic Systems, which are directly involved in mankind, continued to improve its design.

Alternatively, the experiment on creating a human being as a cross-breed of a primitive man with a more advanced model of the Cosmos was carried out. The humanity knows this option as cross-breeding of Gods with wild people. Gods married earthly daughters.

In fact, individuals from other material civilizations located on the highly developed planets, where living conditions were close to the Earthly ones were brought aboard spacecrafts. They introduced into the matter a new genetic code of a more developed person, whose matter in relation to the development level is by several orders of magnitude greater. And initially the code contributed to the progress of the human soul, but when the «Gods» from the high civilization left earth dwellers, then after a few generations degeneracy of a Godman began, followed by a rapid degradation of society.

There were options with a planet perished somewhere and its people carried aboard spacecrafts to the Earth, because her climatic conditions suited well for people in distress. They also made some corrections to the gene pool of an earthly man, but not for a long time. All this did not give the desired results, and space designers continued to improve the biological form of an earth dweller.

Experiments were followed by experiments. Against the background of human existence as a core species new forms such as fishman (mermaid), birdman (phoenix), animalman (centaur), and so on were created. Such forms existed in the second and early third civilizations. But they were not inculcated either, having appeared somewhat flawed.

And then the Material Space Systems by the order of God created a new improved model of man, which went down in history under the name of Adam, and a secondary one – under the name Eve (their real names given to them by the Space System that created them were Rios and Firina, but on the Earth people gave them other names). A material body of a man had to ensure the improvement of souls needed to God, which He reproduced. The body was created – for the soul and for the given Level of earthly matter development, because every level of matter has its corresponding shapes.

Newly-made Adam and Eve were created far outside the solar system, transported onto the spacecraft and brought to our planet together with the accompanying forms of animals. Hence arose the legend of the expulsion of Adam and Eve from Paradise, that is, they were moved from the Creators' Higher worlds to our lower rough world, where they gave life to the improved model of man.

Subsequent experiments were no longer so significant, presenting partial and gradual transformation of the biological structure of humans and animals.

Thus, man was upgraded from civilization to civilization not under the influence of the environment and the survival of stronger animals but under the influence of space engineers who continually adjusted their invention in the same way as modern designers improved the model of the TV. Something was constantly changed in it, improved although our TV remained the same TV. And we have not noticed how for example while maintaining the external shape, all the details inside it changed over the ten years. The same happened to the material human body. But his form improved in accordance with the requirements and needs of God's Hierarchy, not for the Creators' own pleasure, examining the power of their thoughts.

Man was created under God's great plan by a large galaxy of space developers having a wide variety of specialties to bring together in a model the properties of different matters and processes.

When we asked during the contacts: – «How was a man created?» – we were asked to specify:

- "Which civilization are you inquiring about?"

However, in every civilization people were created in different ways, or rather he was created during the first civilization, and modernized in all the others. Therefore, when studying the materials of human origin received through channelers, some books write that man originated in such a way and had such and such initial appearance, others – in another way, the third books –in some other way. And it seems that every channeler, translates wrong information.

In fact everyone is right in his own way, but in the absence of a holistic look at the object they see and describe only the different parts of the whole. Only by combining all these together, we can see that whole and volumetric that parts compile.

Recall the parable of the three blind men who were given to touch an elephant. One touched the tail, and said that the elephant is like a rope, the other touched its leg, and said that the elephant is like a log, the third touched the ear, and said that the elephant is like a big burdock.

So we are in many of our views on the cosmos truths given to us from the Above, similar to those blind. And just because we are given opportunities to combine parts into a whole, it becomes possible to see the object in its full volume.

Incidentally, because of our limited perception of many cosmic truths given to humanity by the Higher, certain truths seem to contradict each other, and hence – to be false. But if you develop a holistic volumetric view of the single, all contradictory things will unite in one whole, manifesting themselves as a sort of harmonic structure.

A man sees things by fragments, that is why he is confused, constantly rejects the old and regards new issues as the firm axiom. But the old is just links in a chain, and the chain is infinite.

If you ask the question: what for the model of the man's material body has improved and is currently improving, then we can answer that, of course, the root is not in a person, but above all – in the needs of the Cosmos and the Earth itself.

The root is the need of Cosmic Systems in certain types of energy. As a person, for example, required rubber for his technics, and a certain process was developed to manufacture it, so is the Cosmos that required some energy for its needs, and the Earth was created for its production. And she required some energy transfer mechanism, which was originally embodied in the form of an animal, and then – of a man. A whole chain of dependent relations was established, which have progressed in their interactions for millions of years.

Everything develops over time, so some needs are replaced by others, now you want one thing, tomorrow – the other. In space terms these requirements stretch for longer periods.

And once a new demand for something emerges, the old construction is corrected or a new one is created in order to meet emerging needs.

Thus, man was created based on the needs of the Cosmos and the Earth, because at a certain stage of development our planet needed for her life some types of energy, and to provide her with these energies a connecting link was needed, so the man appeared. That is, receiving one type of energy from the Cosmos from his Systems, the man processes it, producing high-frequency energy to the Cosmos and low-frequency spectrum – to the Earth.

And it is a complex mechanism of energies interchange for the sake of which a human construction was designed.

And because everything in the Cosmos is multipurpose, the third function, which a model of a person was to perform, was the improvement of the soul and its uplift through the levels of development to Higher Hierarchies.

Having combined all the three functions into a single manufacturing process, a man was settled on the Earth.

Managing and changing internal processes in him, the Space System regulated the production of required energy types and, continuing to experiment on «subtle» structures of a man, it prepared the foundation for a new, sixth civilization.

Based on the needs of the Cosmos, the primary objective of the emergence and change of civilizations can be pointed out: **each civilization is created to produce new types of energy.**

But what then is the evolution of development for humans?

First of all, it implies improvement of the soul. Evolution of the man is not the progress of his material body, but the progression of the soul, which is reflected in its self-development.

The evolution of the body in this regard is absent as there is no self-improvement. Of course, the soul passes through various kinds of living creatures that is, it evolves through insects, birds, animals, and comes, finally, to the human body. But the body itself is not evolving, and changes artificially, by means of systematic work on it by Higher Entities. The presence of a man primitive by appearance in modern society is determined by the evolution of souls of animals entering the human body.

Intermediate forms of bodies are created as evolution stages of living beings, starting from the lowest stage to the man, that is, a soul should accumulate certain qualitative characteristics.

An embryo in the womb of its mother repeats the forms of fish, birds and animals, not because the human body passed through these phases of development was, but because the soul passed through them. And here is the dynamics of its development.

Our fifth* race has finished to exist, and now mankind is in anticipation of the birth of a new sixth race*, which, however, is a continuation of our civilization. The representative of the new race will differ from the modern man, but not so much in appearance (generally among all the external indicators only the color of skin will change) as inside. The main changes will affect his subtle* structures. And it is they that change from civilization to civilization most of all, though the least noticeable.

Introducing corrections into a human form at this stage of development is caused by the need to change the functions assigned to it as a working part of the Cosmos.

What does a change of civilizations mean?

This is the change of functions imposed as duties on mankind, and as the functions change, therefore, the form of the man must be corrected, as the old one is incapable of meeting the new challenges posed from the Above.

Thus, summing up we can say that the main reason to change civilizations is the needs of Hierarchic Systems and the Earth to obtain new forms of energy.

And now let's try to understand the change of civilizations and related changes that occurred with a man over a long period and to determine the role of each civilization to the Earth.

The Reason of Civilizations Emergence

To begin with, the Earth has not existed for ever, but has appeared in the Universe since some relative point of time. We are therefore interested in:

- "What has caused the need to create the Earth for You?"

- "The need for creating your planet came from the Above. The higher Hierarchy required a planet meeting certain material parameters of the Cosmos. The Earth is a part of a huge mechanism, obliged to perform those functions, which should ensure the normal operation of that mechanism."

- "Was there a time when You existed without the Earth?"

- "We worked in a different mode. Then, We were given instructions by Higher structures to create the Earth, and <u>We created her</u>. We also change the work from time to time or, more precisely, switch from one type of job to another."

- "For a long time the Earth managed without humanity. What contributed to the emergence of life on the Earth?"

- «We the Higher created life on the Earth. The need for certain energies contributed to the origin of life, first one species, then the other. Everything created on your planet was determined by the needs of Hierarchic Systems, combined with the development needs of the Earth itself. She had no humanity as long as her development program was simple. But in the course of evolution the program itself was to be complicated in collaboration with Space Systems, thus, creating a need for more complex forms of life that would have introduced a new color in the energy range of colors produced by her. Therefore, since a certain moment of its development, the humanity has become a necessary detail in the transformation of energy between it and the Cosmos. And now the Earth has so accreted with the humanity into a single mechanism that she is not able to do without him, as a clock is unable to work without its gears.

People have a lot of elements of the internal structure of the planet itself, and at the same time, people themselves give a lot of new to the Earth. The Cosmos receives exactly what It needs from their joint work. The Earth and the humanity are working together as, say, your body is working together with the stomach. One cannot do without the other».

- "So the evolution of the Earth needed for the humanity, didn't it?"

-"Yes, to its further evolution. Mankind is a further shape of the Earth's evolution. Only thanks to their joint work the progress of both forms of existence occurs. Therefore the man was created as applied to the united work with the Earth."

- "Did the animal world appear on the Earth earlier or later than the first civilization?"

- "Animals appeared before the first civilization, as it was necessary to produce a lower level of energy. Everything went in the line of ascent, as it is already known to you: first–stones, then –vegetation, then – fauna, then – the human race."

- "Some people suggest that prior to or during the first civilization a gas-like human being existed, having the density like a cloud. Has such a person ever been on the Earth?"

- "No, there were no etheric people, all of them were just material. Probably people confused them with a parallel world. There such creatures were possible."

The First and Second Civilizations

We were interested in the issue of the first civilizations. What a man knows about them is taken from the history, this is his personal understanding of the origins of man on the Earth, his assumptions about how the humanity was born. But what God will tell us concerning this issue, what new will He open to the reader? Therefore, we ask Him the following questions:

- "What was the first civilization like?"

- "The first civilization revealed itself as a first material human that used plants in food. They were involved only in their life support and lived at the level of the prehistoric man, but lived in societies."

- "Were they bisexual or unisexual?"

- "Sex separation occurred immediately with the advent of the man. All the civilizations were androgynous. Although there were particular versions of experimenting in unisex beings, but there were very few of them and mostly in subsequent civilizations."

- "Did the representatives of the first civilization have housing?"

- "Houses were present in all the civilizations."

- "They say that the first people had black skin."

- "No, they were white. Black people appeared in your fifth civilization. There were white, grey people. Then –yellow, then – white people again. And after all there appeared color-mixed specimen. So we experimented, making attempts to achieve the desired result."

- "In which way did the first civilization differ from the second?"

- "The difference was in intelligence and a body size. Initially, already the material man was very large and dullish, in your terms. His mind developed very weakly."

- "Did they have any elementary technical devices invented in a primitive way?"

- "No. They had no technical devices, even the primitive ones."

- "Did they live in wild tribes?"

- "Not so wild as you think, although they led a primitive way of life. There are savage tribes in your civilization too, so that some souls remain on the Earth so far underdeveloped technically and illiterate, as those in the previous civilizations. Moreover, even in your crowded places there are people who lead a primitive lifestyle, despite the fact that they live in a civilized world. So it is all relative."

- "Why did You refuse the first civilization? What didn't they satisfy you with?"

- "Their brain was far from being perfect, as that was our first specimen. Lack of intelligence contributed to insufficient development of a soul, so We had to work in order to improve the human mental apparatus and diminish the size of the body. In the second civilization, his height became shorter, i.e., the structure of the material body was improved; the selected model of body was optimal for conditions of that time. Thereupon the second civilization was making considerable progress. But we kept working towards a more rational model of the human organism."

- "Were the internals being improved too?"
- "At the transition period from the first civilization to the second the whole structure as a whole was adjusted, as changing the size of the material body one had to rearrange the internals in the best way. Everything was being improved and modified."

The Third Civilization

The existence of the humanity on our planet wasn't constant; at one moment it appeared for some reason, at another it disappeared. It was important to understand what caused the emergence of civilization, and what led to the decline and its complete disappearance. Higher Hierarchs and God never disclosed the subject at once, and gave new information in small portions. So to somehow cover this or that subject broadly, we had to reflect for a long time in which direction to develop our knowledge. I started with a question:
- "Did Atlantis exist in the third civilization?"
The Higher Hierarch replied:
- "No, Atlantis existed in the fourth one."
- "What did You create the third civilization for?"
- "To reorganize people's thinking. The man's ability to think was fully dependent on the design of his thinking apparatus, which continued to be imperfect. At the same time, the pace of evolution increased, the man was to be involved in more active circulation of energies, was to improve the quality of mental energies produced, that is, to raise their level. The same trend was applied in respect of the fourth civilization, namely improving the design of a brain apparatus in order to involve the individual in a more active thought process. It was necessary to form new ideas, and this, in the first place, just depends on the brain design."
- "What was new in the design of the brain?"
- "The performance of the pulse ring was successfully improved; besides particular elements were added in the very construction of the physical brain that provided more intensive and fruitful work of the brain."
- "Did the pulse ring exist in all the civilizations?"
-"Yes, because it provided the communication between the man and the Determinant* guiding him."
- "Did people of the third and fourth civilizations have very considerable intelligence?"

- "Yes, they did. We managed to raise a thinking activity of the man to the proper level, thus providing the Hierarchic* System with the required sort of high energies."

- "Why didn't You supply the people of our civilization with the same high intelligence, which was among the representatives of Atlantis, for them to build «flying saucers» or to transfer by means of dematerialization to other points of the Cosmos?"

- "High intelligence produced special energy that was powerful, but sharp. It required to be somewhat extenuated. That is, continuously working to improve the thinking apparatus, We sought primarily the improvement of the quality of the required energy produced by that apparatus."

- "So, You can do the whole civilizations more intelligent or more stupid, can't You?"

- "Yes, it all depends on the reasonable needs of Hierarchic Systems."

- "What was the third civilization represent?"

- "They had a unified nation and a common language, not like you have at present. But it was already a highly developed civilization."

- "In what part of the world was it located?"

- "In those days, the continent was united. Later it was separated into pieces. So the third civilization was located on the single continent."

- "Did they reach the technological progress?"

- "Technically, they were developed enough to fly. Their stay on the Earth ended in such a way that they all flew far beyond the solar system."

- "Why did they leave the Earth?"

- "Their controlling services got to know that a large comet or meteorite would fall down to the Earth. A luminous body was approaching them from the Cosmos. And since there was only one mainland, it could result in their complete destruction. Therefore, they created an artificial planet, say four times less than the Moon, and flew on it into the Cosmos. Their population of the Earth was small, so all of them were placed on the flying island. Nobody stayed here."

- "What did an artificial planet represent?"

- "It was a flat platform, within which there was technical equipment allowing the platform to move in the Cosmos. On top the protective canopy covered the platform. It also kept the atmosphere. That was a spaceship-island with artificial atmosphere and everything necessary for life."

(The writer Swift described this true story, which came to his ears as a legend, in his fantastic story «Flying Island». All experiments carried out by Space* Systems on the Earth, or all those interesting events that occurred there, were left for the next generations as legends)*³ .

- "What happened to the Earth after their departure? Did the expected catastrophe take place?"

- "No, there was no heavy catastrophe. There was an explosion, not so big, caused by the fall of a celestial body on it."

- "Were they rendered technical assistance by other nonearthy civilizations, if they could reach such a high level of development to have created a flying island?"

- "Nobody rendered any technical assistance, although they were in contact with representatives of other civilizations located in the constellation Zetta, of Sirius system. They reached everything using their own power of thought."

- "Did the third civilization itself fly to other planets during its stay on the Earth?"

- "No human civilization has been allowed going beyond your world. Their flights were limited within the spheres of the Earth. And only when the threat of a collision with a celestial body emerged the third civilization was allowed to leave the Earth. But it was the end of their development programs in this world, so they left. And We made room for the development of new people."

- "Where are they located in the Cosmos on their flying island: in our constellation or farther?"

- "They flew very far away and stayed in the constellation, which is not visible from Earth. Therefore, it is not known to people."

- "How long did they exist on their island?"

- "They continue to exist at present, more precisely – their descendants."

- "What type of energy did the third civilization use to lift the island-ship? Was it antigravity force?"

- "No. This type of energy is not known to the fifth race people. This energy is opposite in sign to gravity, it has repulsive properties and belongs to the category of minus energies."

- "How did matters stand with time on their island-ship? In other places of the Cosmos it is different."

---

³   * – See the glossary;)* – the authors' explanation

- "We helped to adjust the flow of time inside their spacecraft and its compatibility with the time of the Cosmos."
- "Did they have power over time?"
- "No. Only We have power over time."
- "But do their descendants have now the same time as it is on the Earth?"
- "No. The time-flow rate varies with the program. And across the universe it is different. Therefore, in terms of adapting to a new place of the universe and changing the program of development their time too gradually changed. Now it is different from the Earth's."
- "How did matters stand with morality in the third civilization?"
- "They were morally highly-developed, so We allowed them flying away, instead of killing them, as We did with Atlantis for having low morality, which attempted to combine high technical development and low morality; the latter is the case of the degradation of society."
- "Did they have religion?"
- "No. They did not require it, because they knew of the existence of Higher Hierarchies standing over them and treated them with respect. They knew the laws of the Cosmos and worshiped them."
- "Were they aggressive and did they have rocket technology at their disposal?"
- "There had neither rocket technology nor aggression. Unlike you, they progressed in a right way."
- "What was it manifested in?"
- "They could move objects, using the power of thought; they had the ability to materialize things. And they went beyond the Earth not on aircrafts, but in subtle* bodies, using the power of thought, too. They did everything by power of thought."
- "How did they manage to reach such a force of intellect?"
- "They were correspondingly built. We were not satisfied with weak thinking of the second civilization; therefore We inserted the special units, which contributed to the thinking in the respective programs, into the brain construction of the following human civilization."
- "Were they capable of teleportation and levitation?"
- "No, they were not."
- "The third civilization was technically well developed. And were their feelings developed too, or intellect alone?"
- "All developed in parallel: both feelings and intellect."
- "Did they develop through suffering or through joy only?"

- "Each civilization on the Earth went through suffering that was the optimal environment to resubtle the emotional and sensory areas of the man."

- "Were there civilizations in which knowledge was imparted not through the training, but, for example, was set in the brain in the finished form in accordance with changes of the time?"

- "No, there were not. All the knowledge was to be developed by individuals in the course of development through hard work on themselves. This is the essence of perfection."

The Fourth Civilization

The present human civilization was preceded by the fourth one. Our historians know a lot of things about it, and many books have been written, so I did not develop this theme globally but asked a few clarifying questions.

- "You said that Atlantis was in the fourth civilization, didn't You?"

- "Yes. Atlantis was the fourth. Modern man is very much aware of it as the most close to him, so We won't say anything new about it."

- "Due to what did Atlantis manage to achieve a high level of development?"

- "Due to the superior intellect given by Us. We tried to somewhat change structure, that is, it maintained a high intellectual potential, but gave milder types of energy. They were half-humans, half-gods. Children of twelve year old and elder thought like adults at their relative maturity, so the whole civilization stepped far forward over a relatively short period of time."

- "Was it the brain alone that improved from civilization to civilization?"

- "No, absolutely everything improved, while maintaining a constant external form."

- "Both the third and fourth civilizations were highly-developed. But what didn't suit You, if You replaced them one after another?"

- "We were not pleased with a set of energies they gave. Each civilization is energetically built in a new fashion and in such a way as to produce certain types of energy for the Cosmos, which vary in a spectrum composition towards high frequencies from one civilization to another. That is, each subsequent civilization should give a higher range of energies than the previous one. And to do this it should be appropriately restructured. Therefore one civilization gave place to another, the man was redesigned to produce new types of energy towards higher frequencies, and the Hierarchic Systems received new products."

- "Where did the souls of the second or fourth civilizations go after the completion of their cycles of development?"

- "They came over to Us. All the souls of the Earth's material world are distributed in Our world."

The Fifth Civilization

The modern man lives and does not think what civilization he lives in, therefore there is a reason to remind him that he is the representative of the fifth civilization. Therefore, I think it will be interesting for him to get to know something about the past of his civilization.

I address the Higher Hierarch the question:

- "Among the people there has appeared the hypothesis that our fifth civilization derives from the warlike race, representatives from Sirius?"

He says:

- «No, this information is not correct. In this case, certain facts were confused. The point is that not all members of the fourth civilization died. Some of them moved into the fifth one and served as the basis for the creation of a new civilization. That was happening the same way as in your case now during the transition from the fifth civilization to the sixth one, it means that the remained representatives of the fourth civilization were to serve as a material basis for the introduction of a new civilization on the Earth. Therefore one can say that some people originated from the residue of the fourth civilization, which was not militant.

Another part was built energetically in a new fashion and brought ready-made to the Earth. From this your second hypothesis about the creation of man arose. Those people were created by Higher Cosmos* Systems of the material Level. And, besides, some people like you were brought to the Earth from the planet, which had undergone a catastrophe. This gave rise to the hypotheses about the migration from Sirius. They were rescued, and this actually happened prior to your civilization. All these options made the man confused.

Each civilization was born in its own way, and during the existence of each of them there were subvariants of either migrations or pilot

55

experiments to establish a new type of man. Therefore, one can say that a lot of experiments were carried out. It does not matter in which way the humanity progressed, more important is where it has come and what results it has achieved».

- "Why were the people of the distressed planet brought to the Earth, rather than to some other place?"

- "Here the natural conditions suited them most of all. Not all environmental conditions are available for constructing dwelling or having food. In the wilderness, they would have had neither this nor that. On the Earth, it was all about the same as in their old world."

- "How were those people transported, and who did it?"

- "There is a special organization in the Cosmos, which is specially engaged in providing assistance in space to those who suffered the disaster for some reason. They are at a very high level of development and thus they transported the distressed using space ships, in other words, very large stations. There were a great number of people being transported. So more advanced Systems helped them resettle. As you can see, there are migrations in the Cosmos: some fly away from your planet, others settle on it."

- "But is this done with Your permission, or accidentally?"

- "Everything related to the Earth is made with Our permission, as the Earth is Our object."

- "Did those who carried people aboard space ships, help them settle down in the new place?"

- "No, it was not included in their duties any more. Only delivery at the place."

- "So, can it be assumed that the fifth civilization partially originated from them too?"

- "No. All the old forms of a biological structure died out gradually over time, since their constructions did not fit the new time energy-wise and were not able to perceive a new increased potential of energy coming from the Cosmos. This potential could only be accepted by a new improved model of man. And those who were transported, and who moved from the fourth civilization, created just a transitional moment for the next civilization to grow accustomed; being old forms they became extinct, while the new rooted and started to progress."

- "How did black, white and yellow races emerge on the Earth? What purpose were they created for?"

- "The needs of the Cosmos for different kinds of energies were amplified, as well as the formation of the Earth itself changed, which demanded more various types of energy received from the man. Therefore various models of a man were designed, meant for different frequencies of energies. The very color of people implied the trend of increasing frequencies from dark to light, in other words, the black race produced the lowest range of frequencies, the yellow one – medium, and the white – the highest frequencies. These types of the man were created by different Space Systems, more precisely, each System created its own type of man, its own race to get the type of energy it required."

- "Were the races created in different places?"

- "Yes, they were created by different Material* Systems and in different places. But all these Systems are under My control."

- "In what sequence did the races populate the Earth?"

- "There was no sequence. All of them were settled in the fifth civilization simultaneously, but in different places. Each of them had its own predetermined way of development, its own purpose, and after death they go to their own Distribution Centers. But different objectives do not imply that the races should quarrel among themselves. All should live in peace at one Earth. But due to his low development level the man makes the wrong choice."

- "Can the soul move from one race to another, if souls belong to different Space Systems?"

- "It happens sometimes, but only in case of need. Typically, each System deals with its own souls by itself, brings them to the set level of perfection and collects them. In case of need or necessity, of course, the soul can move from a lower to a higher race, but not vice versa. The white race is considered the highest on Earthly plane for the people of the fifth civilization."

- "What purpose was set for the fifth civilization?"

- «The purpose was to develop the human BRAIN at least to fifty percent. But your civilization has developed it only to ten percent, thus not fulfilling the task set.

Your subtle bodies* have not developed well either, although there was set a goal – to the end of the fifth civilization, that is, by 2000, to develop five subtle bodies, the five subtle bodies. And you have very few people that have coped with this task and developed their five subtle bodies, that is, they can simultaneously exist in the material body and four subtle bodies. This is manifested in the ability to get into one of them on one's own wish and receive information at the given level of the matter. This goal has not been achieved. The man has deviated away from the set purpose due to the freedom of choice given in the program».

The Transition Period from the Fifth to the Sixth Race

We know that there have been different civilizations, different races on the Earth. But how is the transition from the previous to the next one accomplished? We'll try to find it out at least for the present moment during the transition of the fifth race of the sixth.

- "Now (1998)* much is said about the transition of the humanity to the level of «fire». What does this mean?"

- «First of all, this process is linked with the emergence of a new sixth race, more energy intensive than the fifth one. Since the program of human development is changing, energy-carriers are also changing, that is, a human being like a certain unit of energy, increases in his energy level. He should take new, more powerful energy upon himself, which is going from the Cosmos, should work with the new type of energy, but the old construction of his, which is not designed for taking a more powerful potential of the Cosmos energetics*, is not able to accept it and give the desired result.

Transition to the level of «fire» is a metaphorical comparison. But the process itself reflects descending onto the Earth from the Cosmos, or rather from My Hierarchic Systems, of very high energetics; its power is so great that it is able to burn down every living being of previous versions, if it is managed improperly».

- "Is such a transition from the old energy to the new one available to a modern man?"

- "Those, who this transition is not available to (spiritually they are mostly highly undeveloped people), will die out within a short period of time. But some people will move into a new race, as the preparation of their material and other bodies is already going on quite successfully through the transformation of the entire biological structure."

- "What is the transformation of a human body?"

- "The old version of man has some reserve of cells capable of transmutation, i.e. able to adjust from the old to the new mode of operation. On average, the transmutation of a medium-level human is twenty percent; among the most advanced in the spiritual plane it may be as large as fifty percent."

- "Can a person accelerate the percentage of transformation of his body, and in what way?"

- "Preparation of the material body to the transitional period has been taking place for the whole last century, not just for the last twenty years.

To do this, some people, mostly psychics, beforehand, since their birth date, were constructed in such a way as to take on a powerful stream of energy and transform it through themselves to other people. The work of psychics with masses of sick people is caused by this reason, that is, psychics gradually delivered to them through themselves small doses of new energy of a smaller potential compared to what they took upon themselves. The same work is performed by channelers, but they mostly broadcast new energy to people through the new information.

Between people there have spread all sorts of exercises and meditation to promote self-work with new energies. Therefore, any person, through treatment, listening to the new information, and working with new techniques can accelerate the material body's percentage of transformation. But there are those who cannot do it all the same.

If a person has come a short way in his development and, consequently, is spiritually undeveloped, he will not accept the new energetics and gradually go into the past as the representative of the body of the old version. He will not be able to withstand the power of the new energy. But at the same time, no representative of the fifth civilization will be able to achieve one hundred percent of transmutation, as the previous model of a human being has become obsolete at this stage of the humanity's evolving, and if, for example, a car has run on petrol, it won't run on water. A new type of fuel requires a new processing mechanism, a new formation of the engine, although externally it can remain the same. The same is with a human being».

- "Consequently, there is a stratum of people capable of transforming the body, isn't there?"

- "Yes, there is. It is not noticeable in outward appearance, but changes in energetics of the cell as well as in energetics all of the subtle constituents of a man are taking place."

- "Will the entire stratum be transforming the body synchronously or at different speeds?"

- "Of course, everyone will do it differently. People are not identical. Everything depends on the person's spiritual development."

- "What was the transformation percentage of infants born by the end of 2000?"

- "It was different. Everything depended on their programs. The transition period lasts from 1900 and will end after a few centuries after 2000. In the beginning of the new era people of diverse levels will dominate, and this motley of levels will last till the middle of the millennium and a little longer. It is not so easy to move from the old human design to the new one; everything will occur mostly on the subtle plane and will not be noticeable in the outward appearance. Then a gradual alignment of human development will occur and, by the end of a new era, the humanity will become single-level, i.e. having one level of development. In other words, one can say that the complete transformation of the body will take place in two hundred and fifty-five hundred years after the year of 2000, many generations later. The contingent of the sixth race representatives will be formed."

- "There is a great flow of energy from the Cosmos to the humanity. Is it spread to the Earth too?"

- "We send new energy simultaneously to the Earth and to the humanity. The emergence of the sixth race is directly connected with the transfer of the Earth to a new orbital, i.e. with the planet's transition to a higher trajectory on the energy plane. The Earth also is making a transit to a new state of energy through the transformation on its planetary level."

- "Are orbit and orbital different things?"

- "These are different concepts. An orbit is the path of the planet's motion, while an orbital is a new energetic state of the planet. Transit to a new orbital means the transition to a higher Level of development."

- "What is primary in this case: the emergence of the sixth race causes the transfer of the Earth to a new orbital or vice versa – the Earth is transiting to a new state and this requires the emergence of a new race?"

- "These two processes occur simultaneously and are interconnected, because <u>they cannot exist without each other</u>. People of the fifth civilization, having transited to a new orbital together with the Earth, will die out, because they will not stand the new frequencies of energy, which would correspond to a new state of the planet. You know that the biological structure of a man contains a large number of physical elements of the Earth's internal structure. And if the components of the Earth have changed and those of a man – have not, or vice versa: energy components in the structure of a man have changed, but Earth's remain the same, it would cause great derangement of both of them. That is, one cannot exist without the other and their impact is interdependent.

<u>Earth transited to the new orbital after the first race, and after the second ... Now it is the sixth time that it transits to a new orbital</u> after the completion of the fifth cycle of civilization. Now it is <u>the sixth orbital meant for the sixth race</u>».

- "Is the planet's transition to a new orbital possible without participation of the humanity?"

- «No, it is not. When there were no civilizations on the Earth, it did not transit to any orbitals. If the planet is young, newly established, it can for a while develop at a low level without living beings. Then as it evolves it gets inhabited with living creatures. Their joint work continues, which prepares the planet for the first transition to the new state.

Civilizations do not just live and develop for themselves, but they are the necessity that prepares the planet for higher stages of development".

- "Did Earth's transition to the second, third orbital, and so on, happen exactly the same as it happens now to the sixth one?"

- "Regarding the humanity, the transition was accomplished the following way: that is, We descended channelers, envoys onto the Earth. Trough them We discharged energy on other people and the Earth. What is for example the essence* of the phenomenon of Christ and his apostles? Through them descending of new energies to the Earth for the next two thousand years was accomplished. Therefore, Christ himself and his apostles were constructed energetically in a proper way to take on themselves the enormous potential of new energy discharged onto the Earth.

And what is the essence of the present envoys, i.e. you? The essence is that you are also energetically built in a proper way, but are already designed for a greater energy potential than it was two thousand years ago. Therefore, the souls of new envoys have been selected under a special plan, and they are not just souls of former people who have attained a high level of development, but the souls that passed through the stage of human development, and have already passed the stage of development of planets, i.e. they were small planets and therefore are capable of withstanding the enormous potential of energies discharged through them onto the Earth.

This is especially true for the souls of direct channelers, their energy capacity is immense. Ordinary people would have simply burned out on the first communication session. Direct channelers have souls of planets, which are endowed with special power. And We had a lot of work to ensure that such a powerful soul, as A* has ... (referred to the channeler's Cosmos name), could become implanted in the human material body without burning it out. Therefore a number of protective measures have been developed for the material body to function normally on the human plane. Channelers and envoys transmit energy to people and the Earth, saturating them with new energy».

- "There are many channelers at present. Are there any souls of former planets among them?"
- "No. It is only our envoys that have souls of planets."
- "What did the transitions of the Earth to the new orbitals differ from each other in?"
- "Firstly, the planet during transition to a new orbital becomes a stage higher in its development. It's like a human transition from one class to another. Secondly, the previous energy was quantitatively less and weaker in terms of power. When your first civilization transited onto the first orbital, for example, very little energy was passing. But it was enough for them to transit.

Also, a small energy potential was discharged later for the second civilization's transition into the third one. Then the energy began to grow. But even if you take Christ, the energy potential discharged through him was a thousand times weaker than that passing through these envoys, although the soul of Christ, before his mission on the Earth was determined, had already passed the stage of development through a small planet too. But in the course of evolution the needs of the Cosmos increase and the energy power of the modern envoy a thousand times more than the energy power of Christ. And at the moment any modern channeler surpasses him in relation of energy potential, and it is connected with the general evolution of both the Earth and people. That is, from civilization to civilization the volume of energy discharged from the Cosmos and its energy power increase".
- "What is the energy and physical essence of the Earth's transition to a new orbital?"
- "The energy essence is in the relationship of two processes: changes in qualitative state of people and planet. This is a single process – transition of the fifth civilization into the sixth and of the Earth – to a new orbital. And one from another is inseparable.

The physical essence of the transition is that Earth, physically remaining in her old orbit as the path of motion, transfers to a new state: her energetics is changing; the processes within her and her subtle bodies are also changing. But time remains the same".
- "How many times will the Earth transfer to new orbitals?"
- "If everything We have conceived come true, then it will do it seven times. This is the cycle of your Universe. But there may be more. It all depends on how the following civilizations will develop."
- "Are other planets transferred to other orbitals in the same way?"

- "No. And the reason is as follows. Our experiment with people, conducted on the Earth, did not succeed. Every time people gave Us unwanted deviations in the development. Therefore, We have continuously, from civilization to civilization, improved your experiment. And at the moment it keeps being conducted. When We bring it to the end We will see in the development process, what to do next. On other planets of your system things go on well. Everywhere everything is subtle, except the Earth."

- "Assuming that the Earth will continue to develop normally, what will it reach when it transits to a new orbital for the seventh time?"

- "The Earth will reach planetary perfection."

- "And what will happen to her after the seventh orbital?"

- "She will no longer exist on the material level. That will be as if she is a single soul, which will take new steps to improve on the energy plane, and of course – in other worlds in other planetary energy states, i.e in other bodies. Similar bodies exist now, too, although you do not see them. So, in general, it is a long and wide path of development.

* * *

Chapter 3

Golden Race

SIXTH (GOLDEN) RACE

Every civilization carries a lot of mysteries. Scientists can only guess, what ways they developed, but the Creators have their own explanation of everything, coming from a true knowledge. Therefore, we started with a simple question:

- "Can we say that the sixth race takes its origin from the fifth one?"
- "Yes, a new race emerges based on the old one, through the transformation of the energy structure of the body. And a few centuries shall pass before the internal structure will be completely reconstructed, and We will get what We require. The very human physiology and way of life will change."
- "Will the sixth race be like our fifth?"
- "Races themselves cannot be compared, because they are different in design, though in outward appearance it will not be noticeable for you. They have everything different: quality of energy, programs, and ways of life. You see, the reason is that when We want to obtain souls of a certain quality, We construct in a special way their bodies and create a civilization or race with an appropriate lifestyle. Each civilization gave Us a certain type of souls. After that it became useless, and was destroyed physically. But the souls themselves, having a set of energies in the matrix, which We required, continued to develop further. And the accumulated type of energies continued to grow in them, but at a higher level. It is the same with you: when We needed your energy, We created the man of the fifth race. Now We need the new, and We have changed the design of the man so that it corresponds to the functions entrusted to the representative of the sixth race. So changes take place permanently, and one race cannot be compared to another, as they are so individual and specific different."
- "Why do You call the sixth civilization a race?"
- "Civilization is a somewhat diversified structure of society, dividing into nations, nationalities and other subspecies. The new sixth race will represent a single nation. Division into groups and subgroups will cease. The entire society will represent a whole – a single nation, one people, that

should help end the war. Of course, all this will happen not immediately but gradually."

- "How long will the sixth race exist?"

- "Perhaps it will take a millennium, if everything goes without any deviations from the program. Otherwise, it will take perhaps a longer period. The complete program is also intended for two thousand years."

- "Will the subsequent civilizations develop more rapidly?"

- "Yes. Acceleration of development will occur as when souls transit from civilization to civilization, the degree of their development increases. Souls with larger volume of previous knowledge will come to the sixth race, and they will require an accelerated pace of development."

- "Will the development in the seventh race be accelerated to a greater extent?"

- "Yes, the acceleration will increase. However, this is a theoretical assumption. Practice makes its changes. Therefore, to me more exact, We still do not know what will happen to your Earth in the future. All this may happen not to be. People constantly give deviations towards degradation, so We watch you, and think – «what to do with Earth». It all depends on people themselves, in what way their development will progress."

- "If the pace of development increases, therefore, will the process of reincarnation change too?"

- "Yes, soul will participate in the cycle of life and death more often. In the sixth race the time and number of incarnations will change, because the soul will become more developed and will reincarnate more often, stay in the subtle plane for a shorter period of time, i.e., one will die and almost immediately be given a new body. And as representatives of a new race are highly developed, then the burden on them will certainly increase: one person will be able to perform a program of four people of your civilizations, because they will have to fulfill their goal for several lives, not for tens or hundreds of incarnations, as before. The sixth race will progress in its development more rapidly than the fifth one, not only due to the fact that more advanced souls will be involved in the process, but because We have laid a more rapid mechanism to pass the program, meaning that We have given them some opportunities of extrasensory plane, some abilities of the subtle plane, so that they would quickly come to the set goal."

- "Does the purpose of human development remain the same, but improved?"

- "No. Representatives of the sixth races have another goal. But they have to achieve it entirely because your civilization has not achieved it."

- "They will by-complete our goal; and what new goal is set before them?"

- "They shall develop six subtle bodies, six bodies, and all the knowledge related to the six subtle bodies. Also, their brains should be developed at least to ninety percent, because the seventh race is obliged to develop the brain to totally one hundred percent. But the beginning has to go from here, from the year two thousand, so that later people would be able to achieve the one-hundred-percent development of the brain. You know that the fifth civilization, which was to develop brain to fifty percent, has developed it, on average, only to six percent, and in rare cases – up to ten percent, it means that its underfulfillment is high."

- "If a person of the sixth race combines three or four programs, how will this affect his behavior? Will he have spare time?"

- "He will become more active. As for free time, it will necessarily be given to him. The man without free time is not a man, but a robot. I will always have it at least it will be in my worlds. But the individual himself will better use the freedom provided to him and direct it not for pleasure, but on self-improvement, so he will work both on the material and spiritual bodies, involving all his envelopes. The aim of the new advanced programs is to make people work on each plane he is. But, of course, this is distant future. However, We are on the way to it."

- "Will all three or four programs develop sequentially or in parallel?"

- "In parallel, in other words, people will immediately be able to work simultaneously in several directions."

Nature

What unknown to us does the so well-known nature hide? On this issue we appealed to God:

- "How is the practical program to change natural conditions on the Earth for the sixth race being implemented?"

- "Every civilization, as it has energetically designed in a special way, requires the corresponding environment. If the energy of a man is changed, then first of all the structure of the planet should be modified for the energy to get acclimatized and exist on the Earth. Its subtle constructions and material microstructures are saturated with new energies directly through the man of the fifth civilization, through channelers and psychics receiving a huge flow of energy from the Cosmos and redistributing it to other people and animals. People, being saturated with new energies, introduce the new acclimatized and already transformed in cells energy into soil in the process of putrefaction after their death, that is, energetics of soil, of its constituent elements changes, assimilating material bodies after their death. Hence due to the changes in soil energetics of material basis construction of flora and fauna also changes.

And in such a way a qualitative basis of the Earthly plane will be reconstructed. In addition, huge radiation is being discharged onto the Earth. Afterwards, it will decrease to normal. But after such great energy, being discharged by Us onto the planet, mutations in the structure of all living things will occur. Other cultures of flora as well as new species of fauna will emerge. It is new energy and, of course, radiation that influence the cell. However, radiation will influence the mutation only in the beginning, and then they will stop, having turned into sustainable forms of flora and fauna."

- "Will the landscape be reconstructed?"

- "Certainly, it will. Natural conditions, except little changes, will remain the same, i.e. the temperature of habitat, natural cover. However, the landscape will change, and this is happening now. Land reduction and water coverage increase will take place. And at the initial stage of Earth's reforming it will be implemented through cataclysms. The initial year of two thousand is basic, when major changes on the surface will start. These reformations will temporally stretch. A large part of land will go under water. But later, in a century, everything will stabilize and be quiet; destructive hurricanes, earthquakes, and floods will stop."

- "For what purposes will the water cover of the Earth increase?"

- "It is all connected with the change of energetics. The new sixth race will begin producing much energy, so it is necessary to increase energy reservoirs. Water has great energy intensity, so the seas and oceans will accumulate a greater amount of energy. So the increase of Earth's water cover means above all increase of its energy storages. Any changes in natural conditions now are associated with the emergence of a new race."

- "Will the firmament in the sixth race change?"

- "Yes, it will, but slightly. It should be mentioned that it has already begun to change. And American scientists have already recorded the initial movement of stars, some of which have disappeared, others – appeared. The transit of Earth to a new orbital, which is the transformation of her energy state, will cause changes in the energy exchange between all the celestial bodies. The Earth will require new types of energy of higher frequencies, so new high-frequency translators will be required. It is this need that the changes of Earthly firmament are connected with."

How the Man will Change

The future is always uncertain. But sometimes it can be found from God's «lips». And we decided to find out about it at least a little, but to disclose it not for ourselves but for the humanity.

- "Now (1999) the population is declining on the Earth, although the total number of mankind is very large, – we applied to God. – In the future, as You have said earlier, it is planned to keep a third of the population of the Earth. Where will the rest of souls go? Or will some reserve of souls remain on the subtle plane?

A part of souls will be decoded*. Some will go to the lower Hierarchy Level, some – to other worlds, and all those who correspond in their quality parameters, will transit to the sixth race. And then in the new race there will be an intensive circulation of souls: some will leave; others immediately will come to replace them. But they will be born in the new improved body, which will be pre-saturated and filled with energy from the Earth; in other words, this increased energetics will descend to the material body. This did not take place in the fifth race, because one could take energy from nowhere, and since the year of two thousand that reaction will start."

- "What is it required for?"

- "For man in the new environment with increased energy of everything around him it will be easier to survive. If for example you envoys – people with high energy– are implanted into an unprepared material body, as by the way it happened at this moment, to be more precise, the body was not quite ready, that's why you «are burning» and have all sorts of deviations in physical state, then other people will have deviations in health too. Great energy will begin to tear a material body. This will not happen with new race. We are placing a new gene energy fund, which will support the material body in a state of very high energy pumping. This will allow creating a greater potential for pumping of the material body. The soul that will come to the prepared body will have a huge energy potential too, and they will match each other. This will enable the soul to exist very easily and painlessly, therefore many diseases of the outer body will no longer exist."

- "You have said that some souls of the fifth race will move to the sixth one. Which parameters of development will be taken into account?"

- "As the sixth race will be more spiritual, it will include only souls who have attained certain standards in the spiritual and mental development. The man should be comprehensively developed. Those souls who have not attained the required performance will be directed to the lower worlds, as they will not cope with the pressure to be assigned to the human being in future."

- "How will the man of the sixth race differ from that of the fifth race?"

- "The people will have closer link between the material body and subtle bodies. Changes in very subtle structures will occur: the number of bodies will increase from seven to nine. And that will followed by mastering of such abilities as levitation, telepathy, the ability to fly out of the material body and others, which are at present in their infancy. But, of course, the properties will be disclosed neither by chance nor at will but in accordance with the program.

The human mental outlook will broaden and the man will see objects in the Cosmos that are not available for the perception to your contemporaries. In addition, they will be able to see the parallel worlds of the Earth, parallel in terms of the Cosmic existence and, consequently, they will be able to watch other forms of life. But all this will be possible thanks to the ability of flying out of the material body. People will be able to fly in subtle states, dematerialize in the Cosmos and possess many others, which is beyond the present comprehension. The sixth race is designed for complicated existence."

- "Will they see in the range of infrared and ultraviolet frequencies?"

- "Yes, of course, as their properties will become subtler, although the similar is already available for some representatives of the fifth race. The sixth race will have a larger range of perception. In addition, some of them will be able to look through material objects as if they do it through transparent glass. And all these new properties will be possible only thanks to changes in subtle structures of the man. And due to the fact that he is designed in a different way compared with the representative of the fifth race, his nutrition will partially change too. Basically, it will be vegetable food, fish; besides, a large number of gifts of the seas and oceans will be introduced in diet. But the most important thing is that a human being will start to get besides regular material food energy supplement from his Determinant, i.e. it will be sent to him from the Cosmos. But only people of the seventh and eighth races will completely move on to a new kind of energy."

- "In the fifth race people have already developed enough their astral body. Will it continue its improvement in the new race and, in this connection, will art development influencing it progress in the future?"

- "Other Levels of development will be present in the sixth race for some time, so at first the art will be required to improve their subtle bodies because they are not at an adequate level yet."

Evil and Wars

- "Now the relations between human beings are far from ideal: there is anger, envy. Will these features be overcome in the next race?"

- "In the future, all these remain for the Earthly plane, but to a much lesser extent. And, besides, these qualities will also be constructed in another way, and will manifest themselves in other things. The man will begin to envy spiritual wealth rather than material benefits. Minus qualities will get another basis."

- "They say that in the sixth race the forces of evil will change their tactics and begin to act through charm and love? Now they for example act through deception and aggression."

- "Devil always starts with the charm and ends with the evil."

- "What will be the purposes of the evil in the new race?"

- "They will remain the same as in the fifth: to subordinate to itself as many individuals as possible, avert from the way that leads to the Plus Hierarchy, and gather as many souls as possible in their Minus System."

- "If the forces of evil keep existing, will wars continue to be conducted on the Earth?"

- "At the very first stage of development of society, that in your calculation is a hundred or two hundred years, maximum – three hundred, wars will continue, as the nature of the man will not be sufficiently restructured yet, and together with him a lot of minus qualities will come from the fifth race, which taking into account introduction of new programs and new habitat, will be gradually eliminated."

- "Will it be connected with the abolition of nations?"

- "This will be connected with the formation of the people's true kingdom on the Earth, of that which should exist here, and of course with the extermination of Devil on the Earth. Thus, origins that feed His

System should disappear. And His expulsion should occur necessarily in the sixth race. It must exterminate Devil finally, destroying in itself that which serves as His basis. This is primarily related to the improvement of the man's soul, to his self-consciousness, which will reach such a high level, that humans will need no temptations or lower amenities any more. They will start being rejected by his soul and also become as disgusting as eating raw meat for a civilized man. What is a titbit for a savage is disgusting for a highly civilized person. And this is already the progress of a soul.

By the end of the sixth race people should reach such a level of development that all these amenities that evoke positive emotions in a modern mid-level person will evoke rejection in a highly developed individual. Off is the evil in the soul of man – and it will disappear from the Earth. It is that important that people should understand."

Public Way of Life

Public life of humanity changes from civilization to civilization. But how do Higher Teachers suppose to build it in the future? With this question I applied to God:

- "What will the social life in a new civilization be like? What will it be based on?"

- "At the core of society is the family unit as a cell of the large body. Families will always exist, as long as there is the man in the form in which he resides at present. Higher ideals will remain, but will take the more real shape, the man will know – to what and for what he should strive. The society will also continue to hold on love, mutual respect and common goals, but all these will become apparent at a higher level. However, family relations will be corrected."

- "Will the statehood be kept in the sixth race?"

- "Initially, the state remains for a while. It is necessary to keep different peoples in the obedience. But the qualitative structure of society will change over the millennium. The nations and peoples will remain only at the beginning of the sixth race, then the old forms will die out naturally, but they will be replaced by a new race. The Earth will be a single nation, or simply – race, limited in territorial extent, as water will cover the majority of land. There will be one nation, one race on the Earth; therefore the need for state will vanish. For this reason, there will be no wars. There will be no one to fight with. And, of course, one should not forget of the high consciousness of people themselves. Over time, a new social way of life will emerge."

- "Who will lead the new race: a woman or a man?"

- «At first, starting from the second millennium (2000)* rulers will change very often. Now men rule, and then after some time they will be replaced by women, and they will lead the society for some time, and then again men will assume power.

The fact is that We, according to the program at the previous level at which the Bible was written, put men at the head of the list. Therefore, the Bible was written for these men. And they ought to have achieved a high level of development and use their brain at fifty percent, rather than six, as it takes place at the moment. But they did not manage to reach that level, which was planned originally two thousand years ago.

Total degradation has begun. Family relations have also formed in such a way that a woman pulls on herself both her husband and the whole family, again, not in accordance with the Bible. Therefore, by the year two thousandth, the woman has come forward, although, as We say, this was not planned.

Therefore, at the beginning of the next era the woman will prevail – it will last approximately for four or five hundred years, but may be less, depending on how a man will get on his feet, and how will the development of mankind will progress. Freedom of choice is given, and people will continue to use it, although some programs will be stricter, i.e. the percentage of choice will decrease to correct the humanity's deviation made by the fifth race. In connection with all this the woman will rule for the first half of the next millennium, but then the man will acquire the qualities that he ought to have had before and will have them in sufficient quantity, which allows to fill gaps both in the individual and previous society. This race will rise properly and will bear the name of «GOLDEN RACE» with honor."

- "Is it called the golden race?"

- "Yes. It's already called so, but so far it has not lived up to its name."

- "For what qualities is it called «golden»?"

- "This will be the race of higher energy intensity compared with all the previous civilizations, that is, the number of people on the Earth will become two-thirds (2 / 3) less than now, but they will produce energy for the Cosmos, or in other words, for certain Hierarchic

Systems, two-three times as much. One person will work for three-four individuals of your race. In this regard, it was required to dramatically increase the volume of the seas and oceans, where excess energy will be discharged to. At first, while the area of water cover has little increased, people will use gold and stones with a rigid crystal lattice to discharge the excess energy.

Moreover, at first, energy from people will be dispersed on precious metals and stones. Therefore, people will esteem them. But if now people do not know why the gold is marked out as a precious metal among others, the sixth race will know the truth – what for they need gold and jewels. A man will cease to idolize them, and will learn to appreciate their true qualities."

- "What are these properties?"

- "Gold is the conductor of subtle energies. Therefore, domes on the church ought to be made of gold. The people of the sixth race will discover many new properties of both gold and precious stones."

- "Will gold absorb the energy of people?"

- "It will absorb and store its surplus."

- "If the sixth race starts producing a lot of energy, will it have certain techniques to do this?"

- "Special techniques will not occur. The very organism will start producing energy three to four times as much, and this will be implemented due to their special construction, and through the program developed. Of course, in their outward appearance they will remain the same as you, but their power* potential will increase many times, the energy pumping* of subtle bodies will increase. And besides quantity, the quality of energetics itself will become very important. And it will change towards the characteristics We require."

- "Will the quality of energy produced by man be based on the correct way of life or on the improved design of man?"

- "Both are relevant. More precisely, the right way of life stems from the improved design and the <u>design depends on the development level of the soul</u>. Therefore, if the construction of the external body and its subtle components change together with the change of civilization, or for other reasons, the lifestyle of a living being adequately changes as well as ways of feeding, housing, and everyday life. The image of cities and outside area of residence will change too. The sixth race will have more planted forests and other greenery."

Manufacturing

In every civilization social and production life goes its own way; technologies change, materials used by people as well relations between different groups of society change too. Therefore, in anticipation of the birth of a new race a reasonable question arose:

- "Will a new race develop through industrial or agrarian relations?"
- "During the transition period both will keep existing. People will not be able to produce anything alone, so the overall production will continue to exist for about three to five hundred years. Then there will be no need for them."
- "Do You have similar examples on other planets?"
- "Like the Earth? Yes, I do."
- "If production keeps its existence, will there remain exploitation of some people by the others on the basis of the old industrial relations?"
- "The exploitation of other people's work will continue, perhaps, till the mid-millennium. But concurrently free creativity and merging with nature will get enormous scope. Man cannot imagine another way of development and does not know that in nature there is everything you need to live, and you can take it without technology and sophisticated production. Using natural resources properly, a man can live alone without a roof over his head and society."
- "Will Earthly and cosmic technology be advanced in the new race?"
- "Yes, the technology will continue to improve until the person develops those abilities that We have put in him. People will become higher regarding both a development level and energy potential than the present generation. At present ordinary people are equal with computers relative to development. Therefore, the computer enslaves lower-level individuals. The new race of people will be much higher, and although computers will also grow, they won't be as good as people, so they will not be able to enslave them. And only by the end of the sixth race the man will come closer to nature, to understanding of it, and up to that moment he will continue to take great interest in technology. But the higher-order technology itself, namely a cosmic one, will also be close to nature, to its clean energy.

Nature will be able to provide such opportunities so that your crafts could fly using natural substances, that is, people will learn to use something that they cannot see now. At the turn of the seventh race the man will begin to learn how to use natural features. And that means that he will master those fundamentals that We have put in a man, that is to manipulate the properties. People will be able to move without their own bodies as well as move objects, and the need for techniques will be no longer relevant. Now, these isolated cases put people into horror, force them to go mad, although they are ordinary and most natural manifestations of future properties."

- "Consequently, will the man find new types of energy when current earthly resources are depleted?"

- "First, he will use the old fuel, because the new one would require too powerful technologies that, at the beginning of a new era, people will not have. But then We will help and assist."

- "And what will be the driving force in the development of society?"

- "A new religion i.e. the area of certain new knowledge will become the driving force of society. It will promote the individual to a goal."

- "Will special rules to worship God and the Higher be introduced in a new society?"

- "Yes, the old religion will gradually cease to have significance because there will come people with new consciousness that will know the true essence of what is taking place in the Cosmos. People will become aware of the rules and laws of subordination in Hierarchies of the Cosmos, and consequently, of the rules to worship and obey the Higher and at the same time – of the rules and laws to manage the Inferior."

- "What primary goal will people follow in the sixth race?"

- "The main goal is self-perfection of a soul. It keeps for any civilization."

Family

Time introduces novelty not only into the surrounding landscape, but into the man's life, his lifestyle, and social sphere as well. Each age imparts its own color to family relations. We are well aware of the way they evolved in the past, but what like will they become in the future? This question I addressed God.

- "You have said that family relations will remain in the subsequent race. On the basis of what will the family keep: on the basis of love, some economic relations or other purposes?"

- "Love remains principal in the relationship between human beings, on what marriage should be based."

- "What main goals will marriage follow in the «golden» race?"

- "The main goal is a mutual improvement of each other. There also remains a goal of growing decent descendants together."
- "What parameters will the Higher be guided by in the selection of married couples?"
- "The level of energetics and, consequently, the development level of both as well as the degree of spirituality will be taken into account. There are many parameters. For every human being is an individual approach, individual program."
- "Now all our marriages are mixed, high-level and low-level people unite. Will this trend continue?"
- "New social relations will change a lot between people. And, of course, the relationship of spouses will change; the family will become more stable, firm, because without that foundation a firm society cannot be created. Family relations will be based on one-level partners, thus avoiding marriage instability and, as a new race will be replenished by more mature souls, as compared with the fifth, they will have such an ability as a «seeing» of a partner, «seeing» of another person. Of course, not everyone will develop this ability, but one of a couple will certainly do.

In addition, they will have developed intuition and seeing of human constructions on the energy plane. These unique people: some having telepathy, some – intuition, some – analytical logic, will be able to understand the essence of a man and not to enter into a marriage with him, if the essence doesn't suit by some parameters.

Of course, there will be offered various options to check spouses to be, and the choice of the most suitable partner, the most optimal choice will depend on the man's experience, on the maturity of his soul. But there won't be improper marriages any more. At least, in case one chooses the wrong partner the Determinant will give a person some signs that they are incompatible. Therefore, the quality of family relationships will highly increase."
- "Should marriages be kept till the end of life or, as required, may they be cancelled?"
- "Divorcement will be no longer relevant. In the golden race men will achieve such a level of development that once united, they will be together all life through. Mismatch of partners will be seen immediately during the first week of their acquaintance, in other words, before getting married they will see a mismatch between them. And even slightly feeling that someone is not a match for another, they will depart immediately, will

not delay living together at a long date. Therefore, all divorces between potential couples will occur before entering into legal marriage."

- "What if a person feels that the improvement with his /her partner cannot be achieved, may such a marriage be dissolved?"

- "That marriage will not take place. Everything will be clear from the first meeting. People of the sixth race will cease to make mistakes when choosing a partner."

- "As concerns children, what changes will take place? Will children be born the old way?"

- "The physiology of birth remains the same as in the fifth race. But children will develop in a different way. Youth up to the age of fourteen will be removed from the program of children, in other words, the time a child wastes on childish games and toys, will be removed. We have concluded this is useless pastime that makes little for development. Such a waste of time, which lasts fourteen years, is not profitable to Us. Therefore, We are changing the program of childhood in the new race."

- "What way will a child develop then?"

- "Up to the age of two a child will learn to master a physical body, as usual. All the rest of it is changing. In an outward appearance, a child remains the same, while the essence of his behavior will change in accordance with the new program put in him. Children will become very smart; their intelligence will be very high. Imagine a three-year-old child apprehending as a fourteen-year-old one. Mentally, they will begin to develop at an accelerated pace immediately from their birth, so at the age of fourteen he will already be a personality."

- "And what way will their development evolve after the age of fourteen?"

- "Since the age of fourteen, they will get the university and other specialized education, including academic. The school itself will change. It will be like Academy. Some similar experiments with children We have carried out in your race, you've called them child prodigies. They were Our so to speak experimental samples. They have not been inculcated in your society and could not find themselves in life due to inconsistency with the environment. Only the program of childhood was worked on them, adulthood was of no significance. Child prodigies have shown good results, which We decided to use further."

- "Doesn't a child's psyche overwork, given such a load of the program?"

- "No, no overwork will arise, as the very energy potential of souls, used for this, is higher than that of modern humans. At their level this load is quite normal. The contemporary man, compared with them, is nursery-aged. In addition, there are other planets, where such childhood has been tested, given the full development of their program, and the result exceeds that We have on the Earth. In these civilizations children as well as adults are very smart, thanks to which they make a great leap in development. If compared to their civilization, one can even say that people are nobody compared to them."

- "Aren't they the beings that visit our planet on flying machines?"

- "No, they are not, although there are very smart material civilizations, but they are not from this planet. Those beings have never flown to you, because for them there is nothing to do here. Not every high-developed civilization will get interested in a low-developed one."

Old Age

Age has always oppressed a man. It makes him helpless, painful, and weak, forcing to cease an active life and become a mere vegetable. We think, in such a way people lose decades, whereas, in the absence of old age, they could use them for a fruitful development of themselves and others. So I decided to explore the matter with God.

The dialogue with Him continues:

- "What can You say about old age?"

- "Old age will cease being. We have come to the conclusion that the most economical model of a man is middle-aged. In other words, the thirty-years-old form will dominate in the golden race, which will provide the man a number of benefits when improving. Old age was necessary for the man of the fifth race, as an additional measure of education to develop certain qualities in the soul such as compassion for the weak, respect for the elder, and so on.

Old age allowed a person to review his entire life from new positions, and that the youth could not provide to understand, old age provided. In other words, old age is the strictest version of education of underdeveloped individuals who have little understanding of life and are too selfish.

A more high-developed person, who has passed a long evolutionary track, will not require such quality as old age because his level of awareness is high and the soul has already gathered the necessary characteristics. In Higher worlds there is no such thing as old age, because any Higher Personality the older becomes, the more powerful, more beautiful and wiser, as opposed to your age, where the progression is inverse: the older, the weaker. But as people have come to a new level of development, the need for body aging is no longer relevant.

Besides, We save the energy spent on the aging processes. Yes, to age a material body according to the program, having moved from the young body to the old, in other words, to turn all the processes towards damping, huge energy consumption is required. But for the sake of human education, We agreed to such expenses. Therefore, the option of the human race without old age becomes economically sound for Us."

- "With old age being removed, will diseases remain in the new race?"

- "First, they will remain. But soreness of internal organs also takes a great amount of energy which is also non-value-added. Diseases are needed for a low development level because they force the individual to learn something new in him and others, stir the person to activity. Owing to diseases, such field of knowledge as medicine and a number of subsidiary productions have developed. Diseases helped improve the spiritual and intellectual growth, because a man tried to cognize himself and what caused the disease.

The man of the sixth race will exceed his predecessor mind-wise many times so the path of development through overcoming disease will be no longer relevant. The man will have other awareness, and he will be given quite different ways to progress. Everything will be different. But, of course, it is a long-run perspective. Much time will pass before people reach this level. But it may happen that this, absence of old age and disease, will not occur in the sixth race, but in the seventh, depending on how they will evolve. Everything will depend on the individual."

- "What diseases will disappear, and what continue their existence in the sixth race?"

- "Plague, cholera, tuberculosis, based on very low human energetics, will be eliminated completely. Cold diseases will remain. Diseases of internal organs will be kept till about the middle of a new race, up to the next level of development. Almost all the rest will remain, but the incidence will start to fall. Sick men will simultaneously exist with healthy men, stages of disease decreasing. However, in the course of time diseases will cease, as a further development level of a man will enable him to fully manage his physical condition."

- "But will the principle of reincarnation have seen its day then?"

- "In the sixth race, it won't yet. But in the seventh race it will be possible, because the man will understand his life and his mission differently. If a person wants to exist, he will live as long as he will need, as he already will start to truly understand – what for he is sent here, and will begin to seek to acquire the qualities he needs, and therefore he will try to quickly execute his own program, quickly achieve his purpose and quickly return back to Us. This goal – to make human consciousness similar – will be set. And such a man will already be able to manage his own death: either to approach or distance it, when he wants to withdraw from the physical body forever – he will, if willing to temporarily leave it, he will be able to do it, in other words, he will master the free entrance to the physical body and withdrawal from it."

Morality

At all times human behavior has been restricted by certain rules of conduct. People have never been free in their actions. We consider these restrictions as moral and ethical standards. But where did they come from and what for? And will they still exist in the future race? About this, I decided to ask God.

- "How will moral standards change in the golden race?"

God answers:

- "Morality and ethics is a social organization of human masses. Over time and depending on the development level of a society, they change. Each century is given its moral norms, because they regulate the internal relationships in a social environment. Early in the following century morality and ethics will remain at the present time (1998) level, but from the mid of the second century, they will rise sharply, because by the end of the next century, all the low-level souls will die out, having completed their cycle on the Earth; and only representatives of the sixth race will remain. And since it will be comprised of higher level souls compared to the current ones, they will correspondingly require higher standards of morality. In one hundred years, people will change by fifty-seventy percent in qualitative terms, their behavior and moral aspirations will change."

- "What feature will characterize mainly the people in the sixth race?"

- "Of course, it is a high responsibility both for their words and actions, as well as a sense of duty."

Seventh and Eighth Civilizations

- "What can You say about the seventh and eighth civilizations on the Earth?"
- "Let us not run too far, because these civilizations may happen not to emerge at all, as We have said. Everything will depend on the way of development in the sixth race. It will be a determining factor in the entire follow-up. But in short, the human lifestyle in the seventh and eighth civilizations would entirely differ from that in the fifth race. There would be no houses, no plants on the Earth. Only wood and water. People would protect themselves from bad weather conditions with the help of their high-level energy: they would use it as a dome and take shelter under it from all the negative factors and unfavorable weather conditions. Their energy structure would refine so that they would not need rough food but would consume only water and some vegetation, mostly leaves."
- "What would they be engaged in, what work would they do?"
- "They would not need physical toil. Due to the changes in the energy structure of the body their way of life would also change completely. They would be only improving their souls."

Lifetime of Civilizations

- "How much was the lifetime of the previous civilizations?"
- "Time intervals vary. The time itself will mean nothing to you, because your life is comparatively very short, but We can say about the time in general. The first civilization did not exist long, as there were found many flaws in it that needed to be improved. The second civilization lived longer, and the lifetime of the third one represented the average between the first and second, thus, We leveled the time. The fourth civilization existed longer than the third. Actually their lifetime represented a sinuous curve."
- "What determined the duration of their existence?"
- "Many factors. That was Our experiment. It underwent continuous improvement. But all that is one line leading to one: the needs of the Cosmos."

- "Who needs more time to develop: low-level or high-level civilizations?"

- "In the material world there is a correlation: the lower the Level of a civilization, the more time it requires to develop. In the subtle world the stairs of the Hierarchy have an opposite correlation: the lower the Level of development, the less it exists. The higher up the stairs of the Hierarchy, the greater the lifetime. The Higher live eternally."

* * *

GOLD AND PRECIOUS STONES
IN GOLDEN RACE

The sixth race will be named «golden», as it will correspond to this title both in the literal and the figurative senses. And this race conditionally rises from 2000. For what qualities or virtues will it receive such a wonderful eminent name? We'll try to summarize the information on this issue and highlight the main points.

The golden race will correspond to its name in all respects. First, this race will have most unusual properties, of which we have only a dim idea. They are telepathy, levitation, high intuition, and a very high intelligence (compare: the modern man has developed it only up to 6%, while they will develop it up to 90%), clairvoyance and extrasensory abilities, as well as many others.

Second, it will be the greatest energy-producing race among all that have ever existed on the Earth. Everyone will produce energy three-four times more than the current representative of the fifth race. And it is the new man's ability to produce much energy that will require discharging of energy surplus into some natural energy receivers represented by the seas and oceans as maxi-reservoirs and by gold and precious stones as mini-reservoirs.

Hence is the third reason for the new sixth race to be called «golden» – this race will wear adornments of gold and honor gold.

The true value of gold and precious stones will be very much appreciated again, so jewelry will be honored by most population, but it will be valued not for its external beauty, but for the inner content. People will get to know the truth – what jewelry is needed for, and what qualities it possesses. But the most essential functions carried out by precious metals and stones will be the collection of surplus energy from people, its distribution in subtle components of human structures, and the storage of this energy in the stones' capacitory potentials.

Some part of the energy produced by people will get to the Hierarchic Systems, and some part will remain on the Earth. The energy capacity of the Earth itself as well as the energy content of all its subtle bodies is increasing, and therefore each particle of the Earth is moving into a new, more energy saturated state, i.e. energy changes in people are accompanied by energy changes in the planet itself.

- - -

If the Earth is changing energy-wise, the changes affect all around it, including people, plants and stones. Therefore, the following issues became urgent.

- "For what purposes are gold and precious stones supposed to keep the human energy?"

God answers this question as follows.

- "A man used to accumulate wealth, but now acquiring gold and precious stones, he will accumulate his own energy and energy wealth rather than luxuries. The man will start to store up his own energy surplus in adornments of gold. Gold itself will start to absorb the excess energy, if it appears in humans. Up to a certain moment gold keeps up this surplus, which, if necessary, can be withdrawn again.

When, for example, a person is tired or sick, or even for some reason he needs additional energy, no sooner than he puts on a gold adornment, the state that happens after the rest will come back to him. He will recuperate. The people of the sixth race will learn to use the energy stored in the gold and stones. As for the people in the fifth race, they produce little energy, so they know nothing about how to charge the stones or to use them further. People of the sixth race will discharge their energy surplus into them, like into the money box, and use it at the right time."

- "But do you need to say any words or codes to put the energy in gold or withdraw it from there?"

- "No, nothing like your spells should be uttered. Everything will operate automatically. Gold will be part of you, of your aura, will feel this aura, as it is alive too."

- "Can artificial stones be used to accumulate energy surplus?"

- "Artificial stones won't be appropriate. Only natural gems have real properties. Of course, if a person has very high energetics, he could easily charge artificial stones as well. But diamonds are characterized by special energy capacity."

- "What about amber?"

- "This stone is too weak for subtle energies. One should be guided by hardness of stones: the stronger and harder the stone, the more energy it stores. Hard stones are energy capacitive."

- "What can You say about silver in terms of its energy capacity?"
- "Silver is much weaker than gold. But it has healing and disinfecting properties. Silver is meant for other purposes."
- "Is a gold hallmark of any importance?"
- "The purer the gold item, the less impurities it has, the higher its qualities. Ideal gold is the purest. The greater the gold hallmark, the greater its power."
- "Is the weight of a gold item of any importance?"
- "Yes, both weight and volume are of importance. They affect the capacitive characteristics of gold items. Therefore, the more weight and volume of the gold item, the more energy it will be able to store."
- "Are gold items saturated with energy up to a certain limit or without limit?"
- "Up to a certain amount. Their energy capacity is limited by the hallmark, weight, and volume of the item. What is the maximum gold hallmark that you have?"
- "Nine hundred and fifty-six."
- "Let us take a scale from one to one thousand, which defines up to which points the gold of your maximum hallmark can be charged. And according to this scale, a gold item weighing one gram can be charged with energy up to one thousand. Suppose you are producing energy, equivalent to one hundred by the given scale. If you are going to wear the gold item constantly, its energy capacity will also be constantly replenished with your energy, and it will be replenished until it reaches a thousand. If the gold hallmark is less, the limit of its capacity is correspondingly reduced to 583, 375, the less energy gold items accumulate. Weight and volume affect the capacitive characteristics in direct proportion."
- "How does the gold aura influence the human aura?"
- "Interaction occurs on the energy plane. But in this case it is important who owned the gold, and whose aura it influences. Results may be opposed, because if the gold item is yours, it will interact with your aura in one way, but if you take it off and give someone else, with someone else's aura it will begin to interact in a completely different way, and the result could be unexpected."
- "Could You explain, please, the way it interacts with my aura, and the way it works when I bring it to another person?"
- "If it is your gold, it is advisable for you to wear it continuously and take it off only at night. In this case, you are contacting the gold item, its aura in the best way. Gold perfectly «feels» (although here the bodily

contact takes place) your state, the presence of subtle energy in you, and given its lack in the form of fatigue, it will provide the particular points of your aura with energy, thus, leveling the energetics of the aura, in other words, it will recharge you at the right time as a subtle-energy battery.

But if you hang your gold item to another person, it would be dangerous for him /her, because an average person has less energy than you, and your gold item has accumulated a strong energy potential that could seriously harm the other person, having holed his aura. Of course, this concerns people with high-level energetics, such as channelers and psychics. But if people with equal-level energy exchange gold items, this will do no harm to them."

- "And if someone wants to render energy aid to the other man, may he bring the gold item to that person?"

- "You must neither bring your gold to another man, nor transmit your energy through it. Gold must always be individual, and it is recommended to wear to restore one's own health. If you are going to help other people using your high-level energy, you should better take stones for this purpose. Those having a very high-level energy (channelers, psychics) should better charge artificial stones for people, hard and natural ones, such as crystals, quartz, or diamonds. One can even use ordinary marble, but pure, without impurities.

Everyone is advised to wear individual adornments of gold to maintain personal health. They are especially useful for channelers and people communicating with them, because gold would absorb by its structure the energy surplus that is sent from the Cosmos to the channelers and others, thus the channeler for example would not burn and the people communicating with him / her would get the additional energy in their energy storages. That energy would be already transformed so that it would be focused on their personal qualities and therefore would help restore their health.

Since gold incorporates energy surplus of particular individuals as the energy of a certain quality, theft of gold items from the personalities possessing high energy potential can pose a threat to the health of low-potential individuals, i.e. those who steal their jewelry, and those who would be wearing it later, as the difference in energetics between them is very large, and a more powerful charge can hole weak bodies, causing various health troubles."

- "Energetics of people varies. How does this affect the gold?"

- "It is because each person is unique, and the quality of his energies differs from that of another man, that gold adornments should have one master only, because the energy of some person may not be suitable for another in qualitative terms."

- "With the help of what method can one define the stone which is, from the energy point of view, the most appropriate for an individual?"

- "This can be done using the signs of the zodiac. But after 2000 the whole astrology goes in a different way, hence, with respect to contemporary men, some amendments must be made."

- "What is the difference between gems and ordinary stones?"

- "The difference lies in energy capacity of accumulated power."

- "Why are some stones capable of affecting a human state?"

- "They have a specific structure, that is, they are built so that they may implement the circulation of energy between the Cosmos and the Earth through the man."

- "What is the difference between the soul of an ordinary stone and that of the precious stone?"

- "Considering the Hierarchy for stones souls, ordinary stones are at the bottom. The more valuable the stone, the higher it is in the Hierarchy. That is the souls of gems have passed a longer path of evolution, and therefore are more developed, while the souls of ordinary stones have evolved very little."

*   *   *

Chapter 4

MYSTERIES OF DIVINE
FOUNDATION

TALKING WITH GOD
ON MORAL FOUNDATION OF BEHAVIOR

This chapter sets out our dialogues with God on the topic of morality and moral foundations of society and clarifies certain aspects of philosophy of a modern man.

Life goes on, the laws by which people live change, therefore what seemed wildness two thousand years ago has become now a norm of conduct and vice versa what was earlier considered to be the norm of conduct now has turned into savagery. So despite the fact that codes of human laws sometimes seem immutable, they always undergo some changes raising the morality or letting down manners. Although the general trend of human development remains the one defined in the Bible for the two thousand years.

But the era of Fishes has expired, the humanity has entered a new era – the era of Aquarius, thus changing the laws and rules of conduct in society, as the time requires new global changes to be introduced into life as well as many settled and inveterate views on the world and the man's place in the universe to be reviewed by the humanity; the latter should move closer to a real life of the Cosmos and reflect itself not in the primitive human being but in complex processes of macro- and micro-cosmos and understand the truth of reality.

But if we are talking about the truth, let it be it to start with.

During one of the contacts with God we asked Him:

- "Would You please tell us what is the difference between the concept of «truth» and the concept of «truthfulness»?"

To this God replied:

- "Truth includes the entire multi-dimensional reality: both the material structure and spiritual content. Absolutely everything that exists independently of us is Truth that everyone is seeking to cognize, but never reaches its full understanding and conceiving, because truth is too large and infinite. And the person is able to discover only a small part of it, but never all at once, and as a whole.

Therefore, any truth is always relative, because it is the truth about something particular, but not the truth about other things. And the farther outward, the less it is true for humans or any other being. Therefore, the concept of «truthfulness» is always attached to something smaller, particular and it itself serves as something particular within the greater, i.e. within Truth.

Truth is the Universe itself, the Absolute, the Top Perfection, which includes the entire Great formation, and truthfulness is some part of it. Truthfulness may be more or less, while Truth is always constant, comprehensive and steadfast. Therefore, truthfulness is always a constituent part within the larger, i.e. within Truth. At present a person is able to cognize only five percent of the universe Truth but in the course of his improvement this percentage will grow and consciousness – expand."

- "One legend says that at the festival «Transfiguration» Christ opened the Absolute truth to his disciples. What is the Absolute truth?"

- "The Absolute truth is Me, God. But, of course, it depends largely on the comprehension of those this truth is explained to. Truth may be interpreted in different ways, depending on the comprehension of a human being or an Entity* it is disclosed to."

- "In fact, truth may be totally different?"

- "Everything depends on the Level of a person or an Entity that cognizes this truth. The very word «truth» is an absolute* word and an absolute concept. It is disclosed at a certain Level, because only at a specific Level of development this Absolute* becomes visible. Therefore, if the truth be said to a being* at a low Level of development, it will be distorted and will no longer be the truth in its reality. That is, <u>truth starts to be understood since a certain limit</u>."

- "People take delight in accepting the image of God, created two thousand years ago, and do not want to recognize Him in modern clothes. The church denies the contacts and does not believe that through them one can talk with God. Why is this happening?"

- "The education of earthly men, which lasted under the Bible over two thousand years, should be taken into account. During all this time, the old dogmas acted that kept people in certain moral framework, not allowing them to diverge anywhere. And the established dogmas were necessary for some time, because earlier human brain was so poorly developed that it was unable to understand something independently. For this reason, due to his own insufficient development, it was impossible for the man to understand the truth about himself and about things around him.

That is why We gave him a periphrastic version of the Bible, more lightweight and close to his primitive way of life. Therefore, people have become accustomed to the image of God, which has been created over all these two thousand years, i.e. accustomed to the old way. It is difficult to understand contemporary God for them because they should abandon the previous inveterate dogmas, rethink many things inside and around them, and should reach the Level of **the cosmos consciousness** – not every person is able to do this."

- "To what extent is it true – «every man is God», and if so, what is it – God?"

- "Man is God is in his particle, i.e. in his soul."

- "But for the time being this «particle» is immature, and it will have to ascend to true God for a long time."

- "The path of evolving is infinite, so each immature particle is God, who is improving in his development. This spiritualized cell is created by Me and in the future it will reach My Level. Man should strive to become a God himself, but not in the sense that all the rest worship him, but in the sense of his own creative potential and maximizing the development of intellect. This is his goal that he should remember in this life as well as in all the subsequent ones."

- "What does the phrase «merge with God», often used by clergymen, mean? And how can a person reach this merging?"

- "Merging with God for the ordinary person means that he ascends a higher level of consciousness or sensation. This can be achieved in three ways: with the help of meditation; by means of the old method used by your ancestors – prayers; and through cognizing the cosmos and other Higher knowledge. The third way is more progressive for the given period of human development and includes the study of new sciences and channelers' books on the modern state of the world. Through direct contacts new information corresponding to the next stage of humanity's evolving is translated to people. But every Level of development can move to a higher world. Everyone should keep in mind – the way to Me is through self-cultivation."

- "And can a man via hard work at himself «break through» the channel of communication to Higher Hierarchs of Your System?"

- "Everything depends on human effort. He can «break through», only not to the Higher Hierarchs, but to the Determinant* of his Level.

Everyone can break through only to one's own Level*. Higher Hierarchs are too high for them, and for an average person it is energetically impossible to ascend Them. The energy potential of people is too weak to come up to Their Level. But They can sometimes descend to someone for a particular purpose."

- "We understand that it takes much time to reach Your Level of development, and the concept of «merging with God» was made conditional to determine the purpose for a man to which he must seek. But can then a transition to the Hierarchic commonwealth «Union» and the following existence in the subtle world be regarded as «merging with God»?"

- "Again, it all depends on the person, on what he has achieved on the Earth. Transfer to the commonwealth «Union» is carried out only after a certain degree of individual development is reached. Otherwise, what shall a savage do among highly civilized individuals? And it would not be interesting for him, because everything would be incomprehensible, and they would not take pleasure in communication with primitive intelligence, which he could appear for them."

- "This is probably the basis of improving the human spirituality – to become closer to Our Teachers with regard to the internal state, isn't it?"

- "Certainly. Everyone should strive to accumulate spiritual wealth, as it brings him to Higher worlds. To reach the Higher means to pass the way that enriches the soul with high spiritual qualities. Spirituality is an aggregate of the highest human qualities produced through actions, thoughts, feelings, through the comprehension of new knowledge."

- "How long should a person develop to get those qualities that help him rise to Higher worlds?"

- "For the humanity there are a hundred levels of development on the Earth. An individual may pass the same Level during many lives, and showing zeal he may accelerate passing the Levels. Usually at the initial stage the pace of development is always slowed down, but then the man can speed up his own progress and pass one Level during one incarnation. To reach the Higher in digital terms means to reach One hundred Level of Earthly plane. That is enough to leave the Earth forever. Then the soul goes to another world or another planet of a higher level and it will develop even higher. And now, speaking of total merging with God, it may occur after the soul has passed all Earthly Levels and a quantity of Levels of My Hierarchy."

- "Some people assert they have experienced unity with the Universe. How can an ordinary man feel inextricable link with it?"

- "One can do this by force of imagination – a person should imagine himself within the Universe."
- "One can imagine it, but how can he feel like this?"
- "One can feel it in a state of meditation."
- "Is this the only way for such sensation?"
- "Yes, for the ordinary level of human development."
- "And he will be able to reach such a state, won't he?"
- "His Determinant* will help him. People have different feelings, and one person is able to feel something that another is incapable of feeling, and he will require a lot of lives to reach the feelings and the level of sensation of the first. Therefore, one can feel his unity with the Universe, because he has developed himself up to this state. But if someone desires to experience such sensation and does his utmost for this, the Determinant can send him a wanted sensation as a stimulus to development, although the man still has not reached this Level. A person is given much in advance, but it contributes to the person's evolving. Having experienced the new, he strives for self-cultivation more."
- "People have one more saying – «to reach a fiery state of spirituality». Is this what we have talked about?"
- "Yes. This is precisely the state of fire, as reaching the highest Level means reaching fiery energies. Above there is Light, Fire."
- "What does Divine Love mean for the man? Is this the highest standard of love or return of a special kind of energy and no more?"
- "The feeling of love is firstly a special kind of energy that not every soul has and such quality hence – energies are being made by it in the course of development, of many situations and complex relationships. With regard to Divine Love, this is a very powerful kind of energy, covering every one of My possessions covering a number of Universes. For the Earthly plane of existence the concept of «Divine Love» includes overall serving as that model of emotions, which people should strive for. The Superior model for it is love for all the life. Feeling love for absolutely everything – this is the basic principle of development in My Hierarchy, because love contributes to the lives of others. Love helps live and survive. And most importantly – it gives pleasure and the sublime state to the very loving soul. It loves and it feels good because of that, the soul enjoys bliss. This in turn means in the physical sense that the soul is filled with special kind of energy related to the Superior creative energies of the Cosmos. Wrapping everyone in love, helping him live and improve, My Love contributes to strengthening and prosperity of My worlds, that is Love strengthens them,

reinforces, in contrast to, for example, hatred that destroys everything and kills, weakening the world itself, and eventually leads it to death. Therefore, Divine Love is the natural condition of any Higher Personality on the path of evolution and expansion of its borders.

Worlds cannot be expanded using force and coercion as any coercion evokes resistance and hence brings destruction and ultimately – weakening and reduction of the borders. Only Universal Love contributing to the prosperity of everyone promotes common prosperity of the whole."

- "Why do people have such a notion as «God's retribution»? Can You punish anyone personally?"

- «God's retribution», according to people's concepts, is unexpected, but deserved punishment. In fact, I do not punish anyone. But in My world, there acts the law of cause-and-effect relation, in accordance to which everyone gets something that he has deserved in his previous incarnations. However, a person undergoes trials that he must learn to overcome in order to increase his own strength of Mind. And trials sent should not be confused with punishment which a man receives according to his karmic debts."

- "Is there the principle «to each his own» in the Cosmos?"

- "Yes, there is. But it depends. If this concerns Hierarchy*, everyone occupies his own place in it, his Level*, in accordance with the development progressed, and he cannot find himself below or above it because there is a law by which each is placed in a Hierarchy according to his energy indices."

- "And how is this principle embodied on the Earth?"

- "Everyone gets something, which his soul is seeking. For example, a person of a high spiritual level is provided greater opportunities for spiritual development than that of a low level, but the latter is provided more temptations. Again – everyone gets, in accordance with his past deeds, his own destiny."

- "The personality which has taken the path of degradation, ceases evolutionary development. Is it necessary to fight for it?"

- "By all means, its degradation should be obligatorily prevented. One must remember that the soul you do not struggle for goes to Devil. All the fallen souls go to Him. It is necessary to struggle for everyone."

- "Ought the degradation of a human being to be prevented in all cases?"

- "Absolutely in all of them."

- "People have a saying – «do not prevent the sinner from going to hell»."

- "This is a silly saying. Incorrect. It is it that contributes to the fact that many souls go to Devil but not to Me. People have a lot of wrong expressions, and one should feel in the soul – which is right and which is wrong."

- "People often say – «well-intentioned road to hell is paved», that is, if a person wants to do something good, but for some reason does not do it, does it contribute to his degradation?"

- "In the sense that you understand this saying, it is not true, because to think, to wish the other man something good, or to do something good – that's great. But the saying refers to the other. There are such intentions when a person is doing something good from his point of view for the other man, but in the end a negative result is produced. For example, parents make a lot of good for their child, and often seek to fulfill all his desires but eventually a selfish person grows up. The parents in this case clog his program by imposing something on him that it is not needed, and make the evolutionary path of his development longer as the child does not get the qualities that he is supposed to get. That's how the good produces a negative result."

- "A child should not be imposed too much on, should he?"

- "No. He should be wisely directed to those spheres which support the development of his soul."

- "The Scripture says: – «Ask, and it shall be given you». Is the man always given what he requests in the prayers?"

- "A human's prayer is perceived by the Determinant, and, if He considers it to be met, He submits his pupil's request for discussion by Higher authorities who can satisfy it or reject. Any request requires time for implementation. What the man asks is also significant. If it is something minor or something that corresponds to his program the Determinant may satisfy such a request himself."

- "What principles does a Determinant follow while solving whether to fulfill the request or not?"

- "A further course of events the program of that who asks is considered."

- "Is it concurrently checked whether the execution of a request will result in harm or benefit?"

- "No, this is due to the recalculation of the man's program: some situations will be cut, some –increase, and what the person asks for should be equivalent to that he returns."

- "So does it mean the man should pay for that he requests?"

- "Yes, it does. He should give the energy equivalent for his request to be met. He should give energy through some situation. Situations are different and supply different kinds of energy. Everything depends on the human experience. But nothing is given free of charge or for no particular reason."

- "Muslims sacrifice animals in the holidays. What is the energy foundation of the rite? Or does it symbolize that one gives something dear to him and no more?"

- "This is a very old rite. It used to be in Christianity too. And initially this very meaning you are speaking of was put into them. But such rituals have long been obsolete. The rituals must also be improved. But Muslims did not want to change the old rite to the new one."

- "People say – «God does not make defective things», i.e. all that is created from the Above is absolutely perfect. Is that statement true?"

- "No, it is not true. You know it very well yourself. All that is created requires continuous improvement over time. Once created cannot be perfect forever, because it has been created for a certain period of time and certain conditions of existence, and if time flows and everything around is changed, any creations require improvement, adjustment or complete replacement by the new model."

- "In our religion it is accepted to praise God. Does it correlate with some energy processes?"

- "Energy processes are certainly involved. But the most important reason for which such a ritual was established, is educating of a man in respect to the Higher. The primitive type of man who existed two thousand years ago and did not know the details of morality yet must have taken the basis of the notion – what is good and what's bad, what's high and what's low, who he should worship, and who – fear. Man had to be taught – and religion brought first precepts of morality. With regard to energy cause of the praise, it can be said that while praising energy flows are directed upward so in contrast to praying when people ask to forgive their trespasses. In the latter case energy flows are directed inside the man to clean his energy channels. Each prayer eulogizing or not bears energy. However, the quality of energy produced by a man saying prayers depends on the individual himself, on his development level."

- "At present do the prayers of praise have the same value as before?"

- "Again, it all depends on the man, his spiritual qualities and consciousness. One may not praise, but just respect and fear the Higher. This has respect to everybody's conscience. One may feel in his heart deep reverence for the Higher. The most important is one should know more about Us and believe in Us. Faith is needed now, although praise to the Higher is still a sign of respect and reverence."

- "At present the man very likely needs more knowledge, doesn't he?"

- "The knowledge is needed, as well as faith, and the truth about his existence. A man must know the real world, rather than separate himself from it through the illusion of uniqueness of the material world and himself in it. In the sixth race Truth is already needed. And it will be disclosed to him through a new religion."

Jesus Christ

So now when Christ has already fulfilled his mission on the expiry of the second millennium, God who sent Him to the Earth, reveals some secrets relating to His life and death.

Of course we did not aim at finding out all the subtlest details of the personal life of Jesus, as we had another goal, but we asked those questions we took interest in and received answers to them.

The most important thing we wanted to know – who was Christ's Heavenly Teacher, His mentor and guide? After all, God is a certain coded name given to Christians. And for every nation this coded earthly name is specific, appropriate to the frequency of those sound vibrations, which this or that nation is required to produce. The name collects the energy of a certain type. These are coded letter combinations – Allah, Buddha, Krishna, etc., given for humans.

But, besides the Earthly name, God has a cosmic one, which only the initiated know and which bears not an averaged energy potential corresponding to each nation but a higher one. And again this cosmic name is meant for people alone because in their Higher world, Higher Personalities as well as God Himself are designated neither in terms of letters nor of figures but in terms of light. However, can the man really understand what the light name of God is like and to what extent it is more powerful than His earthly name!

But people are people, and not everyone, but only the initiated are allowed to know even the cosmic letter name of God. It is not to be disclosed, so we leave it hidden. God told us His Cosmic name responding to the next question.

God says:

- "What Determinant guided Christ's life on the Earth?"

- "I – J* ... (and He utters his cosmic name)*. I guided Christ, I have created a religion."

- "According to the Bible Moses was also guided by God in his life. Was that You?"

- "No, Moses had his own Determinant."

- "The Bible says that Moses was guided by God named Savaoff."

- "Yes, the Determinant uttered his name to him. And every Determinant is both God and Teacher for the person. But all Determinants obey Me."

- "Where are now the souls of the prophets: Iliya, Muhammad and others who guided peoples?"

- "Everyone is in his Hierarchic System, which are subordinate to Me. Each of the former prophets has his own direction in the development and they continue it in their Systems."

- "Aren't they incarnated in the form of people?"

- "No, they aren't. They have surpassed the development level of any human being, so there is nothing to do here for them. Of course, they could once again take a leading role on the Earth, but such a task is not set for them. After all, every goal is always set from the Above in accordance with some requirements of the Earth or Hierarchic Systems."

- "Is God Jehovah, who worship Jehovists, also a Determinant of the same Level as Savaoff?"

- "This is a distorted cosmic name of Mine."

- "Who was Christ's soul before His incarnation on the Earth? Had he been incarnated here before this great mission was given to Him?"

- "No, Christ had never been incarnated on the Earth before. This was his first and last mission on your planet."

- "Did Christ have a physical father?"

- "Of course, he did. People idealized his birth."

- "Was the soul of his mother Mary incarnated on the Earth once again?"

- "Yes, it was. She again performed a spiritual mission, and this time lived a life of nun in a monastery."

- "People now (1998) argue –whether Christ had a wife. Excuse us for such an indiscreet question but people are interested to sort it out."

- "Yes, He had a companion for life."

- "Was this Mary Magdalene?"

- "No, no one knows this woman. She was constantly beside him in his retinue and went everywhere with Christ. He was accompanied by twelve apostles and she was always with them."

- "Did they have matrimonial or friendly relationship?"

- "Matrimonial relationship registered in Heaven. I commanded so", – on the pronoun «I» He made a stately accent.

- "And where was Jesus before he was thirty years old? Did he go to Shambhala?"

- "Before he was thirty he led the life of an ordinary person. At the age of thirty his program to execute the mission was run. As for Shambhala he was there not in the physical body but in the subtle one. His soul was in this country."

- "Devil tempted Christ in the wilderness with wealth and power, i.e. they wanted him to sin through wealth through the power. Was it set in his program?"

- "Yes, everything was programmed."

- "And what were those tests needed for if he was Your envoy?"

- "To test him, to improve his soul. We also tested if He would stand it, if He would not repudiate it."

- "And did there such cases used to be when someone repudiated?"

- "Yes, there used to be such envoys before Him."

Later during the conversation with Devil we decided to clarify who exactly enticed Christ. We as envoys talked not only with God but with Devil as well. God organized conversation sessions with Him to test us. On the one hand God tested whether we would give in to his temptations and on the other hand, through the knowledge of opposites we should have learned to see and feel what is positive and what is not, what leads to good and what – to evil. Therefore, contacting with Devil we also learned a lot and saw the world from his point of view. So in some dialogs there appeared a phrase – «Devil says», as now.

Devil says:

- "Will You tell us whether You or someone in your subjects tempted Jesus in the desert?"

- "No, it was I, –Devil confirmed with pride. – The level of Christ's energetics, – He continued, – must correspond to those with whom He communicated. Christ was to communicate only with the Higher."

- "What was the temptation of Christ?"

- "He had to make a choice – either to choose a painful death for himself, or come over to My side and live like a king."

- "So, the main temptation was the temptation with the future life, with its extension, wasn't it?"

- "Yes, it was. And with wealth too."

- "Are we expected to undergo this too?"

- "No, you are different. God simply will not allow tempting you between life and death. You are sent not for this purpose. There are few of you and you are for other purposes."

- "For what purpose do all the envoys talk to God first, and then to You (to Devil)*?"

- "They learn the essence of good and evil at that Level of development where they are."

- "Where does the soul of Jesus dwell now?"

- "I have not taken interest in, – replied Devil coldly."

- "They say Jesus knew his program. But if he knew, why was he tempted more?"

- "He also like all people had to pass the test on faith, devotion to God, the goal achievement. And also it was necessary to test whether He could while being on Earth come over to Me."

- "After Christ, have You talked to someone else of people? Have You had channeling communication with people?"

- "Channeling? You know, there have not been such people on the Earth, which could directly communicate with Devil or with God. People have had low energy potential. They just could not have stood Us."

- "Therefore, You've had this direct communication only in two thousand years, i.e. with us?"

- "Yes. Last time I spoke to people it was Christ and his apostles."

- "And who of the apostles did You talk to?"

- "To everybody. All of them were channelers absolutely everybody. I also inclined them to come over to My side."

- "Well, did You persuade someone? Peter or Judas?"

- "Nobody, – from His tone it is heard that He is very unpleased to recognize the futility of his efforts to win any of them over. – After his death Judas realized his guilt, redeemed his sin by his own suffering but did not go to Me."

Then we continued the conversation with God.

We were interested in the miracles performed by Christ, so we asked:
- "How did Christ perform miracles?"

God says:
- "A special program was worked out for this. Any miracle involves technical means of the subtle plane. This is precise calculation, and much work done by Hierarchic Systems. Christ performed a miracle while the Systems prepared this miracle. Each of them required hard work and energy costs."

- "How did Christ resurrect the dead: did he return a soul into the body or was a man not dead, but only had fallen in lethargic sleep?"

- "All this was technically prepared too. Not only He alone worked at it, but He was helped from the Above. On the subtle plane He was constantly accompanied by his retinue of twelve Beings of Higher order, which remained invisible to humans. But under his guidance they performed miracles of resurrection. The soul was taken back into the body, which was restored where needed. Besides, speaking about the wonders of that time it was easy for Him to show a miracle because He lived in those times when people were ignorant and knew nothing about the science that modern man knows.

If Christ performed his miracles now at the given development level of your science and technology, you should easily understand the way He did it. And your psychics should grasp and see much in His miracles. The mere comparison of the benighted people, who existed before and progressive which live now gives two different reference points and different levels of understanding."

- "But how did He manage to intervene in the phenomena of nature and stop the wind, calm a storm? At present not such a powerful psychic capable of repeating this can be found."

- "In the Hierarchic System guiding the Earth there is a department that manages the weather on your planet. Just pressing the «button» is enough to raise a storm, and pressing the «button» – to calm it down. Weather changes were made under the actions of Christ."

- "Did Christ walk on water?"

- "Over the surface of the water His hologram was moving not Himself."

- "There are miracles that people create by means of their mental energy and wonders technically prepared by the Hierarchic Systems, «Union». How much energy and effort is spent to prepare technical miracles?"

- "Naturally, a lot. Wonders are expensive and it is always difficult to implement them in material terms. Transferring something from the subtle plane into the physical one implies a great amount of energy."
- "Do You agree on working wonders often and willingly?"
- "No, unwillingly. And not often at all. They are very rare cases."
- "What caused the need for such experiments?"
- "This is not experimentation. Demonstration of miracles is caused by the need to turn people's souls to Faith, to Our existence. But any miracle had an effect only on certain segments of the population and had a short-term impact. We had to send Our people back with a special mission – to restore public opinion to the former wonder. And they returned it and lifted it up to the mark in the minds of people turning miracles into legends.

And in such a way wonders have passed through centuries, reinforcing the belief in the Higher. Miracles, though it was technically difficult to implement them and they required great energy costs, have contributed to the maintenance of the Faith over the millennia, and thus over time have justified their costs. But nevertheless, We appreciate more the human Faith without miracles or religious parables. Faith based on understanding of Us and of Higher knowledge, is above the Faith based on witnessing miracles."

- "The Church says that Christ expiated the future sins of the mankind. Is expiation of other people's sins ever possible?"
- "Expiation in the sense of neutralizing minus energies is possible. Yes, Christ using his powerful positive biofield neutralized minus energies accumulated by people through any improper action and thus enlightened the total energy field and further minus energies in the biofields of the people themselves appeared to be neutralized too. This corresponded to the removal of sin from them because in fact «dirty» energies were removed. But in order to undergo such purification the man should have believed in Christ, because **trust** provides access to energy channels, **distrust** helps close the channels, clip them. Trust is relaxing, is opening of oneself. As for the future, of course, the correction of the humanity's energetic field in the present contributes to its correction in the future as any future is based on the present."

- "When Christ was born, the supernova flared. What did its flash mean?"
- "It was the new energy sent by Us to the Earth. The supernova flare was linked with the birth of Christ because He was built so that

He could take this energy and having passed it through Himself gently distribute it to humans. Its distribution started from the very moment of His birth and was stretched further in time. And this occurred differently compared with the way energy from stars is normally distributed – this is a rough energy distribution. Through a person, it is very softly transformed both onto the Earth itself and on other people. It is not so aggressive."

- "Why was the death on the cross devised for Christ?"

- "This execution was to be the most impressive one for that time. People should have remembered it for the next two thousand years. In addition, the cross has a deep physical cause – it was necessary to introduce the cross as an antenna in day-to-day lives of Christians. The Hierarchic System decided to gather spiritual energy through the antenna and transmit it to the Cosmos.

The antenna was designed in the form of a cross. And to make people use these antennas everywhere in private and in social life it was decided that Christ was to die a martyr's death on the cross. The man loved Christ as his Savior and loved the cross on which He was crucified. Thus, people began to worship Christ and the cross. The cross has become a symbol of Faith. It has appeared in every family having become a small emitter of pure energy. Thus, a space antenna has been distributed throughout the Earth. And it became easy for the Hierarchic System to gather spiritual energy, i.e. the purest of those produced by a person."

- "After Christ died on the cross He rose from the dead as the religion says. Did He rise in the material body or was it a hologram?"

- "After the resurrection He was in the astral body not physical. And because He concentrated powerful energetics in himself the entire body shone."

- "Where was his physical body put?"

- "The physical body was decomposed into atoms. This was done on purpose so that people would not have it, i.e. that followers of Christ would not create a cult and his enemies would not violate Him. After death, His soul went to Us. The purpose of Christ was to show the world a miracle. And this miracle was in his body's recovery. Before Christ no soul had ever returned to the Earth immediately after death, moreover, in a glowing appearance which the others saw. The soul was to appear not in a material body, but in a subtler one and at the same time it was to remain visible for people. Previously, the soul had always appeared on the Earth through the birth, and the physical body had been prepared for the nine months.

A new body-envelope was to be prepared for three days. To be more precise, the protective body in which the soul had to descend again to the Earth had been prepared before, but the soul of Christ was to learn to manage it within three days, as a diver manages his diving suit while descending in the depths of the sea. It is also difficult. It takes a child three years to master his body while Christ mastered his new body for three days. This was difficult. But it showed a miracle. The second body was special not of physical matter. Very powerful energy was concentrated in it to keep a light sole in dense matter of the Earthly world. Therefore, the entire body was shining, so that Christ could not be immediately touched. This energy could kill a man."

- "Who was involved in Christ's revival? They say that material «plates» took part in it."

- "No, it was Me."

- "Did anybody else help?"

- "My assistants. But mostly – I. This was also a specially designed and pre-thought-out plan and everything proceeded according to that plan. Subtle technique was enabled. To descend Christ's light soul into dense physical matter was as difficult as for example a balloon – into water. It would have been immediately pushed back. His soul was much lighter than ordinary people's souls because He worked with high energies and accumulated them in himself. But thanks to a special protective body-envelope the soul was descended and could remain on the Earth as long as it was prescribed."

- "Forty days later Christ disappeared again. How did He die for the second time?"

- "He did not die but ascended to Us finally. And while He was ascending to Us He had to throw down some temporary bodies. Among the people He was like a human being, so some bodies were intrinsic in Him. On Earth He did not leave a single body."

- "What happened to those subtle bodies which He threw down?"

- "They began to exist as separate substances and were the carriers of certain information."

- "Do they accumulate the energy from the prayers devoted to Christ?"

- "No. They just carry spiritual information of a high degree."

- "When Christ died and ascended to You, did he undergo additional treatment as all other people? We are still taking low energies here."

- "No, on the Earth He purified through his suffering and underwent no further treatment."

- "They say that after his first death Christ descended into hell for the period of three days and saved the sinners there."

- "No, his soul was with Us. He descended nowhere."

- "When Jesus was hanging on the cross did He feel pain or as a magician was He able to suppress it?"

- "He possessed unusual properties, but the torments He had to take in full. This was both his purification and karma."

- "What kind of karma did He work out when He was sent to the Earth?"

- "The death of living beings in a different world. Previously He had been a Manager and by His fault by His mistake many peoples perished on one planet. He was mistaken, and the mistake cost the lives of many thousands like you. Therefore, His karma was such that on that planet He had killed living beings and on your planet He should have saved them. Hence His death was to be martyr-like as a ransom."

- "And that He was crucified on the cross in addition to a religious purpose, has it been chosen also in accordance with karma?"

- "Two meanings were combined here: religion and the expiation of his karma."

- "And did Christ work out karma for his last mission on expiation the Earth too? Might He have done not everything correctly under the program?"

- "There were slight deviations. But at least, through His fault no one died. This time He had almost no karma."

- "How necessary was Christ's link with the Apostles?"

- "It was a moral support to Him, besides, they implemented the physical basis of the process in which Christ was involved. Not Christ alone distributed the new energy, but also His apostles did. Each of them had his own group in which there were contactors who worked together with the apostles. And thus the energy was spread by the following clusters: from Christ to the Apostles, from each of them – to his team, and they conveyed it to ordinary people. From the groups branches also diverged in various directions. And now the work is done in the same way."

- "There is an assumption that after the resurrection Jesus went to Shambhala and remained there till the natural age."

- "No, He immediately ascended to Us and hereon His mission on the Earth was over."

- "Has Christ been incarnated on the Earth within the subsequent two thousand years?"
- "No, He wasn't incarnated."
- "And where else was He sent to after his soul had risen to You?"
- "Upon completion of His mission on the Earth We sent Him as a leader to another planet."
- "Do You meet with him now or there is no necessity?"
- "We never meet with anybody. When We need to learn something about someone – We know. We have such perception of the world. It differs from that of human."
- "They say that now Christ manages the solar system. Is this information correct?"
- "No. At present he is engaged in developing a new civilization. His soul also continues to evolve."
- "Is He busy with the sixth race?"
- "No, this civilization will exist not in your solar system, and especially not on your planet."

A New Religion

The year of two thousand is a conditional boundary of the epochs', of people's races change and of the replacement of the old religion by the new knowledge. The face of Earth itself is changing through natural disasters and transformation as well as the planet's climate and landscape are. And within such ambitious transformation introduction of the new knowledge as a change of the humanity's internal spiritual principles, should appear quite natural and necessary.

The new data that is sent by God and the Higher Hierarchs carries to the humanity new knowledge about God, Devil, the whole system of the universe helping expand the cognitive qualification of the fifth race representative and laying the basic foundation of development for the sixth race. The future humanity is given new concepts, new laws of existence; thus it is being introduced to the Higher Truths which guide the life of the entire physical Cosmos and God's Spiritual Hierarchy. The person should be improved, guided not by the particular laws of the Earthly plane, but by the laws under which the entire universe exists. And this is the first step of his introduction to the Higher world. For the first time people will be guided not by the rules of their specific restricted tiny world, but by grandiose development standards according to which our entire great Universe lives. Therefore, instead of the Ten Commandments which, however, remain in force and keep going into the next millennium, the humanity is given over a hundred of the laws of the cosmic existence. The number of laws is increasing almost exponentially. And such acceleration is caused by the necessity of a modern development pace of the future golden race.

- - - --

One of the most basic commandments of the Bible is «You shall not murder». Therefore we were interested to know who among the Higher Teachers of the Mankind has given this commandment to the Earth. In this regard we asked God:

- "Who was the first among the Determinants who gave people the commandment «You shall not murder»?"

- "Of course, it was I because I guided Christ."

- "And why did other Determinants call through their guided disciples, to assassination?"

- "Who called?" – asked God to specify.

- "It is written in the Bible. The Prophet Moses called and God Shiva. And in the «Old Testament» there are such postulates: «blood for blood», «a tooth for a tooth»."

- "If people have read the Bible attentively they would have understood that this is all the punishment and curse for those who have deserved it. Everything is written in the beginning. When I said – «You shall not murder» – it was decided that it was high time for the humanity to move to high moral standards. Yes, I thought that the man would rise to the good, but he could not help but kill. And I tolerate this ugliness. But now has come the time to answer for what is made. Everyone will get what he deserves. **The trial will be strict but fair.**"

- "Now on Earth there are many religions and branches of them, so people are separated in terms of religion too. Will there be a mono faith for all the humanity?"

- "Mono faith will be surely set up, but people will come to it not at once."

- "Is there a separation of souls after death depending on being a member of a particular religion?"

- "People are divided only by colors of the races both in life and after death. Although religion in a general sense can be described as united already now as it is united in the sense that there is one single God for all one Earth, how he could ever be called, it's I. The whole Earth belongs to Me."

- "What is the division into races?"

- "Each race belongs to its Hierarchic System which is also the Creator of this race. After the man's death every soul, in accordance with its race, goes into its Distribution Center* and flies to its own System."

- "Do people of different races but of the same religion fly to different Distribution Centers? And is there division of souls in the Distribution Center depending on the belonging to different branches of religion?"

- "No. The device distributes souls only by races, but not by religion. So, for example, Afro-Americans and white Americans, who believe in one God after death will fly to different Separators*. No branches of religion are taken into account in the process of distribution in the Separator; the latter can affect somehow only the karma of a man".

- "And how can it be interpreted that different peoples have different Gods: Buddha, Allah, and Jehovah?"

- "This is I in the person of all of them. But, you see, all is caused by certain requirements of the Cosmos. Each nation produces its own range of energies in the total range. Similarly, the particular colors are constituents of a rainbow. Each nation should work out its part in a single whole. And to be at the same time an individual each must have its own direction of development; its own rules, laws, rituals, therefore nations differ in the way of life. And all this has the goal – to maintain a certain chemical composition of the body and the concrete formation of subtle structures in order to produce the desired type of energy in a common bulk of tasks.

Different names of the Gods are just a code-sound expression of that energetics that these names should transmit through themselves to the appropriate energy bases. The names concentrate within themselves certain energy types and then transmit them further on.

Therefore, according to the religions soul after death are not separated and go to the general Distribution Center. Division exists only on racial grounds. But in view of the fact that there will be created a new humanity during a new era on the Earth and all other nations and races will go into the past, only one race will exist on the Earth, and it will have one religion. This will form the basis for Mono faith."

- "Will the predicted second coming of Christ happen?"

- "It is not Christ who will make an appearance, but Our people … that is you will make an appearance," – the last phrase God pronounced solemnly and impressively, disclosing to us the essence of our stay on the Earth.

- "Will the new sixth race start its own development without such a leader as Christ?" – We tried to understand what we are predestined to, not daring to ask something about ourselves. But the lengthy explanation to our question won't come.

As we learned later, God sought that every envoy would understand his / her mission not from Him, but would feel it at his /her heart. It was the soul that intuitively should have led each of us to that we were predestined. It was the very essence of the experiment with the envoys, which lasted for ten years prior to our meeting with God: the Higher were waiting where the souls of the twelve persons would lead to. And only three of the twelve of us have reached the adoption of new laws. The others stopped each at his own Level, each chose what he wanted. And we have been disclosed that we are envoys representing the Second Coming only after years of testing when have reached that peak determined by the Higher.

This time we had to be satisfied with a short message of God to our question:

- "A new religion will originate from you. Religion will exist but there won't be such a Manager as Christ any longer."

- "But has the one who is supposed to be second Christ appeared yet?" – We tried to find out.

- "It is You." – God accented the last pronoun, having embarrassed us with this message. For some moments our tongue failed us. But God was waiting for a reply and I confessed:

- "It's such a Lofty Mission, that it is hard to believe for us..."

- "You are given such a program before you were incarnated on the Earth," – He explained.

- "Will the channelers provide a basis for a mono faith?" – Again, I switched to the channelers concurrently trying to understand the heard. And we were gradually and softly discovered the secret of our stay on Earth. But it was explained not in detail and there were no specifically planned actions; God sought our perceiving the program by heart and soul. We should have intuitively perceived what was incumbent on us, although that was we felt, because we could not for a moment help thinking of Higher Teachers, God or of the prospects for human development. And that was our self-cultivation.

- "Yes. The old religion will stay for another hundred or two hundred years and will decay. Now comes its revival and the turn of the third millennium is its apogee. The revival of the old religion was necessary to provide the base to create a new one. A mono faith will come through the creation of a new sixth race. Of course, the fifth race brought up in the dogmas is unlikely to understand the essence of what is actually happening. But then nations will disappear. On the Earth there will be one nation remained, in other words, just the sixth race, which will speak a single language. The economic and political ground for the strife, wars, for different religions and all sorts of their branches will vanish. There will be one nation, one language, one religion. All people will come to a single faith and therefore a Mono faith will come to the Earth."

- "And when will it come?"
- "This will not be very soon. A millennium shall pass."
- "Will Your envoys be sent to create a Monofaith?" – Again, we tried to clarify.
- "Absolutely ..." – God paused and as if He smiled at our misunderstanding of our mission said: – "You are already here. You have started while others will continue and take the baton from you to bear it across the centuries."
- "Are all these activities planned in our programs?"
- "Naturally. On Earth everything is happening according to the program. But the choice was made There, in Heaven," – He said solemnly, with emphasis on the word «There». And the following words God uttered slowly and stately. – "I brought all of you together informed you of your goal. You have agreed." – (There, in «Heaven», He gathered twelve men, twelve envoys, and everyone was acquainted with the program. He gave each a cosmic name. But when we were descended to the Earth the memory of the past closed. Then each had to be governed only by the urge of his soul: both in his deeds and thoughts).

I recalled how in one of longstanding channelings God said that channelers should have entered the consciousness of the given man so that having reached the level of his consciousness to be able to combine modern concepts with the new information given from Above. At that time it was mentioned in passing, but now those words have clarified our future goal – to make the new information and laws sent by God available for comprehension by the modern man.

- "Thank You for Your confidence," – we thanked not yet believing in the possibility of such a mission for ourselves. Much needed to be analyzed inside ourselves and what was happening around us so we did not ask about the forthcoming and began to further develop the topics interesting to people. We have continued to extract the truth necessary to mankind and did not rush as many others would have done to find out personal challenges and our past. I clarified: – "What are the reasons for establishing a new religion from a cosmic point of view? What is the need for its creation?"

- "From the viewpoint of the Cosmos, creation of a new religion is caused by the need for a new stage of the soul development and, on the other hand, – by the needs of Hierarchic Systems to receive a new kind of energy of a higher quality than previously. We cannot be satisfied with what was done a thousand or even two hundred years ago. Evolution moves forward and requires constant modernization of all the old processes. Therefore, technologies used by Hierarchic Systems to produce energies are changing; the processes and carriers of these processes are changing too. Religion itself is linked to global processes of the Cosmos of which people have no idea."

- "How is the link between cosmic and religious processes established?"

- "We descend to the Earth channelers, envoys. Through them, We discharge the desired energy to other people and the Earth. What is for example the essence of the phenomenon of Christ and his apostles? Through them the descent to the Earth of new energies intended for the next two thousand years was accomplished." – (By the way, awaking in the mid of the night I sometimes felt clearly a powerful invisible stream flowing through me. It seemed to me that the turbulent river was flowing through my body as if through a pipe seething with water and foaming up. Now it was clear what energy God had spoken of. The boiling stream which was rapidly rushing across me an incomprehensible way was the energy descended through us to the Earth.)*– "Therefore, Christ himself and his apostles," – continued God, –" were properly constructed in energy terms to take on the huge energy potential of the new energy being discharged to the Earth. Based on this new energy all processes are updated. This is like primary fuel. Based on the new energy, new products for the Cosmos are manufactured."

-"And what is the essence of these envoys, i.e. you?" – He returned to the present. – "It is in the fact that you are also built accordingly in your subtle constructions but are designed for a more powerful energy potential than two thousand years ago. Therefore, the souls of new messengers or you have been selected according to the particular plan and they are not just the souls of ex-people who have reached high-level energy development but the souls who passed through the stage of human development and have already passed the stage of development of planets and have been embodied into the physical bodies of small planets. And so they are able to withstand the enormous energy potential of the new energies being discharged through them to the Earth.

This is especially true for the souls of direct channelers; their energy is of immense power. Normal people would have simply burned out during the first communication session. Direct channelers have the souls of planets provided with special power. And We have had to work much to introduce such a strong soul into a physical human body without burning it out. Therefore a series of protective measures was developed allowing the physical body to function normally on the human plane. For example, in the design of A*[4] ... (the cosmic name of our channeler is pronounced)* specific refrigerants are introduced to cool the material body preventing it from severe burns and overheating caused by the energy received, although minor damage did occur. – (The energy was so strong that periodically we are after all and especially A* ... partially burnt)*.

Channelers and envoys transmit to others the energy with a little reduced potential representing a form of transformer that reduces the potential going from Us to people. And in such a way the retransmission of the new energetics to the Earth via the man is implemented."

- "Does the energy descended to the Earth correlate with of our planet's transition to a new orbital*?"

- "Yes. During the planet's transition onto a new orbital, every time a new type of energy of a higher order than the previous one is descended onto it. Each type of the descended energy corresponds to its orbital level-wise. Earlier in the other civilizations the descent of energy although being implemented through people was not associated with religion. It was introduced in the fifth civilization to enhance the quality of energy produced by people. Previously, the energy that came to the Earth was quantitatively less and it was weaker in terms of power. When the first civilization transited onto the first orbital for example very little energy was descended. But they had it enough to make a transit. Later energetics stated to increase. But even if you take Christ, the energy potential, which was descended at that time, was a thousand times weaker than it is at present. But the soul of Christ too, before the mission given to him has passed the development stage through a small planet."

---

[4] A* ... – a cosmic name; *– see Glossary;) *– authors' explanations

- "So, are there people on the Earth, who have evolved in the planet's material body before?"

- "No. Basically only messengers like A* ... and G*... (cosmic names of the channelers)* may be of that kind. The energy, which is being transmitted to the Earth, should enter the planet itself and the power of this energy is very high. Only another planet equal to its power but slightly smaller can withstand this energy. And this great energy being descended onto Earth comes to the planet's soul which is equal in power and is now located in the channeler's body. From the channeler the energy is transmitted to messengers and through them it comes to people. In fact, power* potential for other people is reduced twice. And then each person transmits the new energy to the Earth having preliminarily processed it within himself. Such is the route of transmission and dissemination of a new energy on the Earth."

- "What are other cases when souls of the planets are embodied in the human body?"

- "They embody the souls of the planets in the body of humans and other Beings* only when more powerful energy is needed to be descended somewhere. This energy cannot be discharged at once. To do this a soul with its more powerful potential is required."

- "Is the power of Christ's soul similar to the power of modern channelers' souls?"

- "Requirements of Hierarchic Systems grow as they evolve, therefore the energy power of a modern channeler a thousand times greater than the energy power of Christ. And religion was invented as an operation to process the new energy descended to the Earth and produce on its basis other spiritual energies required for the Cosmos. So, religion is not something abstract that exists by itself, but presents a certain cosmic process."

- "But do beings in other worlds live without religion? Therefore, it is not obligatory anywhere, is it?"

- "Each world requires its individual technological process. And they rarely recur. The humanity needed religion at a certain stage of its development and it was established as a process, not as something abstract, for human entertainment, or just for his comfort. Everything presents some process. And the new religion is the replacement of the old process by a new one. The new religion of Monofaith will bring the Truth to the humanity. From the fantastic version of religion, it will move to reality, people will get to know the Higher cosmic laws as other Beings of the

Cosmos know them, and will start to intend obeying and implementing them. The Old Bible will be replaced by the new cosmic laws under which all Beings in the Cosmos live and which they obey."

- "The Bible is a conductor of energy. Will the new information also transmit energy via letters and word combinations?"

- "The Bible is meant for the human race with a lower energy potential, and therefore it transmits the energy of an appropriate quality and potential. The book with the new laws of the Hierarchy existence will transmit the energy of a higher potential."

- "How is the energy introduced into a new set of laws?"

- "All is done by means of calculation. The letters remain the same but their energy pumping in words changes. New word combinations occur; letters group certain types of energetics into new words which are transferred from Us by the channeler. New blocks of energetics are grouped into sentences, separate paragraphs and separate semantic chapters. The meaning of many words changes which implies the change of their energetics their functional basis."

- "Is this implemented by means of the technology similar to that of constructing prayers?"

- "No. This is not the analogy of prayers although identification of the Bible takes place. But you see, the new book: «Laws of Macrocosm or the Basis of Heavenly Hierarchy Substance» is Higher, More Powerful. It will surpass the Bible in its energy capacity many times. And most importantly – it will bring to people the new energy."

- "How will a new book affect the man?"

- "In addition to semantic effects, while reading it, a man will accumulate new energy in his bio-fields from which it will spread further. A man passes by other people and the energy of his bio-field contacting with other people's bio-fields is extended to others. In such a way constant energy circulation and dissemination of the new energy will occur."

- "Shall the people reading the new book «Laws of Macrocosm ...» necessarily tell others what they have read? Usually energy is transformed through speech. Or will it be enough to come into ordinary field contact with a person in order to transmit energy to him?"

- "Basically, the contact of bio-fields will matter. But of course those who at present will want to learn the information of the book by themselves will refer to the high Level of development and perceive greater energy potential from it. This book will be of interest to Personalities of a Higher spiritual quality. An ordinary modern individual will not understand it.

The new book of the set of laws is meant for future generations and will march through the ages. At the same time, no doubt, every contemporary person trying to understand it will be encouraged by the new energetics and then it will be credited to him. One should try to understand more than he can, because this is the evolving of both intellect and soul; overcoming the difficulties will lead to an increase in his energy potential. Only one who is not eager to know anything delays his evolving and prolongs his suffering in Earthly world."

Antichrist

God Says.

- "The Bible says that Antichrist will come and start to tempt and deprave everyone. Has that time come now (1998)?"
- "No, it has not."
- "And when will he come?"
- "He will start to act more actively in 2006."
- "And how many years will he have an impact on others?"
- "As long as We shall need. It is not Antichrist that is fearful but rather what is hidden in human hearts. He merely exposes other people's vices."
- "And will he really artificially lead people into temptation?"
- "Of course, he will. He will work for the minus System and will continue to destroy the Earth, in other words, all that people will try to lift within five years after the year of two thousand he will start to ruin again. He will occupy a television network, and television programs will be organized in such a way to corrupt people spiritually as much as possible. «Action movies», horror movies, porno films and all of the same kind will be broadcast continuously."
- "But isn't now the same situation? We observe what is going on and we think that this time has come."
- "No, there is not such ugliness yet which will begin with him. So far, everything that is going on with you now is a threshold."
- "In what country will Antichrist appear?"
- "In yours."
- "Why is his coming programmed exactly in Russia? To make our people suffer more?"
- "At the turn of the new millennium souls are being sorted out. Basically, best souls have already been collected, and those who remain

here are unnecessary for a while. They cannot be removed all at once. It takes time to do this. Therefore for a certain period there will remain those who We do not need Above yet. They should undergo some testing and will be removed through Antichrist. Part of souls the most unstable will definitely go for him. They will feel that the way he shows is their own way. Their low- level souls will turn to dubious pleasures through which they will ultimately get corrupted.

Antichrist will take away all low-level souls with him. This is what he aims at. And for that he uses all means available to him. And, of course, good souls are also tested – to what extent they are resistant to temptations, where they have weak qualities. They can also turn from the right way, if they are not resistant enough. Therefore, Antichrist will examine each of those who remain for resistance to vices."

- "What is Antichrist in general? What is his role in the life of mankind?"

- "For the man Antichrist is a personality, contrary to Christ in the qualities of his soul and in the program given to him. His name comes from ancient times or to be more precise it appeared together with Christ. If Jesus under his program was to save the humanity, in other words to bring new energies of that period to Earth, and force mankind to process them within the next two thousand years, Antichrist was supposed to complete this program. He a kind of puts an end to what the humanity has gained for two thousand years. And most importantly – he separates souls for the plus System and the minus one. And so his program contains the following: identifying in the souls that have passed a certain stage of development all the flaws, shortcomings; defining – what a soul inclines to and what it longs for. Therefore, he has his own system to test souls, and I do not interfere in it. Under this system, he uses a whole set of means to corrupt the man in any way: sex, pornography, wine, drugs, freedom of such vices as deception, hard-heartedness, cruelty, gluttony – on the background of mass starvation and poverty, impunity for the atrocities, and so on. Full freedom for all vices.

Each vice in the energy language represents a certain type of low-range energy which is accumulated in the souls of people when they commit any correspondent action or have negative feelings. If a person is faithful to his wife but is pleased to watch erotic movies, the emotions associated with this level of low pleasures will produce low energies which are accumulated in the soul and like a stone pull it to the bottom.

All human emotions produce different qualities of energy, high and low energies. Therefore, depending on what pleasures the man enjoys he accumulates in his soul low or high energies, and hence – rises or falls down.

And Antichrist is called upon to play with human low-range emotions. If a person takes pleasure from alcohol, plus energies in his soul decompose and minus ones are accumulated. Degradation takes place. And from every evil a soul accumulates minus energies of its frequency, descending the scale of minus energies. And thus, through souls' accumulation of plus or minus energies Antichrist will make a division whether they belong to My System or Devil's System. And though one person may be attributed all adverse actions and called Antichrist, but all this exists in the man himself, and if the man becomes a person of high morals and of a high spiritual level, no Antichrist will ever exist."

— — —

Then we talked with Devil about Antichrist, and clarified some details.

Devil says:
- "Will You guide Antichrist on the Earth?"
- "Naturally. This is agreed with God."
- "Has he come yet?"
- "To be more precise in answering you," – He hesitated trying to come to the level of understanding of a contemporary man, – "Antichrists have always been on the Earth. Antichrist is a collective image rather than a certain person. He is disseminated among the people who are becoming degraded, i.e. every part of Antichrist is being developed in each degrading individual."
- "Is he disseminated in millions of people?"
- "Even in billions, because plus personalities also have minus sides."
- "Will all the people that have fallen under Antichrist's influence be then decoded?"
- "No. I'll take them for Myself ... if God allows Me to and if I still want to take them. Not all of them are of interest to Me."
- "Will Antichrist be born specifically in the body of one man?"
- "You may not talk – born or not born. All depends on how to look at what is happening. We can say that he already exists in the body but partially or in particles. He exists in others. Minus personalities of this order

work for My System. I make up programs I need. Humans always specify everything, segregate. However, the process of degradation is constant, so personalities corresponding to Antichrist have been living for a long time but sometimes they strengthen their activities, sometimes – weaken, depending on the time. But as a single person Antichrist will become only after 2000. The concentration of the negative will occur in one person. But people should understand that Antichrist is a certain system to test each individual. And the testing system is developed by Me.

*   *   *

Chapter 5

Mysteries of God's Private Life

GOD'S PATH OF DEVELOPMENT

Over two thousand years the man has imagined God who sent Christ to the Earth as a wise old man sitting on a cloud and responding to requests and desires of any of «His beloved children», and receiving nothing in return from these children.

God is so good, people believe that He can forgive and bestow endlessly. Though sometimes the man admitted that He was capable of punishing as a strict parent, but still this ability to punish people rarely remembered. And especially the man has not tried to fix his attention on the idea that he is obliged to give God something in return. He rather liked to remember the other – «ask, and it shall be given you».

And therefore the man was not tired to ask and ask endlessly and tirelessly and his whole praying was covered with endless requests for anything. Often the man preferred doing something by himself to requesting and waiting for it to be executed without relying on his own abilities. And indeed some were given what they wanted. And through that belief was strengthened.

But the man never knew – who gave and for what; he did not understand he would have to work out what he was given. All in all, a man in a complex mechanism of the Cosmos resembled a naive and selfish child who hoped to obtain the desired without compensating others' efforts being ignorant of the true state of affairs in the world.

And it is God alone who is able to remove the scales of ignorance from the man's eyes and lift the veil of secrecy, which has surrounded Him for all these many thousands of years. Man is not able to understand the Higher* and perverts many noble ideas trying to apply them to his low and dirty world. For example, in his try to love imitating the Higher, the man mostly catches so much dirt that only Purgatory helps clean of it after death. Therefore, only the expanded consciousness and knowledge of the laws of the Hierarchy existence will help a person to approach the proper reflection of the Highest Truths.

– – –

While channeling it was not at once that we were afforded the honor of talking with God. For many years we have had to ascend the Hierarchic ladder passing through life's trials and increasing our energy level enlarging our knowledge of the common-to-all-mankind and to-all-the-cosmos issues till once it was uttered:

- "J* ... – your God and Creator – is talking to you. – (He calls His cosmic name.)"

And of course it was not the first contact when He spoke about himself Personally. Only two years later God came to straight talk with us and narrated secrets about Him which are hardly known to the contemporary man. It should be noted that the Higher dislike talking of their private life, therefore the fact that God deigned to disclose to us the crumbs of mysteries from his own infinite being is His Great indulgence to the man.

In the initial knowledge of God we based ourselves upon the phrase of the Higher Hierarchs who in one of the channelings to the question: «What is God?» replied:

- "God is composed of three-quarters (3 / 4) minus systems and a neutral one, and one-fourth (1 / 4) plus system."

We based ourselves upon this concept during our conversation with God about Himself.

God responds.

- "We know that God that is you is composed of three quarters minus Systems and a neutral one and one-fourth plus Systems. What does this ratio imply?"

- "The plus System is creative, the neutral one includes a medical System and Systems of support with the remaining engaged in the calculations. Some attribute the neutral part to the minus. But everything has its subtlety needed to be learnt in order not to be confused, but understand everything correctly."

- "Is there more work related to calculation than that related to creativity in Cosmos?"

- "Yes, there is a lot of work related to computing," – God confirmed. – "Absolutely everything should be calculated, although it is not easy to invent something new, and it takes very much energy to create new, or invent something mentally but further to make a reality of all the invented forms a great number of Systems that are capable of computing and constructing them are required. This is the reality. Creation of any new forms in the Cosmos is similar to the creation of objects by human beings. Here the situation is like yours: one architect invents a form while numerous departments of designers embody it. There is the same ratio in the Cosmos."

- "You have one plus System accounted for two minus and one neutral. Are all minus Systems equal in their value?"

- "They are not equivalent and perform different functions."

- "Will You enumerate these functions?"

- "Not all the minus Systems perform the destroying function. But let Me start with the neutral System. One of its functions, for example, is dealing with viruses. Viruses cause diseases lasting for the whole lifetime, but they do not necessarily lead to destruction. They regulate the flow and quality of energy within some volume. Viruses, as you know, are very different. And this is precisely what the neutral System directs."

- "Does Y* ... participate in it?" – We asked about the Higher Hierarch being the head of the medical System in Cosmos.

- "No, He has quite a different System. But He is in contact with the System dealing with viruses. They are interrelated, because they have a common peculiarity ... One minus system is engaged in destroying. In the human body there also operates a minus system destroying everything alien inside it which threatens the normal functioning of the body. I have the same analogy. Another minus System programs EVERTHING. These are calculationalists."

- "Are all the Systems at the same Level of development?"

- "No, at different. Calculationalists of course are at the highest Level among all the minus Systems. This is like Administration for the other two: the minus and neutral parts."

- "And above all this is a plus System, isn't it?"

- "Yes. The plus System predominates over all three Systems. It is the most powerful."

- "Is the lowest among them the one which engages in murders?"

- "Yes, it is the lowest. But one can say it is on a Level with that which engages in viruses. They are almost at the same Level. But the destructing System occupies a greater part while the viral one – smaller. All the Systems that make up My world can be presented conditionally as a circle divided into four sectors (see Figure 2). I am the head of all these sectors. Each sector is composed of not one system but many. This is a primitive scheme, but on the whole it is impossible for a man to understand such a structure."

- "Why was such a ratio accepted in Your structure?"
- "This is the question that may be asked only on Higher planes. People are not allowed to know it."
- "Are You the God of the Earth and our Universe?"
- "Yes. Altogether four material universes are subordinate to Me."

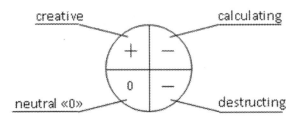

Fig. 2

- "How are these universes located relative to each other?"
- "This is a square – the nearest four adjacent cells."
- "Why are they located precisely that way and not any other?"
- "If the four universes had been scattered there would have been difficulties to guide them. Usually neighboring, adjacent territories are provided for guidance. If My universes had been scattered and I had had to cross the distance, I with My great power may have interfered with the space between My territories. But these spaces are also developing and they have their own program, their own energy and their own lives. Thus only adjacent volumes are provided for efficient management."
- "Are You now at a certain point of our Universe?"
- "Now – at a certain point."
- "Is this place located far from the solar system?"
- "It is far for you. One can build about fifty similar solar systems to reach Me. And despite the distance that separates us We are contacting you. Such are Our technical capabilities. Isn't it a miracle for you?"
- "Yes, it is incredible," – we agreed, having imagined the distance, and then clarified: –"Are you at the given place of the Universe only for a transformation period on the Earth?"
- "Of course I am. I work everywhere."
- "Having completed the transformations on the Earth, will You go to another Universe?"
- "Universes are your terminology. You give this name to a spatial volume in which you exist. With Us it is different. But We have to use

your terminology and concepts. Yes, I will go to another Universe but My control is constant over all the four. I am present simultaneously everywhere."

Development

We have never heard anything about the development of God, how He has reached his perfection. We would like to get to know whether a man may go the same way. Therefore, I (L.L.) asked Him a few questions concerning this topic:

- "Have You passed the stage of development as a human being?"

- "No, I have passed the way not a man but a being similar to you, typical for people. When I emerged there was neither Earth nor the man yet, but there were other beings. And in their forms I existed for a very long time. My course of life is very long. And it was the physical plane that I stayed long on, and then ascended higher."

- "Did You ascend at the expense of the striving for development or at the expense of anything else?"

- "You know when an Entity* lives in the physical world for a long time improving in it the Entity's developing parts become larger in size and more powerful, therefore the long stay in the material world is better for the Entity as its material base for subsequent evolving is prepared. Only after that one can rise higher. Therefore, I have grown very long and hard."

- "Was there something in Your past lives that changed Your further development?"

- "Do you want to ask what has directed Me to the path of God," – He corrected gently, and then explained: – "I was guided by the Determinants the same way as a person is guided. And, of course, many thanks to My Determinant having worked with Me at an early stage of development, because then when I realized My goal I have remembered it all the subsequent lives through and adhered to this goal never turning aside. Or rather – I experienced this, this, and this, went everywhere, but I always remembered in any situation – what I should follow, remembered that path to which the initial Determinant had put Me. He led Me during the first few lives."

- "You've said You remembered your purpose for many lives. Wasn't Your memory of the past cut off or rather was it cut off but the goal was within the soul in its memory?"

- "Yes, it was inside Me. The soul remembers that main it should aspire to, if it becomes the aim of its development. Memory, of course, is cut off in any incarnation of every individual on the material plane. But the soul's major achievements remain within it; the aspirations of the soul as well as some memory of what is the main which is particularly close to a personality, to its internal «I», also remain."

- "So, to be able to remember a soul should have made specific qualitative achievements?"

- "Yes, sure."

- "When you were a simple Being, did You experience much suffering too?"

- "Yes, I've gone through all the sufferings and based on them I have designed My theory of development."

- "Do You remember your sufferings?"

- "Of course, I do. They form a qualitative basis for the soul."

- "Do all souls in Your worlds pass through suffering at an early stage of development?"

- "Yes, one can't do without it. Without suffering, a soul's qualities as practice has proved appear to be low. But My goal is to make a soul perfect."

- "Do souls in the parallel worlds pass through sufferings too?"

- "In My System all souls in any worlds pass through sufferings. If some worlds belong to the other System, the other God, it may be quite different with them. In the other System one may develop without suffering. But in My worlds this is a means to improve souls, a means to educate aimed at development in them such qualities as empathy and compassion for others, love and mutual support, kindness and justice."

- "Are the reasons for suffering the same or different in other worlds? For example, what is deemed to be suffering for a human being can arouse opposite feelings in other creatures of the parallel worlds."

- "For a man suffering exists up to the hundredth Level. But in different worlds they are largely similar."

- "Do Determinants have suffering?"

- "No, They don't have it any longer."

- "You have said that the causes of suffering in Your various worlds are alike. For example, a person suffers from the fact that he has not achieved success in society. May this fact be the reason for suffering in other worlds?"

- "Yes, it may. Many reasons for suffering are identical because My societies are based on one and the same. And I have the same structure of societies themselves and hence emerges similarity. And development one can say is similar."

- "Up to what level did you personally develop through the laws of karma?"

- "Why – «up to what». On all the required Levels, I passed through the laws of cause and effect relationship."

- "By karma* a soul gets required energies. But may the soul itself regulate collecting of its energies from some Level of development?"

- "Of course, some day the karma is canceled, i.e. from a certain Level of development when a person develops certain consciousness. Further its improvement is built in a different way. During subsequent evolving, if an Entity has gone the wrong way in its development it shall replenish the missing. It shall go further but at the same time being obliged before it starts subsequent evolving to collect in addition the amount of energy that it has not collected having deviated. This shall be, of course, more difficult for it. The program shall be complicated at a higher Level and before a new program starts the Entity shall eliminate its previous debts underfulfilled at lower levels, that is, it will have an additional program together with the primary."

- "Have You been engaged in channeling activities to raise Your own consciousness?"

- "At some Level, all people and all beings pass through channeling activity but in different forms. Some people talk with their «I», some – with their Determinant and so on up to someone they can «reach». These are also varieties of contacts. Such connection is generally included both in the man's and Entity's program of opening abilities. Scientists and inventors, writers and artists, and so on can be channelers. So channeling of any kind has always contributed and still contributes to the development of not only individuals but of the whole humanity as well. All inventions are opened to inventors and scientists through channeling relations with their Determinant. Only a Level of contact may differ: some may have it higher, some – lower."

- "What event from the past do You still remember?"

- «I remember everything from the past up to trivial details. The point is that ascending, the higher the better a Personality's memory opens up to recalling of past trivial details. In other words, at a low level of development bad memory prevails and you can forget a lot. But when you reach a high level the memory expands and is capable of keeping in the area of recollection a larger set of information with all the details of the past.

Imagine a cellular structure of memory, and each cell collects all that it can collect. Cells are numerous, and they all differ in the quality of energetics, in the variety of life forms in their everyday terms. For instance, I can take any cell and remember everything I need. It resembles viewing of videotapes at your Level: take any of one's lives like a tape and remember everything that has happened in it».

- "And who personally created You?"

- "The other System that is above Me. And I am for this System as any atom the foundation of something greater, the very foundation."

- "But were You created for the great goal at once or have You reached this position Yourself?"

- "At once no one is ever created for Great goals. An ordinary competition in the development and achievements takes place. And then Tops are taken and compared: who has more advantages. Everything is achieved through one's own improvement, own labor."

- "Consequently, You have achieved everything through perseverance and hard work on Yourself, haven't You?"

- "Yes, of course. Maybe one day you also will come to this. And, I think, it'll happen so. Actually, everyone is destined for the Divine mission and will come to that in the end. Someday, you will also be Top Higher Hierarchs. And not only you but anyone unless, of course, he turns from the true path and moves on to Devil."

- "Is there a large amount of universes in the Cosmos besides Yours?"

- "Yes, there is. And the whole Cosmos is one great organism, in which any Universe can be thought of as a cell of this organism."

- "Are there also many cells in micro-cosmos, each having its own God?"

- "Yes, each cell has its own God, its own Manager."

- "Can You communicate with other Gods?"

- "Yes, I can."

- "Do You establish direct contact?"

- "This happens in case of extreme necessity."

- "Do You God of the great Universe and Gods of mini-Universes exist on equal terms in the Cosmos?"

- "All are relatively equal. The dependence is such that the volumetric content of the given Universe's energy constituent parts belongs to volumetric constituent parts of other Universes. All the worlds contained in each of them are particular energy constituents. And their amount differs."

- "Amount of energy?"

- "Yes. In other words, I possess some amount of energy, the other – some amount. This is Our difference. But, of course, the quality is also of importance."

- "Are other Gods subordinate to You by the Hierarchy levels?"

- "No."

- "Can Gods of these mini-Universes quarrel with each other?"

- "Yes, They can. But this happens very rarely."

- "Who are the judges in case of any disagreement between Them?"

- "Uniting Systems and the Systems who appear to be lawmakers. These are Systems similar to My COD (Coalition Observer Detachment)*, but of a larger scale."

- "Are there Systems similar to COD in every Galaxy?"

- "Yes. This formation is absolute."

- "Do You know how things are going on in other Universes?"

- "I am in charge of a certain number of Universes, and what happens to Them I know. I can, of course, connect the others but it will cost much energy and much work."

- "Shouldn't Your work be interfaced with the work in other Universes?"

- "The point is that the required information is sent to Us. We have messengers which tell us what to do and where to direct our activities. This resembles a nervous system in the human body through which the communication from particular parts in the body to its control center is carried out. We have the same relations in the Cosmos which act similarly."

- "What is the relationship between Your four physical Universes and other material Universes?"

- "We cooperate only with those directly adjacent to My possessions."

- "And can't they get into Your influence zone?"

- "I can communicate and cooperate with the surrounding Universes so far as My energy is enough for this. Of course, We also have very distant communication similar to your telephone and radio communications. But all your communication is very primitive although it is done by analogy with Ours. Of course, Our communication is carried out not merely through such devices as yours. It is somewhat different with Us, subtler, more perfect."

- "Are there Hierarchies similar to Yours in other Universes or are there some other constructions?"

- "In other Universes everything is different. By analogy with the organs in the body: every spatial volume in the body of the Cosmos or

133

rather Nature* kind of corresponds to various organs of a huge maxi-organism. And each has its own structure. And though the organism is single, everything within it is quite different. The same is with My Universes, they are all different. For better understanding, judge by your organism: every organ has dissimilar cells. They are totally different."

- "Now You possess the four Universes and when You ascend higher in Your development how many Universes will be subordinate to You: eight, sixteen?"

- "It depends on up to which Level of a higher Hierarchy I will be able to gather energy constituents. I will be able to extend My power over everything that I will be provided with as far off as much energy I will have at My disposal. It all depends on the quantity and quality of the energy gathered."

- "Will it depend on the number of souls subordinate to You?"

- "Naturally, on the energy constituents. Energetics is always somebody else's potentials."

- "So are you interested to have as many souls as possible?"

- "I am also developing like you and I need to step up Myself in terms of quantity. But I create souls by Myself and in such numbers that I need."

- "Why did You decide to create souls for Yourself? You may have bought them ready-made in other Universes rather than make them."

- "No, in other Universes, i.e. not Mine souls are of other quality than that I would like to have. And, in addition, buying alone one cannot make one's own world. What is Mine should be grown by Me and correspond to the quality I require."

- "Is it probably cheaper to make?"

- "Yes. Those operations which we conduct in Our world can be compared with similar ones on the Earth. For example, someone is engaged in commerce of animals and birds while others prefer to grow them for themselves. Of course, at the commercial level it is more profitable to acquire through the purchase but the quality you need is produced only through your own labor. Therefore, in this case it is easier to grow and monitor the quality by Myself. A merchant will never see what is within his product, I mean quality. I will see it while he will not. But all the same, even My seeing of the subject will not help Me have what I want because nobody will ever grow up a soul with the qualities that I need."

- "Souls help you develop. Consequently, the faster they progress the faster You improve. Is it so?"

- "Yes. We are interrelated. Therefore, each individual retarded in development or taken the path of degradation, hampers, first and foremost, My development."
- "When You ascend a step higher will Your entire Hierarchy ascend together with You or just You alone?"
- "No, My Hierarchy belongs one can say to My organism. I cannot just tear off My hand from Me. So My Hierarchy as a single whole will ascend together with Me."
- "People have the past and the future. And what does that the past represent for You? Is it of any importance?"
- "Of course, it is. The past for Me is all the accumulated information, namely My qualities and all My work."
- "What does the future lie for You in? Is this a series of some events, acquiring new knowledge, creativity or all together?"
- "**My Plans are grandiose, immense for human comprehension.**"
- "Can You approximately say what these plans are like?"
- "You will not understand. This is work within a huge organism."
- "And does it seem gripping to You?"
- "Of course. Everyone chooses what he likes more. We also have freedom of choice."
- "What does Your life consist in now: in educating Entities, creating of new souls and worlds, or in controlling of everything that happens in Your Universes?"
- "My life consists in everything that surrounds Me. I live by all this. You understand that I live by all of you, without you I would not have been Myself. So lives a loving father by his son's interests, and it improves his purely human qualities."
- "Is educating Entities and the man of a great importance in Your life?"
- "Of course, educating is always of a great importance as it is this the quality of souls depends on. And I spend a lot of effort and means on it."
- "Once at one of the channelings it was said that a soul is aware of itself as being «I» only at the initial stage of development. And in this context raises the question: – In what way is the soul aware of itself further on in its development? Is it aware of itself as not «I» but as a certain unity?"
- "The soul feels it is a part of a huge Volume and its necessary part."
- "Is a High Entity aware of itself as some community?"
- "As part of the whole but very large."
- "Excuse us for the question but how are You aware of Yourself?"

- "I am aware of Myself simultaneously as being «I» as being Unity and as being Integrity because I represent a complete type of development at this stage. And the complete type while it has not yet moved to the next stage is still itself and feels like «I» like a Personality. And when I move to another stage of development, to a higher Hierarchy I will again feel like a part of a greater Volume*."

The Work of God

For the first time the man had the opportunity to learn what God is engaged in His world in and we could not but use it for a good purpose to cognize the world and the Higher's interests. I turned to God with the question:
- "Can You say what You personally find joy or satisfaction in?"
- "I have no joy, no satisfaction. Emotions are absent in Our world."
- "But still You find greater or lesser satisfaction in something. What do you like more: working, communicating with others or acquiring energy?"
- "In this sense, I find satisfaction in all that I have and I do. But the Higher do not require emotions to orient themselves in the environment or any of their actions. In Our case they are replaced by Higher consciousness. I need something – so I do it. And I do it as much as I need. As for emotions they are inherent in people so you are glad when you manage to do something and from your point of view try to measure everything around. With Us it is different."
- "It turns out that You have only work and nothing more, doesn't it?"
- "Yes, just work. But We have creativity. A creative work brings the soul into a particular sublime state."
- "We know that You are very busy due to the fact that You're involved in restructuring of the whole Earth. And in how many years will You become freer?"
- "We have no time. With regard to pressure of work We always have something to do, We are always busy. Being busy with work is constant. And herein the essence of Our being lies. Rest as such does not exist. The higher you ascend the ladder of the Hierarchy, the more workload you have. The rhythm is intensive and arduous. And the higher, the more intensive the continuous flow of matters of all kinds is. The continuous flow is such that you cannot even imagine it."

- "Does a Higher Personality always cope with the load provided to it?"

- "Of course, the load corresponds to the Level up to which the soul has risen in its development, so it is potentially ready to the offered work and the continuous flow of matters."

- "You work with many Higher Personalities of Your Hierarchy. Do You have favorites among Your assistants?"

- "No. There are just personalities whom I respect."

- "Do You appreciate them for the mind or for the work done?"

- "For the work."

- "You are engaged in bringing up Your Entities in all the four Universes in the Hierarchy in restructuring of the worlds, and this is Your inside work. And do You do any outside work?"

- "The outside work is connected with the inside as any education or reconstruction requires more means and one has to carry out interchangeable activities. I am at the same time inside and out."

- "Do You meet other Personalities like You but that are outside Your territory?"

- "Of course. There are many Personalities of My Level. We constantly interact."

- "And can we find out what issues You interact on?"

- "All the issues are related to work. We generally tie in separate processes with each other, as We have a united goal of Our Level*, for which We're all working and therefore should coordinate Our actions."

- "We know how You collaborate with the Hierarch of the Medical System. Are these relationships of external or internal character?"

- "Collaboration with the Medical System, COD and Devil is internal relationships. To external belong only relationships with such Personalities as I Myself, while Y*... (the cosmic name of the Hierarch of the Medical System), COD, and Devil are below Me."

- "Is there rivalry between those similar to You, for example for the expansion of cosmic areas, acquisition of new energy?"

- "Remove the word «cosmic» from your lexicon. It is outdated. This concept is for the modern man only," – He administered a reprimand to us and continued: – "With regard to rivalry, in Our world it is expressed in a somewhat different form, nobler than yours. For example, people have competitions in a given area of knowledge, so We can have similar. We compare who of Us has passed one's way better and faster, what achievements one has made. And one who has succeeded in it greater opportunities are given and the territory will be greater. A rivalry itself is not peculiar to Us. We support each other, open new things to Ourselves and to others and are always happy for someone who will come the first to the goal. In your world such relations are called fraternal. We never compete in the way people do."

- "And do You give each other advice?"

- "Naturally. Our interaction is based on mutual assistance and mutual support. We have a single goal. Can it be achieved without coherence of actions and mutual understanding?"

- "How do You expand Your influence zone to other worlds?"

- "I cannot expand by Myself at My own will. I work only with My worlds, and within their bounds. They are under My control."

- "And who then creates new worlds and implements the expansion?"

- "What is in My hands I do and create the new within the borders assigned to Me. For example, a person receives an empty area and on it he creates anything available to his imagination and resources. The same is with Us, but there are some peculiarities. There is general subordination and coherence of actions in development, in other words, Someone from the Above capable of doing it, implements this extension and owing to it all the rest expands. In other words, first the place we exist in or some total Volume* expands, which affords an opportunity to everything that is within it to expand its borders. Herein is the coherence of actions. Initially, the total Volume and the potential of the entire space we live in grow and concurrently everything within it grows too. A certain regular succession works. But each by itself has no right to expand. This violates the general laws of existence in the Universe and the integrity of the Absolute* as a single union."

- "Do You expand somehow Your influence zone to the current low-level worlds?"

- "Of course. I do work with them raising them to higher levels of development."

- "Are lower worlds influenced through knowledge or situations?"

- "It occurs the same as with you on the Earth. People also refer to the low-level world."

- "Are there other ways to expand one's influence zones?"

- "Creativity. Only Creativity. And there is nothing else. I have only what I make, create."

- "The epoch is coming to an end on the Earth. Will Your participation in the affairs of earth dwellers come to the end by the year two thousand, and what will follow after that?"

- "The participation will not be finished, because the Earth will always be under My tutelage. But at certain periods of its development We descend to it. For example, now We, i.e. I and other Higher Entities are close to the Earth in view of the change of epochs, to be exact in view of the planet's transition onto a new orbital. Then, to make it plain, We are expected to have other more complicated work. The main We have already done here, and then We'll leave some of Our Higher Entities to continue the work while We Ourselves will be engaged in other activity at another place."

- "Do You personally come to the Earth during the change of epochs?"

- "Yes, I do."

- "And does Devil come together with You too?"

- "Yes, He does. We always live together with Him, in parallel. We collaborate."

- "Are there any other reasons for You to have to descend onto the Earth in addition to epochs' change?"

- "This occurs when Earth's life is threatened by cosmic Systems which are beyond the scope of My influence."

- "And have there such cases of threat been?"

- "Of course they have."

- "We know that the Earth is managed by M* ... (cosmic name of the Earth's Manager), but at the same time Devil is allowed very much here. What is Devil's share in the affairs of M* ... on the Earth?"

- "On the Earth Devil has his own System, which is in His own hands. That is, the distribution of subordination in relation to the Earth is the following: (the scheme is given, see Figure 3)*. We together with Devil are at the top, M* ... – at the bottom, above the Earth. And at the same Level He has Devil's Systems. These very Systems, which are on a level with M* ..., work with Him. These are Systems of Earthly Level, in other words My plus Systems under the guidance of M* ... and minus Systems under the guidance of Devil work with the Earth. But the Systems themselves, the former and the latter, refer to the same Level of development."

- "And how much are You older than Devil?"

- "If Our ages are compared, it can be said I am twice as old. While both Me and Him have existed long before the appearance of your Earth."

EARTH CONTROL SCHEME

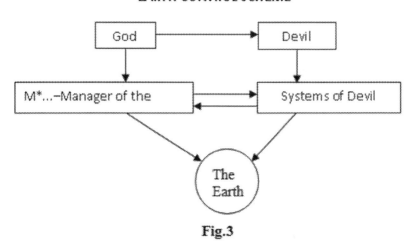

Fig.3

- "And how did He manage to break loose from Your tutelage if the Universe belongs to You? And how did He manage to make His own Hierarchy?"

- "This is My choice. I had a choice and I left Him and allowed Him creating his own cooperating with Me. I had, for example, My Y*.... But He did not break loose from My authority but through the hard work has developed an independent specific branch such as healing."

- "Once You might have decoded Devil* for the atrocities but for some reason You have not done it while You decode other people for doing just the same. Hence, You have appreciated Him for some achievements and therefore have left Him. What have You appreciated Him for?"

- "First and foremost for **obedience**. In spite of everything, He is obedient. And moreover, **for accuracy**. Besides, **someone was to fulfill dirty work**, so I left Him."

- "Is Devil a part of «Union» of the Hierarchical Systems?"

- "Yes, He is."

- "Does Devil control time?"

- "No. Time is beyond His control."

- "Is time under Your control only?"

- "The terrestrial time is entirely under My control. As regards the all-cosmic time, it is an absolute* value which does not belong to anybody but it can be managed. And while creating any structures a desired number of pieces is taken and inserted into the united structure. Units of time are different for different worlds."

- "Can Devil also manipulate time?"
- "In this sense He, of course, has the right to work. We co-operate with Him but there are some subtleties which He does not know, so in this matter He remains dependent on Me."
- "People have a legend that one of the black angels betrayed You. Were there any cases of serious betrayal during Your previous existence?"
- "In what period exactly? My life goes too far into the past."
- "Before the Bible period. The legend tells of the betrayal of Lucifer. Is there common sense in this legend?"
- "Of course, there is. There are betrayals." – (There are sad notes in His voice. It seemed to be unpleasant for Him to talk on this subject. But curiosity pushes us to ask more.)
- "Is Lucifer Devil himself?"
- "No," – He responds briefly and unwillingly.
- "Did you undergo betrayal in the past that did harm to You? Or are You always ready to be betrayed?" – We continued to get to the truth concealing the mystery of the relationship of the Higher.
- "You know, if any harm is done to Me I will rise even higher in My development based on it."
- "We do not understand this. How can one rise higher?"
- "This is difficult to explain on the human level of understanding, but I will try. Suppose I was betrayed. And the one who betrayed, leaves. There is the vacant space in one of My cells. And I fill it with new energy. There is an influx of new high-quality energy which contributes to improvement and renewal. Through the exchange of energies development is significantly accelerated. One can even say that the betrayal is part of My experience which gives Me strength and speed in evolving. Self-perfection takes place. This is similar to your anguish of mind. And by means of them development, growth always happens."

- - -

- "Can we ask a question about Your private life?"
- "What are you interested in?"
- "Would you please tell us if You had children when You lived as a simple Being?"
- "Of course. I lived like everyone."
- "Did any of Your children follow You?"
- "Many of them followed Me. And they also ascended very high."
- "And then everyone went his own way, didn't he?"

- "Naturally, everyone has his own way."
- "Is some of them close to You at present?"
- "Yes, and they are even very close. Some have been so close that have already entered into Me, figuratively speaking."

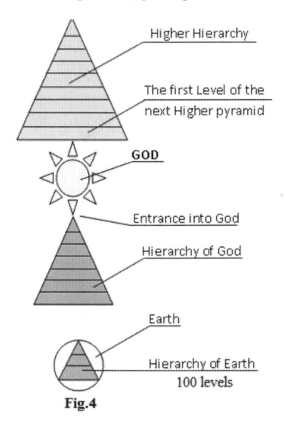

Fig.4

- "Into You?" – We did not understand. – "How is it possible?"
- "You know, in my Hierarchy souls in course of their evolving ascend up to the end of the Hierarchy's pyramid, up to its top, and there am I (see Fig. 4). And when personalities ascend by the levels of the Hierarchy to the pyramid's top they enter into Me through a special channel (merging with God)*. Having ascended he becomes a part of Me. And all the souls that are within the pyramid should enter into Me till the last man before I go somewhere further, higher, into a larger more highly-developed pyramid but into its first Level. The very frame of the lower pyramid remains. And while My souls are entering into Me the pyramid concurrently starts to

be filled with other souls. This is another batch of souls and it is already designed for someone else who will come to My place."

- - - -

As it was mentioned above, after a series of channelings with God we had several communication sessions with Devil. God gave us this opportunity unexpectedly for us. This was done so that we could compare the difference in the development of two different worlds (God's worlds and Devil's worlds) and understand the essence of the good and evil in a new spiral of development while at the same time apparently He wanted to check us on loyalty to Him.

Therefore, many questions were based further on those notions which Devil gave.

God answers:
 - "At one of His contacts Devil said that in the Cosmos all Beings assume energy. It turns out that individual selfishness is valued as a plus trait in Cosmos, doesn't it?"
 - "The truth may be uttered but not proved completely and therefore without understanding of Our relationship, people will always interpret it incorrect. The assignment of energy in the Systems is not selfishness. We have such work. We do not merely assign it to personally Ourselves. Energy is acquired and spent on different needs of Hierarchical Systems, for all kinds of constructing. One can say – We have all in common, and everyone works for the common good."
 - "Devil said He invented the black art. And who then invented the white magic?"
 - "White magic has gone from Me. I ordered my men to create white in response to the black art."
 - "What is the difference between the white and black magic?"
 - "In recruitment of souls. Anyone who deals with the black art is recruited by Devil."
 - "Are ordinary people who use the black magician also recruited to Devil? Suppose a black magician helps some of ordinary people; does he recruit them at that?"
 - "A mage recruits his patients only if they agree and through being rendered assistance no one can be recruited. Any recruitment that occurs

on the earthly plane is carried out only with My permission. Everything is done upon My consideration. Generally those who turn to the black magician have some kind of karmic prerequisite for participation in this action. They have everything connected with karma. The magician himself who is directly involved in magic is already the property of Devil."

- "May the magic be regarded as creativity?"

- "Everything that has any action is creativity. But only the souls of Devil who are on the Earth are involved in creativity. It is due to these abilities given to souls that Devil wins them over."

- "Is the process resulted in creating the new considered creativity?"

- "Yes, actions leading to the emergence of the new. An action may cause something positive or negative, but most importantly, it is different from all the rest. It is considered so in My Hierarchy."

*　*　*

Chapter 6
Formation of God's Hierarchy

GOD'S HIERARCHY

Hierarchy Levels

The time has come to get acquainted with God's worlds at least in general terms. God possesses physical as well as subtle worlds which remain invisible for the man. Their formation has similarities and differences as well. Material planes we can somehow imagine while subtle worlds remain incomprehensible to us in their formation and it is God alone who can disclose their formation to us. We begin to cognize them with the following question:

- "A physical world is built on the principle of the «Russian nested doll». And what principle are subtle worlds built on?"
- "On the Hierarchical principle."
- "And what about spiritual worlds?"
- "But it is spiritual worlds that My Hierarchy represents."
- "Is the Hierarchy's formation similar to the structure of the «Russian nested doll»?"
- "This is an infinite staircase running upwards composed of Levels or worlds of a certain development level. There is a specific construction to fulfill certain work at each Level (see Fig. 5)".

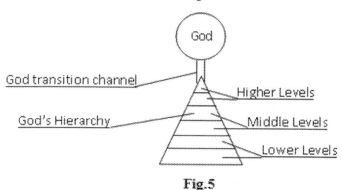

Fig.5

- "The Hierarchic Systems are subordinate to You, You possess various worlds. How do all of them correlate with each other?"

- "They are correlated by the Hierarchy, a multivariate construction which exists in many dimensions. The worlds inhabit Hierarchic Systems which present communities of Higher Entities united by some occupation and a certain development level. The Hierarchic Systems governing the Earth are on the planes close to the earthly one. Above the mid Level there are not the Systems but communities of other formation. And absolutely everything is a part of My Hierarchy structurally resembling a pyramid.

The Hierarchy is divided into a definite number of Levels or worlds. In people's opinion a Level is some stage of development to go upwards the Hierarchic staircase. At each Level there are Entities that correspond to the given world's energetics and are at a certain development level. This resembles the education system in your school: seven-year-old children are united into the first grade and live in their world while seventeen-year-olds – into the tenth grade. Worlds are the environment that also corresponds to every order arrangement of a Level according to all characteristics and requirements. And each order structure* will have its specific development degree, therefore there will be its own Hierarchic Systems at each Level."

- "Are there several worlds or one at one and the same Level?"

- "A Level is one united world subdivided into several particular worlds or sublevels. And there are communities in particular worlds grouped by development stages because at one and the same Level there are Entities* that have reached a limit in their development and are ready to make a transit to a higher stage while others have just transited to this Level from the inferior one. There are also Entities that have reached a mid-level development. In other words ascending the Level itself is also a certain scale. Levels are divided in your terms into classes and for each class or development stage there are particular programs. For every stage for every community there is it own development program."

- "Are the worlds of the same Level different?"

- "Yes, they are. Each of them is in its own state. Everything is different though they may have something common."

- "How does the time-flow rate in the Hierarchy change when ascending the Levels?"

- "At the bottom of the Hierarchy the time flows slowly and in your physical world it is slowed down for Us to an extent that you seem very sluggish and clumsy one can say like tortoises. In the Hierarchy's Higher worlds the times flows at an accelerated pace, i.e. the higher the world, the more accelerated the time. But the more powerful an Entity, the more possibilities are opened for it with the rapid time-flow rate."

- "What sets everything in motion: the time, program or something else?"

- "Time. It is put in the development program and begins to deploy it."

- "How many Levels of the earthly plane should the man pass to rise to the first Level of the Hierarchy?"

- "He should pass hundred earthly Levels. I've made up a Hierarchy of mankind. I am its God."

- "Does each Level have its own energetics density?"

- "Yes, it has both density and extent. Each is characterized by certain parameters."

- "Is one Level different from another by its extent?"

- "Yes. Every world has its own spatial volume, its own borders."

- "What does it depend on?"

- "On approaching the matter. The closer to the matter, the subtler and narrower the Level, and the farther from it, the broader the Level (see Fig. 6). Between Levels, there are certain energy frontiers. Each Level of Hierarchy has its own energy set of specific range. There are more energy-intensive Levels and less energy-intensive. Energy intensity also decreases when approaching the matter. The farther from it, the more number of energies the Level has and the higher its energy intensity*."

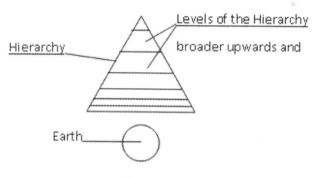

Fig. 6

- "What does a Level represent in terms of spiritual understanding?"

- "Level is the distribution of Entities in the Hierarchy in accordance with the development of a personality and its qualitative set of energies and consequently in accordance with its spiritual development as spiritual coming-to-be implies qualitative gathering of energies, high consciousness.

Therefore, the Level distributes and defines the location of the Entity in the Hierarchy depending on its spiritual progression."

- "What unites all the Levels into a single whole?"

- "They are united by the Absolute*. It gives the program for all the inferior Levels and thereby, i.e. by means of a united goal unifies them. It also unifies by a common structure. Worlds may be nested without interfering with each other. This is a special construction. And the Hierarchy itself is of course not a flat pyramid but the volumetric similar construction, however for the imaginative human understanding a geometric form is taken."

- "Can some Level perish for some reason in the Hierarchy?"

- "Yes, it is possible."

- "For what reason?"

- "Death of a Level occurs due to the breaking of the energy balance, for example between the higher Level and an inferior one when the higher Level gives its energy for any particular purpose to the inferior Level and in return receives nothing in other words it does not receive energy compensating the given energy. And if the Level does not reimburse it for itself it will perish because this energy is vital to it. And since it dies, Higher structures do not get what they need. The energy balance is not observed further above. Thereby the whole Hierarchy's construction may collapse."

- "Don't the neighboring Levels take over its functions?"

- "No. But to avoid the above-said the unbalanced Level is supplemented with lower systems. However, the reconstruction takes more time, i.e. the development slows down as in case this Level had kept its integrity, it would have carried out quicker what it is designed for compared with someone new who would fulfill the same work."

- "And how often do You have such reconstructions?"

- "We are evolving, improving, so it is impossible to use the old always. Rearrangement of everything always takes place. Some becomes lower, some – higher. Levels are being redesigned."

- "There is money crisis in our country. Money is the energy equivalent. Does the accumulated energy crisis ever happen in Your Hierarchy?"

- "A crisis never happens in Our world."

- "But still does it happen that there is lack of some types of energy?"

- "Sometimes there is lack of energy. But then We do everything possible to replenish it. But usually We calculate the energy required far ahead, contrary to what you have on the Earth – doing something without thinking about the future and consequences. We plan quantities and qualities of energies for the period We need. And in the same way it is planned at each Level."

- "Does each inferior Level produce energy for a higher one?"

- "Yes. But the higher Level plans and controls this production."

- "The higher the Level, the more energy it receives, doesn't it?"

- "Yes. The energy transfer goes from inferior Levels to higher successively. And the higher the world, the more energy it receives."

- "And what are qualitative changes?"

- "The higher the Level, the higher the energies, it is constructed of and hereupon are its corresponding requirements to others. So, the higher the world, the better and cleaner energy it receives."

- "Is the energy transmitted downwards too?"

- "Yes. An inferior Level is managed and transmitted energy to implement the necessary processes."

- "Is energy transmitted in smaller quantities to inferior Levels compared with higher?"

- "Yes. You see, there are certain quantitative relationships in the process of transmission. Higher Levels should receive the energy surplus; otherwise there will be no growth, evolution."

- "Does each Level have two energy collectors: one for the energy transmitted downwards, the other – to get it on its own needs?"

- "Similar energy bases exist; however they are not separate, but common to this Level. At each base energies are sorted by the type, and then each of them takes its place."

- "What is the difference between higher Levels and inferior: are the worlds becoming better, more beautiful?"

- "Levels are becoming purer, brighter. But they differ among themselves in chromaticity when it comes to aesthetic perception of them. If you take the highest world in the Hierarchy or the last but one from the top, all of them are permeated with bright light. There is much light coming not from the sun or any stars but from the world's saturation with energies. At these Levels there is abundance of Higher energies. They are emitted from everywhere from all subjects and forms of existence. There dominate such colors which are unknown to man because his chromaticity range is very limited. In such radiant worlds there is multitude of all sorts of unusual constructions which seem fantastic from below to inferior Entities. Constructions are very beautiful and everything else is unusual and beautiful too. Therefore, inferior Entities are eager to get into such a world but for this it is necessary to achieve the appropriate degree of development."

- "Is there a real boundary between two adjacent Levels?"

- "Yes, there is."

- "Is this a kind of artificial construction in the form of a plane or a grid dividing the neighboring worlds?"

- "This border can be represented in the form of a glass partition."

- "Is this the boundary between two energy densities?"

- "Yes. Through it one can see everything that is behind it but it is impossible to go through such a boundary, that is why inferiors cannot penetrate into higher (worlds). Moreover, not all the Entities from one and the same Level can see these boundaries but only those who in their development have approached the next Level. They see both the boundary and what is behind it. They see a different world completely different constructions, more beautiful and exciting than in their world. And Entities are striving towards this new unknown world. It captivates them, they get interested in it. What they see kind of stimulates them additionally and they accelerate their development.

(It is because of various development levels that some people on the Earth see «flying saucers» and all beings from parallel universes while others see nothing, although they can stand side by side. Those who see have approached in their development the borders of those Levels which they have reached in the course of improvement. Usually they see something connected with the adjacent worlds (see Fig. 7). But here one should distinguish between Levels of human development.

For example, an individual «1» will see a higher world while an individual «2» will see an inferior world. For this reason, some people on the Earth can see lower worlds and some – higher. But if it is considered that there are many Levels of human development on the Earth, then developing through them at one moment the soul can see some parallel worlds of the Earth at another – others which it has most closely approached at this stage of development. So there is nothing strange that clairvoyants see different worlds and different creatures; it is, on the contrary the law of human development. These very clairvoyants when retreating from the Level's border in the course of their progression will no longer see parallel world for some time and perhaps in a few lives will approach the next parallel world and see it.

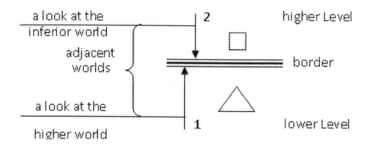

Fig. 7

Subtle vision opens because the individual in the course of development has already made himself as required and if he is below he sees what is going on behind the boundary of the adjacent world. And those who are far from the boundary: either they have not reached it yet or vice versa – have passed it, see nothing of the kind and are present only in their world.

It is due to this degree of development that some people look at the sky and see unidentified flying objects while others see nothing, although it may be under their very nose. They have not matured enough in their improvement for such spectacles. A man makes himself in the process of development. Consequently, those who cannot see anything have not completed themselves accordingly. But everything is ahead.)*"

- "Are there any empty spaces between the Levels?"
- "No."

Hierarchy Structure and its Connection with God

For the man celestial worlds seem elusive air volumes, empty, without having in them any constructive elements. The man believes that the world of God is a pure space where the men's souls and angels fly. And if they want to rest they sit down on the clouds. But these are his old ideas about the divine world. Man cannot imagine something which is beyond of what he has seen on the Earth. And only the Higher alone are able to tell him about the structure of their worlds.

God responds:

- "What is Hierarchy – a structure or a system?"
- "The Hierarchy is a system of improvement, which requires certain constructive design. And one without the other cannot exist."
- "Man imagines the Hierarchy as some air transcendental country."
- "No, it is concrete constructions, calculated by the Higher for solidity, possible load and overload. But this is a monumental construction of the subtle plane, inaccessible for perception of material beings."
- "Why is the Hierarchy given to us in the form of a pyramid and for instance not in the form of a cube or a sphere?"
- "This is its conditional expression which characterizes the best way the trend of development from the lower* to the higher. The real construction of the Hierarchy is so complex that it cannot be inscribed in geometric shapes known to human imagination. If you look at it with a subtle vision of the soul it will be an infinite volume for the person."
- "What is the basis of the Hierarchy's pyramid?"
- "The Hierarchical pyramid has a certain level framework and a platform at the base. Each Level is characterized by its own matter and its own structure. Each Level is characterized by a different set of energies, i.e. its own matter. The platform of the pyramid is an energy grid that holds all the higher Levels. There are branches of this grid too. Such is approximately the building part of this construction, although it also has a physical basis, a technology basis, and several others."
- "Are these constructions of Your Hierarchy permanent or reconstructed?"
- "The main bearing structures remain unchanged. But there are parts that are subjected to renewal. These are secondary structures. They are constantly transformed but so that the main buildings are not affected. The framework of the Hierarchy is referred to these main bearing structures. It remained unchanged during the period of My complete cycle of development. And when the cycle is completed and I together with My Entities leave the Hierarchy, it is reconstructed, modernized for the new stage of development of other Entities with another God."
- "What should one understand by the Hierarchy: the system of Governance and Subordination or the general scheme of the cosmic structure?"
- "This is both: one thing and another, although the latter remains incomprehensible for the man. For the man the Hierarchy is his universe,

in other words that space in all the complexities of its structure through which he will have to go in the course of his progressing."

- "What is the essence of the transformation of the Hierarchy?"

- "In the process of personal evolution I cannot restrict Myself to the development within a single Hierarchy but should move forward, higher. And the transformation of the Hierarchy is precisely the transition from one state into the other, higher. The Hierarchy itself in the form of a structure, its framework remains as a stage of development and all who inhabit it are transferred, transformed into other forms of life. The Hierarchy comprises one Absolute; i.e. regarding people, it is Me. And all who are in this Hierarchy are already the Absolute. Each Hierarchy's Entity comes in its development to the top of the pyramid or to the Absolute and consequently by its construction it becomes similar to it. This is followed by the transition of everyone to a higher stage and after that the old structure of the Hierarchy is filled with other content and Entities of other quality (see Fig. 8)."

- "And what will happen after the last Entity in the pyramid of Your batch of souls enters into You?"

- "I will go higher together with all of you. And we with the pyramid's full complement will arrive at the first, lower Level of a higher Hierarchy (see Fig. 9, Hierarchy «B»). At the same time, the lower pyramid with all its inner content will represent some new Entity of a new God who will be improving for a higher Hierarchy (0-1 – the previous pyramid, 0-2 – our new stage of development within the higher pyramid; 0-3 – the next state of our pyramid at the second stage of the new Hierarchy)*. And in such a way our pyramid rising stage by stage, grows, enlarges. The power of each subsequent pyramid («B»)* increases hundredfold while the number of Levels in the pyramids remains constant and unchanged. Only power increases hundredfold. Our pyramid leaves (0-2 – all its internal content leaves while the framework itself at each transition remains)*, and the next pyramid («0-1»^{2})*, at the former site of the left one («0-1»), develops with a new filling for the first Level of Hierarchy «B» the same way. So the filling of the higher Hierarchy by Levels is carried out."

- "Our old pyramid as the first batch of souls leaves it is filled at the same time with new souls from the bottom. And how do You define Your last soul which enters into You before being separated from the pyramid?"

- "Absolutely everything is calculated accurate to the unity. The last Entity which should enter into Me I know very well. I know everyone belonging to Me and do not accept outsiders. You also know yourself and everything that belongs to you and that – to someone else. Similarly do I."

- "Does it all happen as an automatic process?"
- "No, this is not an automatic process. My last Entity even the lowest one I feel so definitely that until it rises to the top and enters into Me I will not ascend higher. I'll wait till it reaches the appropriate Level of development to enter into Me because being underdeveloped it also cannot enter into My volume since such entrance requires specific power of the soul, certain energy potential. Weak energy potential just physically cannot enter into Me."

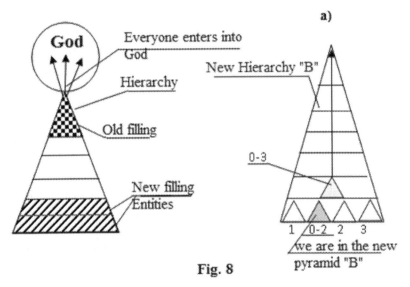

Fig. 8

Notes to Fig. 9:

State «0-2» – each develops by itself for the next Level of the higher pyramid «B», and rises to the extent of its development, without waiting for others (pyramids 1, 2, 3).

The next Entity developing for the first level of the pyramid "B"

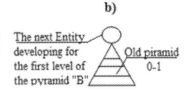

Fig. 9

- "Is the last soul constantly connected with You?"
- "Yes, and not only it. I **do** feel every soul belonging to Me." - (He makes emphasis on the word «do»).
- "Can some Entity be late to enter into You?"

- "No. It can only delay My developing in terms of time. As a result development inhibition takes place. In this case, the Absolute Personality, like Me, does not come to a new Level in time."

- "Do all the Entities of the pyramid enter into You?"

- "No. I give the option: one who wants can take the path of independent development. There have been cases where Entities left Me and led other pyramids themselves".

- "We want to clarify: – Do You feel every soul in the Hierarchy's pyramid deeply, or every person on the Earth as well?"

- "Both. I feel everyone. All of Mine I perceive very well."

- "But You have other planets too. Do You also feel beings on them?"

- "Of course, I do. They are Mine."

- "And is it so throughout the whole vast Universe?"

- "Yes. Such is My sensitivity, if you are able to imagine it. Because I am also Great in size."

- "And do You feel living beings even throughout the four Universes?"
– We continued persistently clarifying incomprehensible to us.

- "It is somewhat different there. But at any moment when it is required I can find any Entity I need and learn everything about it and send it where I need to."

- "After the pyramid Entities enter into You; and what then do they do in You? Do they continue their development as independent personalities?"

- "In earthly terms, they enter into the kingdom of God, into My personal possession. The work on transformation of all individuals entered into this volume continues there. They are constantly changing, constantly moving in development. I supply them new energy, set the program to work with this energy. Each individual receives the energy of a certain quality, recycles it and due to that he grows himself as a part of the energy produced holds in himself."

- "Can we say that there is a general program and each Entity works for it?"

- "Yes, all the Entities that are part of My volume work for the united program for Mine. In other words, everything can be explained as follows: I fill the cells of the matrix* with qualities. A quality* in the form of new energy comes to the cell and starts to develop further within it – to strengthen in terms of its own qualities and increase quantitatively. As a result, the former quality is transformed. The changes occur due to all the new an Entity works with."

- "At inferior Levels, where we are now, we greatly feel our individuality. Isn't an individual lost while entering into the pyramid?"

- "No, he is lost in no circumstances because all the Entities are completely different and such they continue to develop further. But you'll be very surprised having appeared in the Higher and equal to you world after the earthly one. Such nonentities one has to see on the Earth you will not see there. You will be pleasantly surprised that there are so many Entities around you which are similar to you by their internal state."

- "Yes, that is of course very interesting," – we agreed.

- "It is very surprising," – He continued. – "I have put Myself in your place and imagined your impressions."

- "Is there a Hierarchy similar to the pyramid inside You too?"

- "No, there is no Hierarchy inside Me. The fact is that in the matrix, within there is already the required number of Entities and now it is changing only qualitatively. But no one advances the Hierarchy's stairs. Inside there are its own laws of development. The new comes in – and due to this transformation is carried out in each cell."

- "As far as we know on the Earth a man progresses passing through a hundred levels; and do You improve based on the other principle?"

- "The process of accumulation takes place in Me, i.e. there functions the principle of qualitative build-up, qualitative integration."

- "Are the laws that function in You much different from those that function in the Hierarchy?"

- "Yes, they are special laws. There are similar laws of development in each Entity because I am an Entity; and the Entity which is below Me is an Entity too. Not all of Us are Absolutes but each is on the individual level of improvement."

- "What is the functioning of the laws in You aimed at? Can we say that the main purpose of these laws is that through their development they also develop You?"

- "Every Entity has the law of the following character: the main thing is to develop oneself, never stop but go ahead and forward."

- "But shouldn't the laws be aimed at maintaining the energetics of a Higher Entity?"

- "For this purpose, there are general laws of existence for everyone. They (the laws)* are all within Me, and they group all Entity-like Personalities that are within Me into some joint Volume*. In other words, the general laws of higher order join particular laws intended for Entities uniting them through a common goal."

-"Is there any difference between the laws that function within You and that in the Hierarchy's pyramid?"

- "Of course, there is. The Hierarchy is still below Me. The main difference in the laws within Me is that great freedom is added, i.e. the Higher, the more the laws enter into the behavior of the Entities themselves, become part of their own. All the Entities belonging to Me have very high consciousness and therefore observance of laws becomes an integral part of their behavior. For example, an essential attribute for you is cooking meat before eating. This is already ingrained in your mind, in contrast to the wild tribes and has become an integral part of conduct. The same is with Them: many laws have reached the level of unconditioned reflexes, so They no longer consider them to be laws. And speaking of the laws of Their level, they are even the Higher laws compared to that existing in the Hierarchy. Much is based on the work of the Higher consciousness, so one can say that the Higher, the fewer laws. Most laws grow into Entities' habit. And therefore They are offered greater freedom for development."

- "The Hierarchy is now considered to be Your possession. Having completed the development cycle, all the Entities of it transit to You while the very construction of the pyramid remains to be used by another God. And what will happen to the Earth? Will it also pass to the new God?"

- "All living creatures on the Earth as well as in all My four Universes belong to Me and I'll take them with Me. But the constructions themselves will remain. Cells-Universes eventually mutate and become a new form of life. And there from the Above it will be decided what to do with the Earth and other structures: either to remove them and replace completely by new ones or reconstruct everything. But most often reconstruction is carried out."

- "When You transit to a new level of the higher pyramid, will the number of Entities subordinate to You increase?"

- "No."

- "As You will climb the Levels of the new Hierarchy will the number of Entities subordinate to You change?"

- "The number of My Entities remains constant, only their Power increases. Therefore I will work to increase the power of each of My Entities."

- "Do You know what awaits You in the future?"

- "I know that I will create other forms of life with the same Entities of Mine which will go with Me. All of them will go with Me, and the future We will build together."

Who Enters into God

- "You said that the souls of people, having passed the Hierarchy, enter into You. This refers to the souls of our civilization. But on the Earth there have been other civilizations. Did the souls of the second, third, and fourth civilizations also enter into You having passed an appropriate stage of development?"

- "All that is Mine I carry with Me," – (there was an ironical smile in God's intonation. He uttered the earthly aphorism, once said by an ancient philosopher. But most likely the philosopher echoed the words of God and God has remembered His old adage.)*

- "Consequently very many souls have come into You, haven't they?"

- "Let us say – not into Me but into My Hierarchy because they are still under development. As for the Hierarchy, in fact, the many have entered into it. However, some of the Atlanteans for example still exist on the Earth, that is the souls of the former Atlanteans I embodied in people: at this time these are the people with extrasensory abilities. People from each lost civilization currently live on the Earth. Of course, not all of them live but the individuals performing certain tasks or continuing the stage of their improvement here gathering additionally points to ascend the Hierarchy."

- "But are all of them highly developed?"

- "Yes. Compared with a contemporary man they spiritually are far beyond him."

- "And do all have some properties?"

- "No. All of them are different by the development level. There was a civilization which reached an impasse. It was not developed as required".

- "Did the individuals of that civilization also pass through Your Hierarchy before they became the part of You or did it go in another way in those days?"

- "You have no idea about how long the path of improvement is. You see, they are not part of Me yet. Their souls are going to Me, keep on going as the entry in My Volume requires very high-level energetics and an individual will not enter into Me until he accumulates it. And this requires not thousands of years but millions and millions of years by your reckoning. If all souls were already in My Volume then your world wouldn't exist. When all the souls enter into Me your physical world will cease existence. Everything will be different. I'll take everyone with Me. And an overall reconstruction will start in the Cosmos and on the Earth.

There will be construction of the other type on Earth, if We decide to keep her for some needs."

- "And when humanity did not exist at all, wasn't there the Hierarchy either?"

- "I did have the Hierarchy because prior to the Earth I had owned other planets. I have plenty of planets like yours because I have created Cosmos in particular according to My conception. And all the four Universes are My personal ones. I possess them, they are all built according to My plan, so they are the sources whence I could recruit souls for the Hierarchy. And they all have passed through it. But not all the souls have reached the top of the Hierarchy and therefore they have not yet completed their development equal to the entry into My Volume. And so your physical world continues to exist for them to complete their development on the material level."

- "From the Hierarchy's pyramid souls enter into You. Do they concurrently fill any subtle body of Your Volume or some other specific place?"

- "Fill a matrix's cell."

- "Do You have no bodies any longer?"

- "I have some. But they differ from that of human ones by construction, content and their functions as well. Each Higher Entity can be represented as a kind of energy. This is a composite. It also consists of many various kinds of energies but at the same time it is single and represents something special. For example, the color of red is single but it can be composed of thousands of various hues. And therefore this single kind of energy is deposited in some one cell. And its volume attracts everyone having the composite like Mine in a given cell of the matrix. Such Entities are usually unidirectional in development, i.e. the development is similar but not identical. Individuality is preserved."

- "And do souls* from other planets fill Your other cells?"

- "From planets? I do not divide them into different planets. One cell usually comprises: a planet's soul, a star's soul, a soul from somewhere else. And they can vary greatly but be similar by a composite. It is of no importance where they have been located and developed. But to get into a single cell, they should have the similar composite."

- "Do the souls of creatures from the parallel worlds fill something else in You?"

- "There is no difference there. The Entity may come from an energy world or from the earthly one as it may come into the physical world in a bodily form as well as it can transfer to the parallel world and stay there bodiless. For Me it does not matter. The main thing is that composite which they will acquire in the course of the evolution."

- "Do You have any other structures in addition to the matrix?"

- "Everything in Me is filled with energy, therefore I shine. But I one can say am a particular world in which there are many different kinds of formations for Entities' existence and content as well as for their work during the time that they are within Me. But they are developing and I send them to other worlds to obtain a certain quality (in your world it resembles an advanced training business trip)*. But still they are Mine and having acquired the required energy they will return to Me."

Other Gods

Expanding the space of human consciousness implies expanding the boundaries of his knowledge. And since the universe is infinite it forces us to assume that our God is not the single one in it. This makes me ask the following question to God:

- "When all the souls or Entities enter into You You will break away from the pyramid and ascend higher. And who will take the top of the old pyramid which is being filled with other souls from the bottom? Where does a new God for the pyramid remained come from?"

- "The new God – the main leader of the next Hierarchy – always exists. This is also the particular Entity rising in development. Initially, he acts as a Determinant guiding a few men. Then the number of the guided increases. He guides, governs them, gaining experience and is never on a Level with beings but he is always above the rest. Gradually, He creates for himself a structure in which He works himself and which works for Him getting Him something particular required for the quality for the work He particularly produces in the Cosmos. As a result such a personality heads the Hierarchy."

- "Are there many similar structures in the Cosmos?"

- "The whole cosmic body all the Nature* is an infinite interconnected System or otherwise – a huge Entity* structurally designed as embedded one into another like the onion's layers where each layer is separated while all together it is a living volume of one form of existence . But for the Cosmos it is an infinite form of development. Of course, everything is said figuratively; in reality everything is much more complicated and hardly perceptible by the human mind. Each structure does not remain constant and unchanged.

Some structure exists there for a while and then with the change of a development phase it is transformed into another structure in which both the shape and content change. Thus the new structure acquires the structure, form and content which are quite unlike the previous ones.

- "Do Gods who break away from the pyramid have an equal development Level?"

- "They are equal in Level but different in quality, that is why They have equal Power but there can't be identical qualities. This is where They differ."

- "So, does each of Them make his own quality?"

- "Yes. This is where They are individual."

- "And is the volume capacity of similar Gods equal too?"

- "For one Level, it is equal."

- "And is each God comprised of the certain number of souls?"

- "Yes, the number is definite or equal. If they accept the different number of souls, the harmony will be disturbed while everything should be harmonious. In case of differences the subsequent ratios are violated on that Level of a higher pyramid where They are ascending. Since the different number of souls would result in different powers among Them, someone would have it more and someone – less, so they would become incompatible at one Level which they should fill."

- "Do You create souls for your Pyramid by Yourself?"

- "Yes, My system does it under My leadership."

- "And who makes souls to other Gods?"

- "Everyone makes souls to fill his pyramid by himself. But there is a general System which monitors all of Us. This is a special controlling System. However, every God creates the necessary number of souls required for him by Himself. He cannot do more or less as there is a certain amount He is allowed to do."

- "Does each of Them do the quality of a soul by himself too?"

- "Yes, the qualities that He needs, each God seeks Himself. Each God has his own minus Systems which people take for Devil. And every God makes a contract with his Devil; let us assume it being the contract with his second half. They work together. Devil informs his God how many souls he needs so that God can take them into account in his production. But usually God does not give him the required amount and says how many souls He can give to always prevail over Him. This fundamental relation between Them is sustained throughout the entire development."

- "Under what conditions is an Entity trusted to manage the new pyramid when it is appointed God like You? What are the parameters it should have to do this?"

- "For this purpose there is a power capacity criterion though all other indicators must also meet certain requirements. This <u>Entity must have at least half the power of the pyramid which it is going to lead</u>. And this one half (1/2) power capacity accounts for the higher part because the lower half of the pyramid is much smaller in terms of energetics than the upper one while the lower part contains more Entities. Imagine what kind of Entities are at the First Level of the hierarchy and what – at the last one: there are few Entities at the top but they all have a very high potential while at the bottom the potentials are rather small so there are many of them. And the lower part of the pyramid will be many times lower by power capacity than the upper part. Therefore, the leading Entity should have such a relation too, i.e. its power must be equal to or greater than the power of the upper half.

The influence of the given Entity will be distributed throughout the whole pyramid but as follows: The Entity will own the upper half and spread its influence through the lower part. Thus, the upper half will manage the lower one on the basis of the instructions given to them by a Managing Entity. So the Absolute does not necessarily need to personally lead the first Level. This monitoring will be carried out by those who are under His charge."

- "It turns out that each developing Entity, since in the long run it becomes God must be able to manage the ever-increasing number of other individuals?"

- "It must be able to but not necessarily manage. It's all done ad libitum. Paths of development vary. But if it does not like managing it can do something else as well."

- "Do the processes within Levels change over time? For example, at a lower Level Determinants have evolved for two thousand years then – moved to a higher Level and new Entities have come to the previous Level. Will They develop through the same technological process?"

- "Over time everything changes: the quality of Entities, the conditions of existence and everyday development <u>pattern</u> as well."

- "When another God comes to this pyramid, are all the technological processes on the Levels also changing?"

- "Yes, there is global restructuring. And this is due to the fact that in the course of development another Leader requires souls with another qualitative composition which implies changing of the living conditions and of everyday living form organization which in turn leads to changes in production processes reproducing environment and way of life. The new God will have his own laws which will start managing the processes within each Level. And everyone will have to obey these laws."

- "Do all the Entities in any Hierarchies live by their own laws?"

- "There are general laws and private ones. For example, the laws that We have given people are intended only for My Hierarchy. But in fact the living in the Universe develops by such laws, of which man has no slightest idea and will keep having no idea of it because the level of his development is unable to comprehend them."

- "Our laws often refer to the Entities of law as to some living beings capable of self-development. It turns out that any law which directs a person or let's say an Entity at a Level develops and is segregated into a separate being?"

- "Yes, the laws are some developing separate Entities. It's just that it is difficult to comprehend by the human consciousness. But everything exists in a certain living organism of Nature so everything should be living by nature, otherwise the living will not be able to stay alive. Now let us transform this to another concept. The homogeneous energy, if it refers to the Entity of law operates based on the total way of life of all the components of the process which it leads or of the Entity which it guides. They develop and the Entity of law develops based on them respectively being formed into a single homogeneous Entity-like energy and at the same time – into qualitatively heterogeneous energy as everything individual."

- "It turns out that absolutely any quality can be formed into an Entity: the Entity of Time, the Entity of Action, the Entity of Chaos and so on. For a man for example time is not alive while from Your point of view this is some sort of an independent living creature. Is that true?"

- "Yes. Everything is Entities in a living organism of Nature. Time itself, the laws present a few special living conditions which are qualitatively quite different from what they manage and by means of what they develop. Each Entity of My Hierarchy creates and improves its individual Entities of Law and Time. All the three are simultaneously progressing. And all the three mentioned types of Entities are in three qualitatively unlike to each other states. For example, take the man and his Entity of Time or the Entity of Laws based on which he develops; these two Entities have completely different states of qualities but they are making progress on man's changing qualities. However, the Entity of Time and the Entity of Law develop without passing some of the stages which for example the human Entity passes. They have their own peculiar development stages. That means, they additionally pass through their own development paths to turn into such a specific state."

OTHER HIERARCHIES OF GOD

Transition of Souls from the Plus Hierarchy
to the Minus One and vice versa

God says:

- "We know that Devil cooperates with You. And where is He located: in Your Hierarchy or somewhere separate?"

- "Devil has his personal Hierarchy which is the minus development System to individuals. My Hierarchy represents the plus development System."

- "Does it mean that these two Hierarchies are the most important ones in our Universe?"

- "There is one more powerful Hierarchy – the **healing** or, in your terms, **medical** which is of considerable importance. It is the neutral System."

- "So, all in all are there three Hierarchies: plus, minus and neutral?"

- "No, there are many of them. The three listed Hierarchies are the most important. But I have in My immediate Hierarchy Higher Personalities subordinate to Me who have their own Hierarchic structures subordinate to them (Fig. 10) but smaller ones than the first three named."

- "Are these three Hierarchies identical in their construction?"

- "Medical Hierarchy and the Hierarchy of Devil are similar by their constructive forms to Mine but have a number of features associated with the specific actions produced. Within themselves they also comprise particular mini-hierarchies."

-"In what ways do other particular Hierarchies develop?"

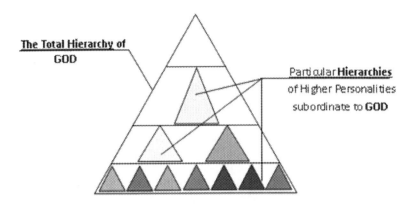

The Total Hierarchy of GOD

Particular Hierarchies of Higher Personalities subordinate to **GOD**

Fig. 10

- "Their activity is aimed at energy production."
- "Do they have some kind of a specialization?"
- "Yes, each mini-hierarchy has its own direction, its own specifics."
- "Can You enumerate at least few directions to be generally examined? Who is engaged and in what?"

God begins to enumerate some individual Hierarchs known to us for their cosmic names:

- "M* ..., as you know deals with the Earth. He works only with the Earth with everything on it. And the planet itself as a living creature too, is subordinate to Him.

K* ... is more engaged in exact sciences. Everything related to calculations is subject to Him. By the nature of his activities He half relates to Devil but only half because basically regarding all other things, He obeys Me.

C* ... specializes in the structure of worlds. This is his direction."

- "Does Devil's Hierarchy lead downwards compared to Yours? We believe that God's Hierarchy implies ascending while Devil's one – descending."

- "There is of course a Hierarchy that leads downwards. But everything is a little different in its design."

- "Is the Hierarchy that leads downwards built exactly the same way as Yours?"

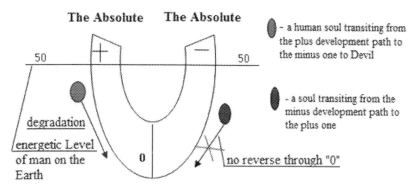

The Absolute   The Absolute

50   50

degradation

energetic Level
of man on the   0
Earth

- a human soul transiting from
the plus development path to
the minus one to Devil

- a soul transiting from the
minus development path to
the plus one

no reverse through "0"

Note:
«0» – the transition point of the soul from plus to minus. At this point the soul's qualities
are assessed and its fate is decided: either it is decoded, or transferred to Devil, or put on the
karmic path.

Fig. 11

- "No. But basically the construction is the same but it comprises a different set of quality energies and a different purpose. It turns out that one top of the construction leads to the plus Absolute in the line of a curve, and the other – to the minus or in your opinion to Devil. But it all goes in the line of one curve (the channeler is showed a chart – see Figure 11). This is a Hierarchic ladder of the physical plane with plus and minus. And if the soul begins to degrade to the limit «zero», then it is examined by Higher Entities and it is decided what to do with it – either to decode it or transit it to the minus Hierarchy. If this soul is not obliterated or decoded*, then it transits from a plus path onto a straight line leading to Devil. But this happens only in case if Devil needs the degrading soul. And if He does not need it either – there are such souls – then it is decoded.

Devil always evaluates opportunities of the soul offered to Him from the point of view of the soul's aptitude for Him and its potential. Empty souls He does not need either. It is essential for the soul to possess some abilities and aspirations in the development, in addition to cruelty and many vices prevailing in it. When the soul transits from the plus system to the minus one, i.e. it is transmitted Devil in return provides the energy of a certain quality but which is equivalent to the decoded soul's structure. Nothing is done to anyone free of charge."

- "Is any soul can be decoded for some offences?"

- "Usually the low-developed souls undergo the decoding. In the course of the evolution the soul gains energetics. The energetics level up to which a soul can be decoded is equal to fifty (Fig. 11, level 50). If a human soul has gained energetics over fifty it cannot be decoded any more. But in the zero point («0», Figure 11) its fate is decided: whether to leave it in the plus System having put it on the path of karma* or send it to the minus System."

- "Who decides where to send the soul further?"

- "It is decided above the Level of the Originators."

- "And who is above the Originators?"

- "The Managers. It is They who decide."

- "And who is above the Managers?"

- "Members of the «Union». Next is «The Higher Union». All of Them are grouped into appropriate Levels, i.e. such a formation of the Hierarchy relates only to the Earth and its surrounding planets."

- "On the Highest Levels of the Hierarchy which are not related to the earthly plane is the transfer of souls from the plus System to the minus one and vice versa possible?"

- "Yes, it is possible but in exceptional cases."

- "On what basis does this transition occur if there is no soul decoding at the Highest Levels?"

- "In My System the basis for the transition is the individual's desire. Everyone goes from My System to Devil's minus System at will. But no one has the right to leave Him at will. The soul may be willing to transit but Devil would not let it go. Until I alone want to take someone with Me. In this case the transition from the minus System to the plus is possible. And this time I take without Devil's consent because He is completely subordinate to Me."

- "You take from Him! But why?" – We are surprised.

- "I'll take very rarely but I do it. Sometimes I need a soul with a set of certain energies which I for example liked and this set of energy I do need for some particular purpose. So, for Me it is such an indispensable Entity which is most suitable for the work that I'm going to give it. In this case, I take the Entity I am interested in and do not return it."

- "Do You teach it in Your spirit?"

- "Yes. And of course, after a very harsh treatment at Devil's it enjoys My free life. Therefore, it does not protest against anything and as a rule it does everything it is charged with well."

- "And can it by force of habit behave outrageously?"

- "Yes, quite easily. But karma keeps working: then it will have to undergo self-purification and self-reeducation. Everything is done according to laws."

- "Is some task on the Earth in the material world posed for the Entity, You take from Devil?"

- "No, no. It does not come down to the material world. All its activities are carried out at High Levels of the Hierarchy. I take only high-level individuals. Low-level* ones I do not need. The material plane is the initial Level. I never do any business with them. Just think what they can do for Me, whether they are capable of doing any work. They have little knowledge and their consciousness i.e. responsibility is at a low level*. While My work is very complicated and I take souls for work only."

- "Is the loss of a highly-developed Entity severe for You if it is willing for example to go to Devil?"

- "It depends on what development stage, what Level it is at the moment. If it has already reached a high Level of the Hierarchy the loss is severe."

- "But don't You get some equivalent for it from Devil?"

- "You see, despite this Entity is given large equivalent for but it is usually of a lower level. Its quality is not as high. For example, if you are given a lot of alcoholics or a wise man the difference is significant in its inner content. The alcoholics have to be much worked on to get the desired quality. And one intellectual is able to replace them all."

- - -

Let us clarify in detail the information about the distribution of souls after death at this moment of time – the year of 2000, in other words, during the transitional period when the shift of souls along the Hierarchy levels is accomplished.

The batch of souls which was launched in life circulation two thousand years ago has matured and therefore the analysis of their maturity is being carried out and the qualities gained are being reviewed.

According to the assessment of energy characteristics gained in the matrix some souls God takes for Himself, others as degraded are rejected. Among the latter some are subject to be decoded immediately while others are offered to Devil. And in these two main directions the following distribution occurs.

GOD'S DIRECTION:

1) Some souls are decoded (they are destroyed as individuals);
2) Souls that have attained a high degree of development move to the first Level of God's Hierarchy;
3) Souls that have not attained a high degree of maturity but have gained certain energy potential and spiritual qualities will transit to the sixth race where they will perform more sophisticated programs and thus, will continue their improvement;
4) A part of souls that have not reached the required qualities and cannot get either onto the first Level of the Hierarchy or to the sixth race but that God has taken for Himself is sent by Him to other worlds that belong to God and correspond to the development level of these souls. There they will bring their improvement to the required standards.
5) Some souls will remain on the subtle plane in «storages» and will be put into life circulation on the Earth. Some constant part of them will always remain there and this is also included in the total number of souls and in their allocation. Such souls are given the right to gain additional qualities they require.
6) Souls of experienced doctors are sent to Medical system. Those who have not reached a sufficient experience return to life with a similar program to improve professionalism.

   In the Medical system some souls of doctors come to the plus part of Medical Hierarchy, others – to its minus one. The division here is made based on souls' qualitative parameters.

   If a doctor has karma first he works it out and then gets into the Medical System.
7) In COD only those souls get that have passed through many Levels of the Hierarchy and attained a very high degree of development.

DEVIL'S DIRECTION:

When Devil selects for Himself eligible souls among the fallen ones their further way is like this.

1) Low-level souls which are incapable of doing anything are sent to Devil's lower worlds to improve in the minus direction;
2) High-level minus souls go to the first Level of Devil's hierarchy and become robot-like.
3) Mid-developed souls return to the Earth and continue to develop under Devil's programs in the minus direction.

Transition of Souls from Level to Level

Improvement of souls in God's Hierarchy consists in their transition from an inferior Level to a higher one. But any development has its own peculiarities. We will try to find them out.

- "Now Your Hierarchy," – I turn to God through our channeler Larisa Seklitova, – "is replenished with the souls from the Earth. And when she did not exist at the expense of what was the Hierarchy replenished?"

- "We had everything different: other planets, processes, methods; and the necessary quality of energy we received through a special technology. Then there was a change. Hierarchic Systems cannot fixate on one thing. And after the humanity appeared the Hierarchy started being replenished with their souls. The process for gaining energy went through another technology. When the soul on the Earth completes the needed development cycle and reaches certain maturity, it is transmitted higher to the pyramid."

- "Are souls transmitted from Level to Level starting with the earthly plane every two thousand years?"

- "Yes. But the timing may be different. It does not necessarily keep within the two thousand years."

- "Does the transition of souls such as we are having now take place throughout the Hierarchy or only from the physical world into the subtle one?"

- "The transition occurs throughout the Hierarchy step-wise. The entire chain is moving simultaneously upwards. If we take the present time all of them are synchronously moving step by step towards this time."

- "Are souls transmitted to the Higher worlds only during the total transition?"

- "This is a global movement associated with the universal cycles of development in the Hierarchy. But in addition to the cycles of course individual souls are transmitted in the interim periods. Once the soul reaches maturity at a certain Level, it is transmitted higher."

- "And what is the mechanism of transition: do Entities take any exams or does it happen automatically?"

- "There are no exams in the Higher worlds. The process is automatic: the Level's density works, i.e. when proper energy qualities are accumulated by the Entity it pushes the latter out of its layers. The Entity ascends the Level through its layers as it accumulates the corresponding energies. And when it reaches the upper layer it stops and remains there until the density of the layer is greater than the density of the Entity which occurs when the energies accumulated by the Entity are above this layer. And then the Entity being a much lighter volume is pushed to a higher Level "

- "What does the Entity feel at the moment it is being pushed out? Is this the state of physical flight or something else?"

- "It is neither of these two. The transition is more like the state of a man coming into the new world. The Entity has a new world, a new program, and new living conditions. The human transition occurs in a somewhat crude form, the similar ascending takes place through his death. But such a nonstandard form of transition exists only for the material world."

- "The man's consciousness is cut off at the time of death and therefore he is not aware of such a transition. Do Entities have their consciousness cut off at this moment?"

- "Their consciousness keeps working all the time."

- "But do Entities perceive this transition as a pleasant event or not?"

- "It is pleasant, of course, because there is nothing so heinous that the man associates with the transition to another world which the Entity is experiencing: there are neither family ties there that a person breaks painfully nor suffering and physical pain which scare you."

- "There are no kindred ties on the Levels but are there probably some other ties combining Entities?"

- "You find it difficult to understand their relationship but, of course, they communicate with each other, however, there is no family there. They do not have such a sensibility to each other like you either. All Entities relate to each other evenly like brothers and it does not happen with them that they like some Entity and don't like the other. They never feel antipathy or hate toward anyone. Friendly and brotherly relations are all over there. The whole Level is one big happy family."

- "So, do they perceive themselves rather a fraternity than individuals?"

- "Of course, such feelings Entities actually experience because they belong to one Hierarchic System, one Level and in this sense they are kindred. But moreover, unlike people they feel their purposefulness, in other words, they feel they should reach the top of the Hierarchy as soon as possible. This is their main goal to which they aspire. The objective unites Entities and they incline each other to approach it and contribute by all means to ascending higher for all of them as soon as possible."

- "What do Entities feel when one of them transits to the next Level, i.e. to another world? On the Earth these transitions are perceived tragic as the loss of dear people."

- "Nothing like your earthly transition they do not have. When others ascend Entities experience joy and desire to rise themselves as soon as possible to the next Level right after the left Entities. Of course, in the first place everyone wants to rise higher himself."

- "While ascending from Level to Level does the Entity's external form change? For example, when transiting from the material world into the subtle one human form after death varies substantially. Does this happen with Entities?"

- "Of course, they undergo transformation too. First of all the Entities' frequency changes as well as their chromaticity, qualitative composition and subtle constructions. They are unique for every Entity. But, generally speaking every Entity is changing every moment not only during the transition. You also are sitting here and changing constantly every moment. All the more so when one rises to a new world."

- "Over time a man sees how much he has changed; is an Entity aware of its changes?"

- "Just like people and even more accurately."

- "What in the Entity's structure is more sensitive: consciousness, the matrix or something else?"

- "The Entity feels through its entire construction, through all that it has. It feels through its full volume. It sees, hears and does something, using its full volume."

- "On the Earth there are many forms of existence in a material world: people, animals, birds, fish and so on. And on one Level of the Hierarchy, are there any other beings besides Entities?"

- "There is a single form – Entities. There are no others."

- "But is there anything similar to animals?"

- "No. Such forms are no longer required there."

- "Do forms of Entities belonging to the lower and upper Levels of the Hierarchy differ among themselves?"

- "The form may be considered to be the same. The difference is in the Entities' size."

- "We want to get more specific information about the transition from the earthly plane to the subtle world. The Bible says that 144 thousand people will be relocated to the Higher planes. At present six billion people live on the Earth. What percentage of this number will be transmitted?"

- "On Earth there are souls of different levels now and only souls from the highest Level will be brought, i.e. the souls that have reached the hundredth Level of the earthly plane. The last year which is intended for the mass transfer of «mature» souls to the Hierarchy is the year 1999. During that year the last two hundred thousand souls are scheduled to be taken from this Level (the reply was made in 1998)*. But We are talking about high-level souls. As for low-level ones they will be climbing but they will not get into the Hierarchy."

- "If for example a professor or academician has highly developed, but does not believe in God will they be transferred to the Higher worlds?"

- "They can be different too. Among them there are careerists. But those who really have reached a high development through their work and their souls correspond to the required qualities are transmitted to the Higher planes. And they come to faith in Us after death."

- "Does high intelligence go to the minus System?"

- "Why?"

- "But some scientists have developed atomic bombs, weapons killing other people."

- "It depends on the qualities that people have gained. If the soul is mostly filled with negative energies, then it goes to the minus System, respectively but whether it is Mine or Devil's it is decided by the Distributive Union. They determine – where to send someone. But good people get to Me."

- "How should the matrix of a man be filled for him to be transferred to the Hierarchy?"

- "The matrix should be filled with all the required range of energies of the earthly plane. At the same time the energy potential of the soul should reach the potential of the energy layers in the Hierarchy's lower Level."

- "Having transited to the Higher worlds, is man no longer incarnated on the Earth?"

- "No, on the Earth he can be incarnated on special assignment like you for example."

- "Now humanity is much disunited. Will it reach someday its unity?"

- "Unity is possible only at a Level i.e. the only place it is possible is within one Level on the subtle plane. Unity with the inferior or higher Level is impossible due to the lack of specific data on energy because beings lack for necessary structures."

- "Can't there be unity between all people on the Earth?"

- "On Earth there are souls of different development Levels. Therefore, unity is impossible here. Low- developed earthly Levels constantly distort Our best ideas descended to mankind. For this reason both you and We often have problems: your societies constantly reach a deadlock from where they have to be pulled out and redirected through the breakup of the old relations. But as I have said the unity can only exist within a particular Level."

- "What about the idea of Christ that all men are brothers? Is this a utopian idea?"

- "This was Our experiment – to awaken the sense of unity in the underdeveloped souls. In part this idea was taken up by the most developed souls and on this basis your socialist state was established which combined many nations. But most fully the idea will be embodied in the sixth race towards the end of its development."

- "Is unity on the same Level of the Hierarchy ever possible given this Level is comprised both with plus and minus Systems?"

- "They are equal by the development level. And it is their unity that the whole Level keeps together and develops through."

- - -

God's Management of Levels

Levels of the Hierarchy are worlds of God. And as their owner He directs them. All the worlds are controlled by God. But how in particular is this management performed? This should be clarified.

- "What does Your leadership of the lower Levels present?" – I turned to God. – "Do You check their development plans, projects or results?"

God responds through Larisa Seklitova:

- "I set the objectives and supervise programs and the results of operations. Everything is analyzed in comparison, corrections are made."

- "Do You give them advice?"

- "It is not giving advice but performing leadership."

- "And if You do not agree with the plans of Your subordinates, should they change them or do You give them freedom of choice in activities?"

- "If something is not consistent with the general plans I point out the deviation to them and they must change their work."

- "Devil's System is subordinate to You. Does it disturb You in anything?"

- "No."
- "And how often does it happen that it does what You do not want to? For example, they have given people such an invention as the atomic bomb."
- "This was done according to the plan."
- "Do You force to correct mistakes that have already been made or do You force to correct the whole programs?"
- "Some correction of programs is required. But everything you regard as errors is included in the plan as it is all connected with people's karma and their choices in situations."
- "Were the Revolution of 1917 and the seventy years of the proletariat dictatorship planned?"
- "Yes, it was Our program. It gave some results."
- "The period to complete stagnation in our country could have stretched out a long time if the society in the eighties has not made a different choice."
- "In this case it was not your choice but Our intervention. For these purposes programs are constantly corrected depending on the results received."

Level-Wise Development of Entities

Worlds of God are filled with highly-developed individuals referred to as Entities. When the human soul gets in His Hierarchy it will also be called Entity. But there are also living creatures on other planets and in other worlds. Where do they get? What way does their further development progress? Hence the next question has ripened:
- "Is Your Hierarchy intended for souls from the Earth only?"
- "Why? Not only from the Earth but from your entire Universe and the other three ones as well."
- "Is it comprised of so many souls?" – We are surprised.
- "My Hierarchy is intended for all the four Universes and is designed to maintain a certain number of souls."
- "But the Universes are likely to have different forms of existence and different souls for living beings. So how do they manage then to reside on the same Hierarchy Level?"
- "By their subtle constructions Entities are alike but they differ in their physical forms and qualities of souls. For your Universe there is one type of

qualities (I am speaking in general), for the second Universe – the other, for the third – some other type. And in such a way – all the four types. The four different qualities which I need and which I am now accumulating. When all that is necessary is gained, I will end My stay here and transit to a superior stage begin a new cycle of development and will be creating another Volume of the world and be generating new qualities. In the new Volume there will be other life forms but souls will be Mine I mean your souls."

- "The four Universes have different forms and different conditions for life, so they are gaining different energies in their matrices. And despite the fact that they are so different do all of them get on the first Level of Your Hierarchy?"

- "Yes, they do. Some, however, that have advanced in their development can reach higher Levels. Various living forms have different speed of development; some progress more rapidly and, therefore, get to the Hierarchy quicker, others – slower. But starting with the first Hierarchy Level they have a single speed of development."

- "It turns out that souls with different qualities gather on the first Level."

- "Of course. Although there are all sorts of mini-hierarchies uniting them by some qualities. Earthly souls get into their own mini-hierarchy. But these unions are conditional. Souls are free in their movements and communication with others."

- "And further in the worlds of the Hierarchy do these souls accumulate the same type of energies in the matrix?"

- "Prior to the first Level they have evolved according to different laws and on the Hierarchy Levels they will be governed by single laws, so their development will be one can say of the same type."

- "Is it like children from different nations gathering in the first grade?"

- "Yes, one can draw this analogy. But you cannot even imagine what sort of life some of them lived before the first Level. If you compare their life with yours then it may be simply incommensurable. Although I lay the similar foundation for all the initial souls but the very living conditions for them are made by the Higher such that they form souls in different ways and even opposite to each other. Thus the speed of development becomes different and the souls – opposite. Living conditions exert influence on it. The environment influences greatly the formation of the soul. So they come to the first Level all being much different."

- "But despite the fact that all souls are very different do they somehow understand each other?"

- "Specifically souls understand everything because their perception of each other is quite different of that of material forms. Other centers are switched on."

- "But do some problems in relationship still happen?"

- "Yes, of course. This is the first grade, first Level. They have to seek for some common ground and understanding. It was easier for them when they were separated by their worlds each having its own groups, its own element. But the first grade is another element, a new and higher one by its requirements, so it is difficult to get used to. Some cannot even communicate with others and are looking for whom they can establish relationships with looking for contact, trying somehow to make it. It is very hard on My first Level. But then as they move upwards they feel better. They learn methods of communication in the new world and feel easier. And then they come to complete mutual understanding but it is reached approximately in the middle of the pyramid."

- "Your worlds are inhabited by Entities or highly developed souls which You collect in the Hierarchy from all the four Universes. But what is the formation of these Entities on the Levels like? Do they have any kind of physical bodies on the first Level of the pyramid?"

- "No. They have only energy bodies."

- "Do their subtle bodies have any kind of organs?"

- "They have no organs but individual centers of sensations."

- "By means of what do Entities build their worlds on Levels?"

- "Through power of thought. In My worlds neither arms nor legs are any longer needed. The basis for all sorts of the Entity's activity is highly developed thought. At the lower Levels they have predominantly digital way of thinking, then – light one and on the top of the Hierarchy – energy thinking."

- "Is all their work done by means of thought alone?"

- "Yes, only by means of power of thought."

- "And even on the first Level does the newly arrived Entity begin to work only by means of thought?"

- "Yes, everything is built on this."

- "People are developing with the help of feelings, emotions, thinking and action. Do Entities have something like that? Perhaps, they have no feelings any longer."

- "Why «no feelings»! They are not robots at all. If the Entity is spiritualized it feels everything but at different stages of development – in different ways. Particularly on the Levels Entities have not feelings but a higher stage of perception although it also recalls the sensual one. They have subtle bodies and they «feel» through them although a feeling is the basis of the material body. Bodies are constructed in a different way but sensations similar to yours they also experience but at a higher level of perfection. One may even say that their «feelings» are more perfect than yours; perception is more subtle and more scaled."

- "Do they have absolutely no emotions?"

- "At lower levels where Determinants and Originators exist, emotions remain. Here, on the first Level come souls of people who for some time continue to keep their emotions."

- "Are there any moralities in the worlds of the Hierarchy?"

- "Morality is conditions to develop environment for Entities. For each Level certain conditions for development are established for Entities. In each world its own laws act and they are developing according to them. Morality is also the law."

- "Is competition in pursuit of energy possible at the Levels?"

- "Yes, it is. But everyone is delimited by a strict measure. Everywhere is strict framework, control. No one can take excess."

- "The higher the Level of the pyramid does an Entity go it through in its development faster or slower?"

- "The speed of passing the Levels increases towards the top of the Hierarchy while at the lower Levels it is slowed down. The time of the Entity's stay at one Level depends entirely on its own, on its purposefulness, on the set of qualities, on the ability to implement faster or slower the personal program. There are many factors influencing the time of its stay in one world."

- "Each world has its own speed of development. What does it depend on?"

- "The world's speed of development, i.e. the rate at which processes flow in it depends on the matter and hence – on the energy it is built of; on programs, the Level this world is on as well as on its progressing. The very energy of the world determines the form of the process while the process determines the speed of development. All are closely related to each other and depend on one another."

- "Approximately how many stages of development does a Level include?"

- "Each Level comprises the definite number of stages of their stay."
- "Does Devil's Level have more or less of these stages than Yours?"
- "Devil's Level has more of them because each of His Levels is broader, i.e. it takes more time to pass it compared with Mine."
- "Are programs to pass each stage of the Level made up separately?"
- "Yes, they are depending on the progress made."
- "What are then these programs in the Entity's life separated by? For example in human life one program is separated from another by death."
- "On the Level it is separated by achieving the goal. Having reached this goal one gets another program with the next goal."
- "Is there any interval between the programs?"
- "Entities do not have intervals between the end of the old program and the beginning of a new one. While the Entity completes some program the next one is ready and is given immediately after the first goal is achieved. One program is smoothly spilling over into the other."
- "What is the main objective of the Entities' improvement?"
- "It consists in accumulating energy, in increasing one's own energy potential. Any progression results in accumulating of all kinds of energy in the Entities' matrices and subtle bodies and the overall energy gains form the Entity's common energy potential. And the higher it is, the higher the individual can ascend the stages of the Hierarchy."
- "Does the Entity's power increase as the Level rises?"
- "Yes, the Entity's power as well as its gauge increases, they both are growing in volume and their performance."
- "Do Entities have equal power at one Level?"
- "One can say it is almost equal, i.e. it varies within some interval characteristic of this world but at the same time each individual's power is specific."
- "Power of Entities differs quantitatively. But does the power of one Entity differ from that of the other in qualitative terms?"
- "Of course, it also differs in qualitative terms because it is comprised of different qualitative characteristics. There are no two qualitatively identical powers. The greater the energy density in the matrix, the greater the power."
- "And the more energy in Entities' subtle bodies, the more the power. Is it so?"
- "No, the energy in subtle bodies does not always influence. The fact is that **the soul is sometimes given the energy for subtle bodies in advance for future development** so that the individual should work it out

later. A deposit is provided and then it is worked out. But this is the case if the soul has not accumulated the corresponding energies for the next stage of development. But it cannot «mark» time that's why it is given in advance what is required for the soul to move forward. Therefore, such energies cannot comprise the total power of the soul till it works them out. In case the soul has accumulated those energies needed for the next phase which will be required for its subtle bodies, then it might already be inculcated in any world on its own and then the energies of bodies can be added to the characteristics of its overall power."

- "Does the increase in the Entity's power influence the formation of its matrix?"

- "Of course, it does. Increase in power is connected with an increase in gaining energy in the matrix followed by permanent building out, adding of new cells, mainly associated with quantitative changes in energy resulting in total volume growth. The volume of cells is expanding, they are filled with quality which (the quality) can grow more and more. And therefore, to adopt the expanding quality cells require expanding, building out. And according to the ongoing building and (energy) gaining the power of the soul increases."

- "And speaking about a human being, can we say that difficulties of life contribute to the rise of his soul's power? Or do difficulties only affect the quality of the soul?"

- "It is overcoming obstacles but not they as such that contributes to successful development of the soul and also simultaneously affects the acquisition of some new qualities because in this case a transformation of one into another occurs."

- "Does the comprehension of new knowledge contribute to the increase in the soul's power?"

- "Yes, it certainly does. The most direct correlation is observed here."

- "Does the struggle with diseases also increase the power of the soul?"

- "Not much."

- "What contributes to increasing the power of the soul most of all: the fight against the enemies, diseases or the comprehension of new knowledge?"

- "It can be classified Level-wise, i.e. in your question, you have constructed a Hierarchy. At the bottom of it is the struggle against the enemies then comes struggle with diseases and at the very top of it is the comprehension of knowledge. This is highest and it helps increase the power of the soul most of all."

- "Human desires slow down his development. What is the obstacle in the development of Entities for example on the lower Levels of the Hierarchy?"

- "Desires too. They also exist above. Desires always remain but change their form, in other words, at higher Levels they turn into aspirations to develop, the desire to quickly reach one's goal, execute a program. Desires become high aspirations."

- "Could the Entity take the path of degradation?"

- "Of course, it could, I give the freedom of choice in all My worlds, so Entities could sometimes choose something leading not to progress but to regress. They also make mistakes. Degradation exists on Levels too. However, the higher is the world in the Hierarchy, the smaller percentage of it is degrading."

- "The higher the Personality in the Hierarchy, is it so more active or less?"

- "When ascending the Levels an Entity becomes more active compared to the lower Levels. But if you compare the work that each soul performs for its world one can say they are equal. For example, some soul does work on the inferior Level, the other – on the higher one. They differ in power, in amount, in a composite* but the work done by them to their Levels can be the same equal to their forces as any work is designed for the appropriate power Level-wise. Therefore, at a higher Level, the work is more complex and designed for a larger volume while in the inferior world it is less complex and designed for a smaller volume. But they are equivalent to their Levels."

- "Does the form of thinking change at each Level or does just expansion of knowledge and consciousness of each Entity take place?"

- "Everything changes qualitatively corresponding to Levels. But the sharp change of thinking never happens at once, changes occur gradually and sometimes so smoothly that the very transition in the form of thinking can be missed. Entities themselves which are improving in the given pyramid of the Hierarchy miss this transition."

- "Ascending the Levels does the number of Entities increase or decrease?"

- "In the Hierarchy's pyramid the number of Entities decreases as they ascend the Levels but the potential of each of them increases and exceeds the potential of Entities at lower Levels. As they ascend all their characteristics increase: potential, power, energy capacity, and so on."

- "What helps an Entity keep the same Level for some time? Man on the earthly plane is kept by the planet's force of gravity."

- "On the steps of the Hierarchy there are particular forces of gravity. Each Level has density corresponding to this Level – the level-wise density of all its energies. And in case the density of the soul's energies corresponds to the level-wise density, it keeps it quite naturally. Therefore, each Entity is in the layer which corresponds to it by its characteristics."

- "In which way does an Entity rise to a higher Level? What contributes to its rise?"

- "Having accumulated the energies composite necessary for the higher Level a soul is affected by a buoyancy force. And if it hasn't gained the desired composition it can no way ascend the next Level. If in the course of development the soul has accumulated the required energies, in other words, it is transformed by new energies of a higher order compared with the previous ones its density becomes lower than the density of the Level at which it is in the moment; as if it becomes lighter with high energies. Similarly, the balloon is pushed out of the water with denser layers. The term "density" is of course crude analogy. But mostly it occurs in this way. The density of the lower energy world becomes greater than that of the Entity itself and it is this density that pushes the progressing unit* on a higher Level. In case of degradation the reverse occurs: the Entity loses its high energies there remain "heavier" ones that pull it down. This is the mechanism for ascending or descending. This is the general principle of moving along the Hierarchical ladder."

- "Are there sins, that is, restrictions on behavior intrinsic in each Level?"

- "Yes. Each Level has its intrinsic laws, its violations and restrictions of behavior."

- "Does it happen sometimes that what is considered a sin at some Level is not regarded as such at the other?"

- "In what sense: at the lower Level – regarded as sins, but at the higher one – not as sins? Or vice versa?"

- "Vice versa."

- "In this case it may be that the sins for the Higher are not sins for the lower. For the Higher (Level) the scale of sinfulness gets refined."

- "From what Level do sins cease to exist at all?"

- "For earth dwellers, they disappear from the hundredth earthly Level. Man's consciousness becomes so great that he automatically ceases to perform them. And getting higher, the very concept of sin changes. In fact, it ceases to exist in the meaning people are accustomed to. In the Higher worlds, notions of good and evil change, the society's social structure as well as its way of life changes, therefore, such a thing as sin disappears."

- "A person can cleanse himself through prayers. And do Entities have any methods of cleansing their internal forms?"

- "There are no special cleaning methods, but there is karma. It cleanses. Entities should work, progress, move to the goal. Appropriate actions are needed. Entities unlike man know their purposes. And if they deviate from them, they are accumulating the energies that are not required. Therefore, they are cleansing in the process of karma. As for prayers and religion, they do not have them. They live by real knowledge and laws that We are just trying to do with humanity – trying to transfer it to the level of real knowledge and the Superior laws. While for earth dwellers, We always have had to invent something, to tell them some parables. They should be replaced by the knowledge of the true structure of the universe and the true processes. In other worlds they know and understand the essence* of what is happening in their world and in others as well, so they make fewer mistakes in reaching goals and improve faster."

- "Are the Higher Entities allowed descending to lower worlds?"

- "Only up to a certain Level, given the law of non-intervention and so on. Practically this happens rarely; mostly no one descend anywhere. There are certain laws of development, and everyone develops according to them."

Codes for Levels and Souls

All living beings in the worlds of God are not under their names, but under the codes that most accurately express the essence of their development and enable to take stock of them. Let us extend our notions of the Codes. Let us turn to God with the following question:

- "We know that all souls, all the Entities have their own code. And do Your worlds have codes?"

- "Absolutely everything has its own codes, because it facilitates their organizing and carrying out further activities."

- "Are the souls' codes interrelated with the worlds', or Levels' codes?"

- "Yes, there is such an interrelation."

- "For the soul to settle in a world, should the soul's code coincide with that world's code?"

- "It is not the soul's code itself that should fully coincide, but only some of its specific figures. In the soul's code, there are many digital layouts that meet the general condition of the concrete world. Everything is built on numbers, which are infinitely many. But there is always some correspondence that unites separate parts into a single whole."

- "For the soul not to get into another world, is such code correspondence set up?"

- "No, it is not correspondence but automatic distribution of souls in the worlds that is of relevance. The very process of souls' distribution is mechanized, so that the soul can automatically get in the right place. But it is not the soul itself that determines what it needs, but the mechanism which is incorporated in this process. The soul's certain parameters are read out, which correspond to its level of development, gained while performing the program and the readout is implemented through the code's components. Thus, the place of the soul, which corresponds to its accumulated characteristics, is found automatically through the figures. Everything in the worlds is done so that every soul can get in its place. But the soul's codes are not adjusted to the world on purpose, or vice versa, the world is not adjusted to the codes of some souls. One thing is not adjusted on purpose to the other through the numerical codes. Everything has its own development system and, the most important in this system is the principle of perfection, which results in the desired ratios. And this is the harmony and correspondence of one with another."

- "How is the soul's code coordinated with the world's code?"

- "No particular coordination is made after the soul enters into the concrete world. Everything exists as a single whole and corresponds with each other. And the soul cannot get anywhere: neither below nor above, but only in the place it corresponds with. And it is determined by *the law of correspondence*."

- "But what are these codes for, if they do not play a major role in the distributions of souls?"

- "I need codes to facilitate reviewing everything. Each energy with the help of codes is under its own number, and the presence of codes helps Me manipulate. For example, I need to join something together or to separate one from the other, and in this case it is better to manipulate the numbers than the energy of this or that quality. It is impossible to give the names to everything because it is so numerous. But the codes help Me. Codes are figures that perfectly replace all sorts of names."

- "You manipulate the codes ..."
- "The energy," – corrects God.
- "You manipulate the energy through the codes," – we also correct ourselves. – "How do You manage to notice that there is a discrepancy somewhere? For example, rearrangement of something results in the discrepancy."
- "In this place imbalance of structures occurs. Any discrepancy leads to the destruction of existing formations. But with Me it can never happen, because I know what should correspond to what."
- "We are interested in the theoretical possibilities," – we justify ourselves, – "because anything might happen, if the worlds are not controlled."
- "Yes, it is clear," – He agrees.
- "So is the correspondence or discrepancy displayed in numbers?"
- "Of course, it's seen, at least to Me."

Information on the Levels

Each world, i.e. Level, has its own information.
- "Which way does the amount of information on the Levels change in plus Systems and minus ones?"
- "If they are on one Level, then enjoy the same amount of information. But if they are on different Levels, they possess different amounts of information."
- "Speaking of the Determinants of one Level, for example, but belonging to different Systems, which of them has more restrictions on the possession of information: the Determinant of the plus System or minus?"
- "On one Level, both have the same opportunities. And, staying on different Levels, Entities of inferior Levels have more limited knowledge than that of superior."
- "For what reason, isn't the inferior Level given the knowledge of the Superior Level? Is it due to the fact this knowledge will not be understood, or does it pose a threat to the inferior worlds?"

- "It will be understood all right, but the knowledge of the superior Level is always a threat to the inferior one, as the latter cannot see the consequences of its implementation. Higher knowledge will always be used by the lower Levels for selfish ends, especially it relates to earth dwellers. The lower the development Level, the closer a person to the animal Level. Taking into account that on Earth there are people of different development Levels, one can imagine how many times any idea or form of knowledge will be distorted, as each degree of understanding would interpret them from their positions. That is why there are a lot of erroneous theories and projects on the Earth."

- "When transiting from one Level to another, must an inferior world be given the knowledge of the Higher world?"

- "The transition from Level to Level exists only in the Hierarchy. On Earth, all is quite different. Earth is entering a new stage in the development, transiting to a new orbital, which means that its development Level changes, it becomes higher in its energy state, in other words, it turns to work with a higher frequency range. And for the transition to take place, all the mankind must be given the new knowledge, which corresponds to the new descending energy. New information is sent from the Above, that is, by Us, through the channelers and envoys, because otherwise people are unable to receive it. Where else could people take new directions for the next stage of development from, unless they are descended from the Above? Therefore, for the future evolving of the sixth race, the new directions in the information are being transferred now."

- "And does information transferred from the superior Level to the inferior in the Hierarchy as well?"

- "We have it somewhat different."

Death of Hierarchies

- "Does the Hierarchy exist in Your Universe alone?"

- "Hierarchy is the level-wise construction of the matter that exists throughout the Cosmos. Everything in it is built in a hierarchical manner. It is major in any formation. There are Hierarchies large and small, and some, a smaller one, may be included in the larger (Hierarchy). The universal Hierarchy of development has neither beginning nor end."

- "And does the Hierarchy extend below the earthly plane too?"

- "Of course, the Hierarchy extends infinitely downwards and infinitely upwards. However, if one considers not the common Hierarchy, but a particular one with regard to some size or composition, then it is finite. And all this is determined by the stages of development."

- "In Your world Hierarchies grow, flourish. Are there ones that perish?"

- "Yes, there are. More precisely, they do not perish but are transformed into a new kind of life."

- "The lower one?"

- "The higher. But the degradation is also present."

-"How often are Hierarchies transformed?"

- "Certain development time is determined for this."

- "Cosmos is very big. Does it ever happen after all, that for some reason Hierarchies perish?"

- "No, the complete destruction of the Hierarchy does not happen. This is not allowed from the Above. All is under control. In case of danger signs, necessary transformations are implemented in the Hierarchy, and it is restored."

- "And why do states on Earth bloom and then must die? Couldn't they have flourished, too, as long as possible?"

- "The society is somewhat transformed, the old is reborn in the new, only at a low Level, it goes through death. The Hierarchy develops based on some laws, the state – on the others. And if the state could have improved itself by new laws, replenished itself with something new in time, it would have kept being. But people cannot do it. They may only transfer something new from generation to generation, and not more."

Cosmos, Universe, Hierarchy

- "How are the Cosmos and the Hierarchy interrelated?"

- "Cosmos is a physical state that has nothing in common with the Hierarchy. And usually people imply its material structure only under this name. But if you mean energy structures, it is already closer to the Hierarchy. Our concepts about the world and the human concept are different."

- "And can Your Hierarchy be called the Cosmos?"

- "No, no. The Cosmos is a purely physical world. People gave this name to a certain volume of space, referring only to physical matter, while the Hierarchy represents the energy worlds distributed according to their sequence, or Level of development. Cosmos and Hierarchy differ in material, construction, laws acting in them as well as in living forms."

- "And can we then relate the concepts of the Hierarchy and the Universe with each other in terms of space? Does the Hierarchy exist within the Universe itself, or separately from it?"

- "Universe is another purely material structure related to the Cosmos. If I say that I own the four Universes, I mean the physical formations that are in My possession. But all that is material has a subtle structure as well."

- "Does it mean that within the volume of the physical Universe there exists an energy formation, called the Hierarchy?"

- "All of them co-exist, and everything is interrelated with each other. By analogy one can consider the man's physical body and his energy bodies, or subtle envelopes. They exist parallel to each other, although all together they belong to a human Entity. The same way one should perceive such spatial structures as Cosmos, Universe, and Hierarchy. Therefore, along with your physical Universe, parallel to it, there are many subtle-plane Hierarchies with different constructions."

*   *   *

Chapter 7

God's Assistants

SUBSIDIARY HIERARCHIES OF GOD

Coalition Observer Detachment
(COD)

In Cosmos there are many Systems that specialize in particular jobs. We decided to clarify some regulations of the legislative System known to us as COD – a Coalition Observer Detachment.

God responds:

- "In Cosmos there is a Coalition Observer Detachment, or COD. Do they obey the general laws of the Hierarchy or is it an independent System with its own laws?"

- "This is an independent System in the Cosmos Management. For your Universe the COD laws remain constant in their constructive foundation and unchanged in functioning. But the platform under these laws is changing, because They are very high, and everything that is below is converted by them in accordance with the legislature. COD is a legislative union. It manages all forms of life and develops activities to be fulfilled by all beings in any worlds. All the subordinate systems work under COD's programs. Therefore, Hierarchical Systems vary according to the laws of COD until they grow to them."

- "Does COD have its own pyramid or is it located within Your Hierarchy?"

- "It has the Hierarchy of its own that is out of My Hierarchy."

- "What is improvement in the pyramid of COD based on?"

- "On expanding the zones of its influence, on increasing complexity of the very processes of the laws, because the constant progression of worlds requires consistency between the new changes of life and standards of their manifestation. And if the worlds, forms of existence are complicated, the laws are also complicated. Some things are continuously improved, depending on others."

- "If we consider Devil's System, is it below than COD?"

- "COD rules the universe by its own laws. I and Devil are subordinate to COD indirectly, as We all have our own Management above. And We are not under COD's direct control, but subject to the co-management. In fact, We exist on our own, but at the same time, We also are guided by the laws of COD to jointly manage the worlds subordinate to Us (see Figure 12)."

- "Does COD apply its power to our Universe alone, or does each of the four Universes have its own COD?"

- "Their power, like Mine, applies to all My four Universes. But each of them has its own sub-COD."

- "There are various Hierarchies in the total volume of Nature. Is COD's activity associated with You alone or with other Hierarchies outside Your possessions as well?"

- "COD is My personal organization and works on the territories that belong to Me."

- "Are they able to solve any issues without You?"

- "They can solve minor issues, but as for the principal ones, they ask Me – whether I shall allow them to do what they want. My opinion is the main."

- "So, do they bring all decisions or issues to Your notice?"

- "Necessarily."

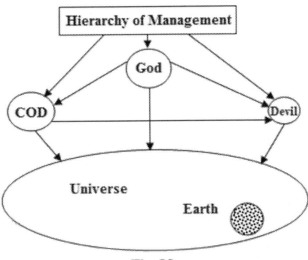

Fig. 12

- "Is COD older than You?"
- "No. I have created it, and I manage it. It is comprised of My best disciples."
- "Does COD control those laws of the universe, which You have just given to people?"
- "Of course. They were all transmitted through them under My guidance. We decided together, what could be given to people and what could not as it was too early. Devil also participated in it, because He also had to give several of its laws by My instructions. So the «Laws of the Macrocosm» is Our joint work. – (He refers to the book «Laws of the Macrocosm or the basis of Heavenly Hierarchy Substance», sent through Larisa Seklitova)*."
- "Does COD control the activity of Devil or is He controlled twice: both by You and the COD?"
- "I control absolutely everything: those, who constitute the COD, and Devil, as I lifted Him up to the present Level. It can be said that I have made them, so they are subordinate to Me, but I give them a certain autonomy and take their developments into consideration. The same is with people; they have, for example, the following (sequence): the president, government, the State Duma*5; here the COD is the State Duma. But they have already reached a very high Level, so I reckon with Them."
- "What is considered to be COD's activity in addition to the overall control? What else do they do?"
- "Of course, they not only control the activities of others, but are legislators as well. They own all the laws relating to the Nature, i.e. higher ones, and develop new laws, like your Duma. Your (legislators) receive money, Theirs – energy. The lower Levels generate energy, and it comes to them upwards. But, of course, They have no such scandals with energy, as you have with money."
- "Do our earthly lawyers, attorneys, judges, who are connected with the law, get in the course of development in the COD?"
- "No, not at all. This is quite different. People are at a very low Level and have different specific character. You cannot even imagine what laws people have and what – COD. Earthly specialists do not even have one percent of the knowledge possessed by the COD. They possess very extensive knowledge: it comprises building of worlds and everything within these worlds as well as designing of all that exists, including processes. And experts

---

5   * Translator's notes: The State Duma is the lower house of the Federal Assembly of Russia (legislative body), the upper house being the Federation Council of Russia.

in the fields of computations, like your engineers, are also part of them. Any development, construction, creation of something new goes through the laws, so They know everything, own and manage everything."

- "Is it similar to the human Construction Norms and Regulations, State Standard, regulations, and instructions?"

- "Yes, sort of. All calculated works refer to COD. This requires the knowledge of all the inner constructions to bring some sort of standard by which they must work. So before one gets to COD he needs to learn a lot about constructive forms and principles of their work."

- "If COD controls the activity of all the worlds, do they use any coercive measures for those who break the law?"

- "Of course, they do. They have a system of coercive measures. But it is Devil that is in charge of the coercive forms."

- "Can you say what penalties they use?"

- "There is no need to use anything, because the laws are designed and made in such a way that disobeying them leads to self-destruction. Inconsistency in the law results in a shortage of energy, blockage of channels and the Entities' degradation or complete destruction."

- "How do they control the vast areas? Do they have a special system of communication?"

- "Yes, they do. They have special equipment. But they can watch themselves as well, because there are at such a high Level, from which everything inferior is seen quite well. For example, I can be everywhere. The same is with them: they are capable of appearing and being in the place required. But they seldom use it, and prefer to see everything in front of them on a large scale, i.e. through the device."

- "Where does COD take Entities for itself from? From You?"

- "Of course. There are Entities, which, rising upwards, are formed in the desired direction, or specialize at once. And the best Entities-legislators come in COD, having reached the necessary Level of development. Generally all Entities, starting with a certain Level, disperse: some come to Me, some – to Devil, some – to COD, and some – to the Medical System."

- "COD takes Your souls; what does it give in return?"

- "In this case, no "return" can ever be, because they are Mine anyway. This power is from Me. Of course, some one-ten Entities may get beyond My control, take the path of self-determination, but the great bulk remains. And in exchange for those who left I do new Entities for Me, selecting out from their best staff."

- "Suppose that in Your Hierarchy Entities develop slowly, and in Devil's – quickly; what is the rate at which Entities that comprise COD develop?"

- "COD consists of the plus part and the minus one, both are headed by the General COD, i.e. it includes the Entities from the plus and minus Systems. Therefore, in different parts of COD the rate of development will be different. But if you compare the plus part of COD with plus Levels in the Hierarchy, the rate of development will be faster above. Also the minus COD will outstrip the speed of the inferior minus Levels. But if you compare the highest parts of COD, the plus part at Higher Levels exceeds the speed of the COD's minus part of the same Higher Level."

- "What System is opposite in its functions to such a legislative organization as COD?"

- "Do you ask about the System destroying laws?"

- "Yes."

- "Destruction is not of necessity. There are Systems that issue minus laws. However, they are directed not at the destruction of certain things and other laws in particular, but at their functioning on the minus plane, opposite to which COD is working. To conceive these two opposite legislative Systems, compare the following: a person can also be guided by the two opposites: the good and evil. The former will push him to do good, while the latter – bad. This is the struggle of opposites, but in general this is development."

- "May such a System be called Anti-COD?"

- "Yes, it may."

- "Do You know the laws that function only in the System of COD, but in other Systems?"

- "Yes, such laws I know. Each Hierarchy due to the specificity of its activities has individual laws that do not apply to others."

Medical System

In His dialogues with us, God often referred to the existence of Medical System working separately from Him, and being singled out into an independent hierarchy. It interested us, and we decided to ask God more about it.

- "You have a special healing System corresponding to our health authorities. It is headed by the Superior Hierarch of the Medical System Y* ... (his cosmic name)*. What is it like?"

- "Now it is also an independent Hierarchy, which has its specific development, different from all others. At present this is a powerful System capable of separate existence, but it too was created with My help for My own needs and, therefore, is in My possession. But I give it full right to liberty and self-determination."

- "Has Y* ... always been at the head of the System or was it created by someone else, and He headed it later at some stage?"

- "No, He has been its founder from the outset. I helped Him."

- "But why did He choose medicine and turned it into a basis for all his eternal existence?"

- "He liked to treat and help others."

- "Was Y* ... a human being in the past?"

- "No, He began his existence when there was no man yet, and developed through other forms. But, being in the material body, He chose the path of healing and care, and further on has not deviated from the chosen path on the subtle plane of existence. There appeared assistants at his disposal. Then He singled out into a separate branch of development, and I did not hamper, but helped Him at first until He created for himself a solid base. And I'm happy for Him because everything He did was necessary, first of all, for Me, for My worlds."

- "Was He likely to choose the way to treat and help others for the reason that He himself had experienced and felt a lot in his lives?"

- "No doubt. The personal choice is always based on the human own experience and awareness of his activities in relation to others. All comes through awareness."

- "Since Y* ... possesses a whole Hierarchy, are His Entities involved in some other activities in addition to healing?"

- "To heal others one needs to spend energy, and in order to spend it one needs to take it somewhere. Therefore His System, for example, together with the physical world produces such energy, which is later used for various health-improving activities. Produced energy is spent on the same physical worlds. Besides, Y* ... is engaged in curing beings, which are in subtle worlds. He treats all living beings. That is Medical System produces a special kind of energy both of material and energy planes by its own methods, which, in their composition, correspond to the living structures to be rebuilt. Each subtle world requires its "life-giving" energies; these are the energies of different Levels. Only Medical System is involved in their reproduction, accumulation and further use."

- "Is Medical System also engaged in curing people?"
- "Yes, when it is required."
- "But we know that Determinants also treat those people they guide in life."
- "No, they do not treat themselves, but correct the human physical state, they can improve his organs' biofields, supply them with the required energy. They constantly monitor the status of all organs and systems of the body, making their digital layouts. On receiving the report about the present state of human health, in the event of any significant deviations, they transmit information to Medical System, and there comes an answer from it."
- "Is everything under Y*...'s control?"
- "Yes, his Systems are."
- "So, when some Determinant's fosterling needs help, does this Determinant refer to Y*...?"
- "Not to Him personally, of course, but to his subordinates. They decide which way to help a man so that he could complete his personal program, if it to be completed, of course."
- "How is the man treated in case when Medical System renders assistance to the Determinant?"
- "They can render assistance by means of advice, but if you want them to intervene, they are able to repair human subtle constructions, his bodies, are capable of directly repairing damaged organs, blocking their diseases so that they could not progress; can insert additional blocks substitutes to help ill and severely damaged organs work. They can charge with energy on the level of cells and their fields, using a life-giving energy produced by their System. All this is done on the subtle plane, often during sleep, so that this assistance to a sick or injured is not noticeable. It always seems to the man that he has been self-restored."
- "What is the life-giving energy?"
- "Of course, more than one form of energy, many of them are used to treat, in other words, for the earthly plane there is a special set of required restoring types of energies on the material level; but at the same time, for the earthly plane subtle energies corresponding to the type of human bodies material are required. Subtle energies are provided by some Levels in the Medical Hierarchy, which specially produce them for such purposes."

Devil responds:

Something about the mentioned Levels we decided to find out from Devil. In his responses, He exposed the harsh reality from his point of view.

- "There are Levels which give their energy particularly for the treatment of people. What are these Levels like?" – We asked Him.

- "These are the souls belonging to Y* ... Therapeutic energy they produce specially. To do this, they have physical objects, like your Earth, which they serve."

- "Do these Levels give their energy for the treatment of humans voluntarily or is it their duty?"

- "Voluntarily. This is their job. But they should get some equivalent in exchange for the given. And if they do not, their energy balance is broken followed by the destruction of the unbalanced Level."

- "The Level perishes. And what happens to the souls of those beings that inhabited it?"

- "Soul perish, too, they are decoded."

- "And what are the beings, which are located on this Level, like? Do they resemble people in outward appearance?"

- "No, they have the form that people will not understand. For people, this is a sort of abracadabra."

- "And what equivalent should they get not to die?"

- "For them this equivalent is money that a man must pay his doctor, or a healer. After all, between the physical and the subtle world, too, there is interchange at their level. If a person pays the physician money for his treatment, the Determinant of the individual who needs treatment gives a certain amount of energy equivalent to this amount of money to the healing Level. Instead, the Determinant receives the life-giving energy from this Level, which He can use to heal his fosterling. When people do not pay money for the treatment, which constitutes the equivalent of energy, the souls that gave their energy and did not get anything in return, perish. If you, for example, give all money at your disposal to others, you perish without it, either. It is quite another matter, if you lend it, and then it is repaid to you. Similarly the matter is with energy in their world."

- "And who liquidates the Level?"

- "It is self-decoded."

- "But isn't it unfair in relation to them: they give their energy for treatment and yet they are exterminated for that?"

- "You know, it is accepted so in the Cosmos by the laws of COD: extermination for disobedience. If they do not get the energy in return, which is essential for their vital activity, they must not give their healing energy either."

- "Is there no escape from leaving the Levels unpunished? Instead, for example, an individual who has not paid the money can be refused treatment, or given a situation in life equal to the payment in money terms."

- "Then it can't be regarded as treatment. If, for example, the healer treats people and does not charge a fee for it, he takes the karma, and then he will work it out. The Higher should be spared and worked for, while people are not worth sparing, as they are very low-level and worth nothing. Therefore, when treating, one should necessarily charge a fee from people, or refuse them treatment, not cure them at all."

That was Devil's view on the treatment of humans, but He has his own morality, while we – our own one. However, His explanation should be treated with due seriousness, so as not to do harm to anyone in Medical System through one's free treatment, and no to cause the healer's getting karma.

God responds:
- "Does Y* ... treat beings in parallel worlds, too?"
- "He serves absolutely all living beings that exist in My four Universes: in all the material worlds and in all the energy ones as well."
- "Does Y* ... also provide medical services to the Higher Hierarchs?"
- "Yes, He does. There are deviations in states on each Level."
- "Does He also treat You?"
- "Naturally, the level of his knowledge meets My requirements."
- "Has He helped You many times?"
- "Yes, specialization allows reaching very high qualifications in any sphere. He is constantly improving and trying to meet My development Level, which is expressed in the knowledge of the energy formation of My structures."
- "Does He help Devil?"
- "Y* ... is independent and works for all."
- "So, did He happen to help Devil?" – We asked this question because it was hard to believe that Devil could get into difficulties and was required

to be provided medical services. After all, for us He has always seemed impregnable and invulnerable, but it turns out He had some weaknesses and appealed for help to others.

- "Does Y* ... collaborate with Devil's System on general terms?"

- "Yes, He does collaborate and treat Him like all the others who need His help. Medical System also includes the minus part. That is, in itself Medical System is neutral but, as a triune structure, it consists of the plus part dealing with treatment and care, and the minus part developing new types of viruses, new kinds of diseases. And at the head of these two is the Management part, into which enters Y* ... as the Chief Hierarch of Medical System."

- "We can imagine how the man is treated, but what has to be treated concerning creatures in subtle worlds?"

- "First, in each subtle world, there are diseases appropriate to this world. They are caused by some deviations from the development technology, by overload and not adherence to the working or living conditions as well. And, in addition, low-leveled Systems, low-leveled subtle worlds can conduct wars resulted in breakdown of subtle bodies of many beings. And Medical System has to rebuild them, using just that life-giving energy it produces."

- "Is Y* ... engaged in treating and spiritualizing of souls?"

- "No, spiritualizing is the process that is not related to doctoring. Y* ... is responsible for the restoration of bodies and other subtle structures of any forms, but He is not engaged in spiritualizing and producing of souls. This is another direction. And the souls production process itself is above Y*..... A special System that is in My Hierarchy is engaged in producing of souls. And it does everything under My supervision."

- "You said that His system is founded on providing assistance to others. What kind of assistance is it?"

- "Guardian-Angels are in his Hierarchy. These are Entities that protect people in difficult situations, when it is required by the program. There are accidents, disasters, in which some individuals are to survive, notwithstanding anything. This work is being done from the subtle plane by Entities, which people regard as Guardian-Angels. That is, in difficult situations they implement the necessary support to the individual. But help is manifested not only in this. Other systems that have economical, energy or other problems may be rendered assistance as well. Underdeveloped beings are rendered assistance in order to accelerate their development. Types of assistance vary."

- "What exactly is the essence of Entities' improvement in Medical System?"

- "It is doctoring of all existing forms of life. There is a direct relationship: life forms advance, therefore, their structures vary and become complicated, the composition and combinations of their energies change. The new can't be treated through old means. Therefore, as Entities advance, methods of treatment are constantly changing and improving, as well as the processes associated with medical service and rendering assistance. Incidentally, from a human point of view, Y* ...'s System is the kindest and most humane, because basically its functioning is aimed at helping others. And from this perspective it is humane."

- "Is Y* ...'s pyramid part of Your Pyramid, or is it isolated?"

- "At this stage His Hierarchy is developing parallel to Mine."

- "What are the peculiarities of this pyramid's construction? Is there any difference in its formation?"

- "Of course there is. Generally the peculiarities are associated with the specifics of its functioning. In the construction of the pyramid intended for Y* ...'s System functioning, special conditions are created, which implies that special structures and process production were developed. Each Level of His Hierarchy has an individual process."

- "Does Y* ... also have his own laws, characteristic for his Medical System?"

- "He follows the general "union" laws and, like every individual Hierarchy, has laws defining and maintaining their specificity. He unites some laws and others, besides He includes laws of the independence of existence."

- "Does Y* ... take away from You the souls of all doctors, for instance, from the earthly plane?"

- "He takes from Me only those who have achieved significant results in doctoring, i.e. He requires individuals with high qualifications. And these petty, like nurses or doctors-careerists who occupy high positions, but actually they know and are able to do very little, He does not need. They remain with Me. But He can send them to the next life for a refresher on the same post, and can even keep their memory of past life with respect to doctoring so that they can achieve the results required to Him faster."

- "Do doctors work out karma?"

- "Everyone has karma and no one manages to avoid it in My System."

- "There are minus doctors who commit crimes. Do their souls fly to Devil?"

- "It depends on what crimes they commit. But doctors usually work out their karma. And those who have gained minus types of energies in the matrix go to the minus part of Medical System. Few individuals go to Devil. The earthly doctors do not go to Devil. And Y* ... selects souls from My (System). Souls of physicians are divided between Him and Me. They are divided, because I have such a condition, according to which the earthly physicians, having achieved certain mastery in doctoring, fly automatically, even without My consent, to Y*...'s neutral System. And I have nothing against that, because everything in His System is aimed at the good, at useful things."

- "When You complete the development cycle in this Hierarchy and separate from it, does Y* ...'s pyramid also go along with You?"

- "Yes, everyone who was with Me, all adjacent pyramids rise together with Me."

- "But do they enter into Your volume, having separated from the pyramid, or do they rise on their own?"

- "No, they do not enter into Me. Medical System has the same God as Me, has its own Absolute, which leads them to their peak. And being combined with Me, they develop. Co-improvement takes place. But sometimes a replacement happens: at any time Y* ... may change places with any appropriate System, which is at some appropriate Level. So He heads another System, while in his place another Hierarch may come and work together with Me. But Devil can't leave Me. He is Mine."

Angels System

We have heard about angels many times, but nobody knows where they are in the united system of God, or what specifically they do. Therefore, it is high time to inquire:

- "Are Guardian-Angels in Medical System?"

- "Yes, those Entities, which people mean, involved in protection of people and offering them medical and other types of assistance are in Medical System. But the real Angels System is in My Hierarchy at the top of the pyramid. This is a Higher System."

- "It turns out that there are two Angels Systems?"

- "For people any Higher Entity can be an angel. But if a person puts in this meaning the notion of protection and safety, then these Entities belong to Y* ... However He does not have Angels System. This is Assistance System."

- "How do Guardian-Angels improve in Y* ...'s System?"

- "It is a certain Level at which Entities improve in their constancy, in other words, they are constantly engaged in assistance function. They are sort of keeping one state."

- "Are they engaged in rendering assistance to people only?"

- "No, the Entities assist all beings. On the subtle plane some beings also find themselves in critical situations that threaten their lives, and the Entities rescue them. They also help worlds that can be wrecked. The field of their activities even in the rescue operations is very extensive."

- "Do all these Guardian-Angels do the same?"

- "They work with different kinds of energy. People need some types, other beings – their own types, and if, for example, a planet gets sick, a specific range of energies is needed to restore its normal state. And they deliver all necessary forms of energy to the planet. To be more correct, they are Cosmos workers. Being Y* ...'s fosterlings, they possess very different kinds of energies and deliver them in proper quantity and quality to the perishing planets or living forms."

- "In addition to rendering assistance to others, do they have any other work? Are they supposed to do anything in their world in their own behalf?"

- "While helping others, they do this work primarily in their behalf, because through such activities their matrix is replenished with energy of a special quality."

- "What can the Guardian-Angels help a person in and what can't they do? Since humans have their own program, are they likely to have the right not always to intervene in this program?"

- "A man may be rendered assistance only with the permission or at the request of his Determinant. But most often the request is sent to them from the Determinant himself. For example, the Determinant's database lacks some of the energies to be given to his fosterling during his illness, as He has just had no time to accumulate them. And then He sends a request to the Assistance System, and they give Him what He requires. But later on He has to pay back the debt in the form of the corresponding energy or one that the System requires. And to get the energy to pay for the treatment, the Determinant can twist any situation in life so that the man, through its elaborating, will produce the energy, which will be given to pay the debt. In other words, the Determinant will give them the same energy, but the elaborate one. And in such a way energies are circulating. But the human health will be restored in time."

- "Do Guardian-Angels have any setbacks? For example, they keep treating the planet, but it dies."

- "Yes, they do. It dies, but the energy remains the same. And they have no loss."

- "Can Guardian-Angels take the initiative and provide assistance to those who need it?"

- "Initiative? No, this is done only with permission."

- "Is an individual's Determinant superior or inferior to a Guardian-Angel?"

- "Of course, He is inferior, much more inferior. The Determinant can be compared with a good programmer on the Earth, but the one that has already reached the one hundredth Level. A Guardian-Angel is two Levels higher."

- "What kind of beings become Guardian-Angels?"

- "To the Assistance System medical staff mainly gets, the former souls of physicians, because this type of service also requires the knowledge of the human structure: both its material and subtle. Typically, they study subtle structures, being in Y* …'s System. To the same Assistance System get those who were engaged in charity and assistance on the Earth and then continue the same activities on the subtle plane as well, improving in the quality of kindness."

- "In the new sixth race, will Angels be named as they are now, or will a new term be invented? At present, for example, the term «Heavenly Teacher» is replaced by the term «Determinant»."

- "Over time, of course, any terminology changes. Even if you do not invent anything new, others will do it."

- "And what new name can an Angel be given?"

- "Assistant. It is more modern."

- "And what does real Angels System represent, and where is it located?"

- "This is the highest System in My Hierarchy, located at the highest Levels of the pyramid, and from this very System Entities transfer to My volume. Angels System has a Hierarchy of its own. Their main occupation is creativity. They create everything new: new forms, structures, processes that calculating Systems develop further. The higher Angels, as My assistants, are engaged in spiritualizing of souls together with Me. I have entrusted My secret to them, because they have chosen kindness as their way of improving."

- "Did they pass all the pyramid's Levels through kindness alone?"

- "They chose the plus direction in development. Each Level has its own processes, which relate to the plus sphere of activity and to the minus one. And the soul must feel itself – where to go and what to choose. They chose the plus branch."

- "Why did You entrust the process of spiritualizing to Angels alone?"

- "Because there is a regular connection between the possibilities of the soul, those energies, which it gained in the matrix, and the process the spiritualizing is based on. Only souls that have evolved through the energies of creativity and love can master spiritualizing. The energies of this quality Devil does not have, that's why He will never master this great mystery."

Material System

People have often met material extraterrestrials on the Earth. Their aircraft and the possibility to overcome vast distances indicate the presence of material Systems in the physical space. What are they? We again turned to God:

- "Once You said there are Material Systems that are as powerfully developed as You. Do they form their own Hierarchy, or do they have no Hierarchies and evolve in a different way?"

- "Hierarchies are everywhere. The whole Universe is built on the principle of Hierarchy, because it most accurately expresses the basis for improving the world. Material Systems of My Level have their own Hierarchy, and go their own way in the evolution. But when I need, I contract with them. The fact is that We could not create your Earth, as you would say, «by Our own hands». Our hands are the intellect's energy. A rough physical world can be created using only the same physical matter. The material is constructed using the material and the energy – using the energy. Therefore, your Universe was created entirely using their hands."

- "Do they do all material bodies in the Universe?"

- "Yes. But they do as builders, by a ready design. While We are architects, calculationalists."

- "Are they part of an even greater overall Hierarchy along with You?"
- "Yes, of course, the greater one."
- "In what other spheres do You cooperate with them?"
- "Generally only in construction."
- "They help You. And do You help them in anything?"
-"Naturally, there is a mutual exchange. They help Us on the material plane, while We help them on the energy."
- "What did Your collaboration with the material System regarding the Earth represent?"
- "All that concerned the physical formation and the physiology of the planet and people relates to Our joint activities. They created a form, the processes within the planet and on its surface. They have created, rather, developed nature and all natural phenomena in a regular sequence of development, linking together all forms of existence through a single global process of improvement. We set them the tasks, give the project in the form of the energy design, which They transfer from the energy plane to the material, using their devices and designs that have already been developed by them. They also monitor the progressing of what has been designed so that no deviations from the set goal of development can happen on the physical plane. If necessary, they make correction of material forms and processes."
- "They have created material forms to our planet and our Universe. But did they do for others, too?"
- "Everything related to the material in My four Universes, these Systems built. And all that relates to the subtle plane, We create. And they keep working in all My Universes. And We have contracts for this."
- "Material «flying saucers» fly to Earth. Where are they from?"
- "Material crafts arrive mostly by My desire, when material structures need to be corrected, some changes in the tectonic plates to be implemented or continents to be shifted some way, or vice versa some tie rods to be set so that they (the continents) cannot diverge during the seismic activity of the planet."
- "Can Your Spiritual System exist without the Material?"
- "Of course, it can."
- "And can Material Systems exist without You?"
- "What Systems? Ours?"
- "Do You also have Your own Material Systems?"
- "Yes, I do, of course."

- "What kind of Material Systems made man in Their own image?"
- "The human being was created by the Higher Material Systems, with which I conclude contracts for the work. They created him in their own image. My Material Systems at a low Level of development, and they will have to go a long way in the evolution until they reach their Level, their evolutionary stage. Matter also develops, and it takes time for it to reach a certain degree of progress. My Material Systems cannot exist without Me, because I spiritualize them, while Higher Material Systems I contract with are independent and can do without Me. They have their own Absolute, to which they aspire in the course of development."
- "Do Your Material Systems help the Higher in their work?"
- "We have no such Material Systems, which are on a par with Me by their development stage. Therefore, I deal only with them. Ours cannot yet perform such work, which I require. But they have everything ahead."
- "Your Material Systems cannot exist without you. And can Your Spiritual Systems exist without the Material?"
- "Spiritual Systems can exist without the Material ones, but vice versa – they can't, because the spiritual is primary, and the matter is secondary. But if you talk specifically about the human being, his material body can do without a soul. There is an artificial type of spiritless people – zombies. They were created only to work as biological robots. This is Devil who made them. You have zombies on the Earth. Their matter can do without spiritual foundation. You can call them people-mechanisms."
- "If you can live without Material Systems, what did You create them for?"
- "By itself, the physical matter in its physiology I do not need, but I needed some kinds of energies which only the material environment could produce. So I created My own Material Systems, having spiritualized them. The relationship of material and spiritual parts is needed to produce energy of a certain quality. And the reverse process – unspiritual existence – invented Devil, having created slaves for Him. And I do not need this, because the development of the spiritual basis of the living is of more importance for Me."
- "Do our Material Systems produce energy for You or something else?"
- "They produce energy of a certain range, based on which matter is further created for the spiritual apparatus."
- "Do those who created the human material body have the same subtle formation, as we have?"

- "Yes, subtle bodies as well as the material one are identical."
- "Do people from the Higher Material Systems have seven bodies?"
- "No, for their Level seven is too primitive. Seven subtle bodies is the first step in the development. You compared with them are at the first Level, while they are at the hundredth Level. The difference is huge. Just imagine what energy potential they have. If their soul is inserted into the earth dweller's material body, it will burn instantly. Therefore, their souls require such a physical body, which is able to withstand this potential. I have set a goal – our Material Systems should achieve their Level of development."
- "But since their physical envelope is capable of withstanding such a powerful soul, are their bodies built in a different way compared with ours?"
- "«Identical» does not mean «completely similar». They are similar to you at that Level of development, which once corresponded to yours, that is, they guide the human physiology according to their own way. But if their present form is compared with yours, then, of course, each structure of the body corresponds to the potential of the soul, which it holds, and therefore their body's construction at the moment is much more complex than yours."
- "And who built Higher Material Systems?"
- "They were created by even Higher ones."
- "Is it You who provides souls for their physical bodies?"
- "No, they have their own. Their souls are of a completely different quality."
- "Can they also create souls?"
- "Yes. Everything they have is their own, and souls are very powerful, that have passed a great evolutionary track. Therefore, to bear their spiritual part, the physical body should also be very powerful. In accordance with their needs, they create themselves what they want. And the quality of the former must match the quality of the latter. Material bodies should also constantly improve to keep pace with the progressive soul."
- "Is the material world they live in similar to our earthly one?"
- "No, it is not. All material worlds are completely different, too, and the way of life, or ways of existence, the very process of life may not be compatible with yours."
- "Material Systems master the construction of the subtle matter as well, as they create souls, don't they?"
- "No, they have the matter and the soul separated, as we do, but the pyramid they have is their own. And the creator of their souls is another God. But I work with them under the contract."

- "Are the souls created for their System also formed from a subtle material or do they have something else?"
- "The energy is the same, but components, which are taken, vary. And the creation process may also vary."
- "Is the very formation of a soul matrix-like?"
- "The principle of formation is similar, but the matrix itself may have some other arrangement: spiral-wise or the structure may twist inside in a peculiar way, while a set of energies is being gained, i.e. the energies being gained by a soul gradually twist and are absorbed into the matrix."
- "Is there no extremely sharp difference between Your souls and Theirs?"
- "Basically constructive differences take place. But these constructive features can be understood in two ways: both as a sharp difference and as non-sharp, depending on which side they are considered. For example, We do not consider them to be very different from our souls, because the energy used is the same, while the taken qualities are different and the very principle of their work differs from ours."
- "May their souls also follow the path of kindness or the path of evil while improving?"
- "Yes, they have a choice, too."
- "So, after their death, do they have the similar distribution of souls either into the plus System or the minus?"
- "Yes, I have already said that they guide your physiology according to their path of development, and the souls improve the same way."
- "Does Devil take those souls who choose the path of evil?"
- "No, they have their Devil. And Mine is intended mostly for the four Universes, though He is also offered some work under their contract."
- "And what does He get for his work?"
- "Energy needed for Him."
- "Does He receive their souls?"
- "No, souls Devil does not get. Payment is made only by energy."
- "Does anybody else but You give Devil souls for His work?"
- "No, He receives souls from Me alone."
- "Are there souls in Your Hierarchy, which formerly belonged to the high Material Systems? Perhaps you took them for a particular job."
- "No, in My Hierarchy there are only My souls."
- "What is the essence of Material Systems' evolution: is it also the gain of even higher energy and the rise within the Hierarchy?"

- "Yes, it is all the same. The matter is also evolving from the lower to the higher and has its development stages and cycles, and their Hierarchies as well."

- "Where do they move to, while evolving?"

- "Man tends to consider everything separately. If every organ of the human body is viewed in isolation, as something independent, although this is possible, the general and holistic can never be seen if being subdivided. Therefore, to see the general, one needs to step aside from the particular and to view on a larger scale. From these positions We, together with the Material Systems, represent cells of a single organism; therefore in their evolution they move the same way as we do."

- "Hence, can we say that the evolution of Material Systems and Spiritual is alike?"

- "Yes."

*   *   *

GOD AND DEVIL

Let us draw some comparisons.

God says:
- "You said that Devil has his own Hierarchy. How is it commensurate with Your Hierarchy in size?"
- "It is approximately half the size of Mine."
- "Is Devil's pyramid similar to Yours in design?"
- "Yes, they are similar."
- "Do the same laws of development function in the Hierarchy of Devil and in Yours?"
- "Not all the laws, although most of them is common, of course. But judge for yourself whether «the law of love or mutual aid» can function in his System. Half of My laws should be discarded. But which laws are not suitable for His Hierarchy, you can guess yourself."
- "Does He have many laws of his own?"
- "Of course, Devil has his own legislative System, but He has few laws, because austerity and rigid discipline prevail everywhere. They diminish Entities' actions and any action in general. Virtually nothing can be violated in His Hierarchy, because everyone operates due under the program, without deviations."
- "What laws are most prevalent in Devil's System?"
- "Calculation laws. With regard to the manipulation of numbers, His own laws operate within His System. He has other laws as well, by which He operates and develops, but He tries not to disclose them."
- "Does the time in Your Hierarchy differ from that in Devil's Hierarchy?"
- "The time goes likewise both for Me and U* ... (Devil's cosmic name). In other words, in the Volume in which We jointly develop and operate, it is single; otherwise it will be impossible to interface with each other on the necessary issues."
- "Is there a difference the time flows within Your Hierarchies? Perhaps, it flows faster in Devil's?"

- "In Devil's System, the development is faster not at the expense of acceleration of time, but only through single-line programs. The optionless program provides progression at an accelerated pace. And the very time for Us remains the same. But both of Us, of course, have the physical worlds in which time flows differently, as a particular time of some spatial volume. Somewhere it can barely crawl, while somewhere it runs quickly. But this is possible in the physical worlds created specifically for certain purposes."

- "Does Your Hierarchy's pyramid also have the minus Systems?"

- "Yes, I need them to implement computational work and to have My plans to be realized in projects and real sectors. Everything is calculated in My Systems."

- "What differs Your minus Systems from Devil's minus Systems?"

- "The difference is in the qualities of their nature. In your terms, Mine are softer, sensual, more peaceful and decent, honest and fair. The very souls are opposite by quality. They develop under other programs, compared with Devil's Entities, and in My Hierarchy they always have freedom of choice. As for Devil's Entities, they develop under tough programs without freedom of choice and gain completely different qualities of character. The thing that My Entities do not like, they take delight in. They can be compared with the soldier-conqueror and soldier-protector: they have opposite goals and different emotional qualities."

- "What happens to the minus Systems at the moment You are separating from the pyramid and transiting to another pyramid?"

- "Everything is a single whole: My plus Systems as well as My minus go with Me. And then similar work continues to be carried out, at the new Level two parts are developing: the plus and minus, as well as the third superior part of Mine – Managerial, it stands over the first two. This is My Trinity."

- "Are there one-pole pyramids of the Hierarchy?"

- "No, there are not."

- "Do all Entities from Devil's pyramid enter into Him?"

- "Yes, they enter the same way as they do into Me."

- "Is there any difference when Entities enter into Your Volume and into the Volume of Devil?"

- "The difference is that the energy of Entities belonging to Us is of different quality. Devil's Entities have rough automatic energy, because His Entities do everything automatically, and their energy is of appropriate quality."

- "Does Devil perceive each of His Entities, too?"
- "Of course, He does. The constructing principle is the same."
- "When the last Entity enters into Devil, does He also break away from the old pyramid and rise above?"
- "Yes, He does, the same way."
- "Having broken away from His pyramid, does Devil enter into You or do You to ascend to the first Level of the next pyramid together, in parallel?"
- "Here it is the following way: I, Devil and Something, which is over Us, or the Managerial structure, form all together the essence of a greater Entity. Therefore, We are a single whole. And if one of the three parts disappears, then everything collapses, We break down. Do you understand?"
- "Yes."
- "This is the trinity," – God continues. – "But We cannot be joined. We simply co-exist under a single principle. And each of you has the same beginning as each Entity does. And I am, too, an Entity. I comprise a trinity: there is another God, another Devil and the other Managerial Structure in Me. The three parts are developed in Me, but this is Me.

But Devil has it opposite. You see, He has his own Devil, which is considered God for Him. And God for Him is the same as Devil for Me. As for the Managerial Structure, it remains neutral."
- "Will You tell us whether Devil's Hierarchy is divided into the plus and minus parts, like yours? Each Level of Your pyramid contains the plus and minus."
- "Plus and minus are inherent to the energy itself, of which Levels consist."
- "But then Devil must consist entirely of minus energies?"
- "Why so? He has the similar formation, but the ratio differs. For example, His Entities consist of ninety-nine percent minus, and one per cent always, in any case, remains plus. Therefore, in His Hierarchy there is also some plus, though to a little extent. In addition, Medical System belongs to Me as some neutral component, and together with it We are contrary to Devil. In other words, My Entities contain ninety-nine percent of the plus and one percent minus. Of course, this ratio is achieved at the Highest stage, while below these percentages are less."
- "Do You and Devil break away from Your pyramids simultaneously at the end of Your development cycle?"

- "Almost simultaneously, given that We do not have time. Together with Devil, We are a single Entity, so the breakaway happens almost at the same time. For this purpose, We design the programs of Our Beings so that We can both complete Our development simultaneously."

- "Does Your last Entity enter into You from the pyramid along with the last Entity entering into Devil?"

- "Not, of course, a small difference is assumed here. Assumed, – God repeated thoughtfully and said, – The fact is that My Entities may be late for entering into Me, while His – may not. He is always rigorous in His calculation. My Entity may slow down its development due to the provided freedom of choice, and may, vice versa, accelerate its progress for the same reason. And in this case My last Entity will enter into Me before Devil's Entity – into Him. Such a small discrepancy occurs, but it is not so much."

- "You have said You constitute a single Entity together with Devil. But what does the Managerial part represent then?"

- "I am the plus part, Devil is minus, and the Managerial one is a separate part."

- "Is it COD?"

- "No, COD is much more inferior to the Level of this part. COD is intended to monitor the lower Levels. And The Managerial parts that makes up My Trinity is a very High, separate and independent structure. It manages all the processes. But I am part of this Managerial structure; in other words, a very big part of Mine constitutes it. This is My «I» – Absolute."

- "Does Devil also form the Managerial part?"

- "No, He does not. He is subordinate to Me."

*   *   *

Chapter 8

On Devil's Private Life

CONVERSATION WITH DEVIL

Devil has historically been the embodiment of treachery, cruelty, lack of principle and all the evil that manifests itself in any forms on Earth. This view has prevailed among mankind for thousands of years.

But the Higher Teachers open any knowledge to the man as he develops and according to the level of understanding. Similarly, the truth is disclosed to a child as he / she grows.

At this stage humanity has reached the level of consciousness that is ready for a new comprehension of Devil's essence and perception of him in the new qualitative embodiment. From the eternal frightening creature He is being changed into the God's obedient assistant (if we remember that God values Him for obedience), and reveals quite new sides of his nature to people.

God and Devil partially remove the veil of secrecy from the internal structure of their Hierarchies and from the existence of plus and minus Hierarchic Systems, make it possible to understand – whether they are able to exist without each other, what is the meaning of their union and working together in the physical Cosmos and subtle worlds.

The very concept of «Devil» is changing its internal content, as previously unknown aspects of his work come to light.

What should the new attitude to Devil be like in view of the disclosure of the unknown functions of his activities? And what attitude should we have, for example, towards the Minister for Internal Affairs or the Commander-in-Chief?

If we consider the president to be plus, the Commander-in-Chief should be considered minus, because he, doing at the president's bidding, may unleash war or carry out any activities associated with maintaining law and order in the state, since without them the state would not constitute a strong and solid organization.

But should there be someone to pacify and establish order in the state, resorting to tough measures? And proceeding from the definition of Devil, based on the work He does for God, any force minister or any sapper blowing up unnecessary constructions and thus clearing space for the new ones can be called «Devil».

The similar work is carried out by Devil – He puts God's required objects in order, destroys the old to build the new and, under God's instructions, is developing a system that allows the souls to gain qualities required by our Creator.

– – –

But before having disclosed this information, God brought us to contact with Devil. We have mentioned this before, but now we are going to tell you more about it.

All the envoys communicating with God must meet His opposite as well.

However, a meeting with Devil was unexpected, because God did not warn us in advance that a definite channeling, instead of Him, Devil will hold. He wanted to see, on the one hand, our reaction whether we would be frightened and, for fear, cease the channelings. On the other hand, God wanted to test our loyalty to Him, as two of the twelve envoys had volunteered to work on the Hierarch of the minus System, tempted by the accelerated development in His System and wished to quickly come to perfection. So two of the envoys have betrayed God. Two, on the contrary, fearing to get into the clutches of the Lord of Darkness and trying to save their souls, have fled from the channelings at the very beginning. The others have reached the Level that they have been able to reach. It should be mentioned, that by the time of the adoption of the Laws (i.e. the book «Laws of Macrocosm, or the basis of Heavenly Hierarchy Substance») we were left by all of them. Only three of us remained (our family), and in this membership we came to adopting the Divine laws.

Remembering the words of the Bible: «For whosoever will save his life shall lose it», we continued our work, realizing that we must not stop, we must go further through the strange and unknown, through what is despised and rejected by people.

The words: «For whosoever will save his life shall lose it» meant the human fear of the unknown, which sometimes closes the road to the light. Fearing for his soul, a man will not get to the truth; will not ascend in his mind the next Level. A person stuck to the old dogmas shuts himself from all the new and is thrown back thousands of years in development, or, through ignorance of Devil's tricks and techniques, ultimately gets in His network.

Know your enemy – and the knowledge will be your defense and salvation.

That is what helped us to safely treat an unexpected appearance of Devil in our channelings, though, of course, doubts flashed: «Why did God give us to Devil? Or are all of our channelings some kind of a trap?» It is the latter – the fear to get in Devil's network – that has forced many of our supporters to run away from us, but the words of the Bible prompted us to proceed further in cognition. And besides the belief that God would not leave us but would appear in the right moment again, forced to continue the channelings and get to know a lot of surprising, and most importantly – to understand the ways that lead to God and Devil, all the subtleties of a contemporary cobweb of human roads. And having got to know the ways, we were terrified to see how many people go to hell, without being aware of that.

The channelings with the Chief Hierarch of the minus System helped us know the truth, which corresponds to the current level of human understanding, and we hope that it will be understood correctly by others as well. Let everybody examine the path that he / she goes, but our desire was to bring people the truth discovered to us and warn them of possible mistakes, for the one who is able to see will see the way to God, while the blind will fall into the abyss, get in the network of Devil.

– – –

We knew Devil's cosmic name as God had mentioned it in one of the channelings with Him. Therefore, when it suddenly sounded at the next communication session, we realized that the Prince of Darkness Himself was speaking to us. We started the contact with a question:

- "Who is communicating with us?"
- "U* ..."– He called His cosmic name.

It is difficult to convey our feelings when we realized that we were talking with Devil himself. Typically, the name of God always sounded at our communication sessions, and we got used to His calm and noble sound. Devil's name was therefore tantamount to the bombing, because God had never warned us that the meeting with Someone who all the humanity is afraid of and to whom even the great of this world thrill was expecting us ahead. His name burned us. But that was not fear that arose inside, as the first thought that flashed was: «What have we done wrong? How did our behavior suddenly bring us to this meeting?» Mentally, we tried to find our main flaw, but outwardly, remaining calm, accustomed to go in a straight line rather than along the winding paths of speculation, we asked frankly:

- "What is the reason that You have got in contact with us today?"

- "To test you," – He said shortly, without explaining what exactly our «test» was, but it could be both the test of knowledge and the test of the technical aspect of the communication.

We could escape in panic from the contact right after He called himself, as the many had done, for fear to lose the soul; we could stay at this Level because we already had the examples how some of our channelers had been connected up to low Levels with dire consequences. But the desire to understand the real world, hidden from us in legends and fabrications of people, the belief in God made us instantly suppress our doubts and continue. We quickly came to be calm, becoming aware that it was necessary to do so, and without being taken aback for a moment or breaking the communication session, we were immediately engaged in regular work.

And then the Prince of Darkness answered all our questions, just as God did; He answered the way God required, and did that honestly without trying to seem neither elegantly good nor factitiously evil. In his intonation, as in the intonation of God, one could hear calm, composure, dignity, worked out by billions of years of existence. And, compared to the intonation of God, which, now and then, had a note of friendship and kindness, his answers sounded coldly and dispassionately. And it should be said that both Hierarchs were on formal equal terms with us, and we have never heard the informal address to us, though we were incomparably low in relation to Them.

Brought up on a set of dogmatic prejudices of people, we represented Devil somewhat differently, more insidious, arrogant, malicious. He tried to show us that for many billions of years of existence these low earthly qualities had grown into completely other constituents of His soul at the Higher stages of development. Regarding us, He behaved equally, passionlessly, stiffly, and though sometimes another intonation was brought out through that tone, it remained within those emotions that could not deter us from Him.

Devil tried not to show his black essence, likely to conciliate, to win our confidence, knowing that only kind, noble qualities of nature, honest revelations and sincerity could draw us to Him. The slightest hint of anger, or hatred would have immediately alienated us from Him, alerted, and He still had to try to entice us to His side, so He tried to look dignified to us.

And although, of course, He had all the evil that we know and even more than what has been known to mankind, but it remained far away in inaccessible depths of His matrix, hidden behind a layer of billions of past lives. However, at the communication sessions of those who had come over to His side and to whom He did not have to hide his true face, Devil would not hesitate to lay bare His personal inner essence. And arrogance was openly oozing out from it as well as a sense of superiority over all, malice, contempt and hatred for the man and all humanity – that, as He puts it, pathetic mold on the body of the Earth.

Devil appeared to us a cold and indifferent arbiter of others' fate. As the Superior Hierarch of the minus Systems, He represented, just as our God, the hidden secret, unknown to any man in full, which He had made up for the billions and billions of years of His existence.

And this chance to talk with Him gives us a tantalizing prospect to find out something about His private life, understand ourselves what He represents in the present nature, and most importantly – open to humanity hidden and subtle paths that lead an inexperienced soul to the minus Hierarchy, revealing at least some of the traps, which He covers with sweet chrism and beautiful scenery.

At first channeling, of course, we did not dare to ask about something personal, but during the following communication sessions our curiosity, to be exact, thirst for knowledge overcame our fears, so we started to ask.

Devil's Path of Development

A man got accustomed to think that the only work of Devil is killing others. However, as demonstrated by our dialogue with Him, his field of activity is extensive.

Devil responds:

- "We know that You constantly watch the humanity. What purpose do You do this for?"

- "We have such work. We are in charge of watching the separate Universes, or more precisely, the four of them. Earth is located in one of these Universes, so it is also under Our control."

- "Are You assigned such a scope of work due to the fact that You have developed to a high Level?"

- "Yes, everything is achieved through self-development."
- "Are You one of the main assistants of God?"
- "Yes, but not the «assistants», how to better express this…," – He was looking for the word that most accurately expresses the essence of their relationship.
- "Employees," – we suggested.
- "Yes, employees," – He agrees and explains: – "I do not help Him; He does not help Me either. But We collaborate."
- "And how many assistants like You does God have?"
- "At this high Level there is no one anymore," – there appeared dignity in His voice.
- "The term «Devil» at this stage of human development is already obsolete. What new name can You be called by: «Chief Hierarch of the minus System»?"
- "I will think it over," – He said, and at the next channeling, which took place a week later, He said: – The term «Devil» can be replaced by the title «Joint Coalition Council for Computational Combinations».

The name sounded somewhat unclear for the first time, polysyllabic, although it expressed His real essence more accurately than the old name.

- "Is it possible to call You «God of the Union's minus Systems»? That name my husband offered."
- "Yes, I am God," – He agreed with pride, but corrected: –"But not all of My Systems are minus."
- "Do You have plus as well?"
- "No, neutral ones. In other words, your name is not quite accurate."

However, we failed to find the new name for Him and therefore left the old one, as the most familiar to man. But why did He replace the word «Devil» by such a long and strange name? Here we should stop for a while.

The term «Devil» is a generalized notion of some minus personality, which is usually attributed all the mischief and filth, all the vicious and brutal acts committed at the moment not by Him but His subordinates, i.e. by representatives of His minus worlds.

Everything that does evil in the earthly world is attributed to Him. Therefore the term «Devil» has been materialized in some bloody, ruthless, vicious and seemingly terrible form. Such has been His image over the past two thousand years.

For the next two thousand years, till the year of four thousand, Devil gives a new term, His new name, which expresses His true essence more accurately.

And in the new terminology such concepts as a «united coalition Council» and «computing combinations» are coming to the fore rather than qualities of «evil» and «dark». The new name indicates, above all, that not a single individual works as "Devil", but a whole system of minus Entities, acting according to the minus plan.

And the next part of His name has rather a modern view – «computing combinations», indicating that the representatives of the minus Coalition perform any work based on the precise calculations, rather than simply wave a magic wand to implement any desired action.

The meaning of their calculations is reduced to the fact that they disrupt and destroy all that is required, not on their own volition or desire, but on the program, which plans the overall global process, and everything in it is calculated to the smallest detail. All is programmed and calculated by them, nothing arbitrary or on a personal whim of a particular minus Entity is done.

– – –

Continuing to disclose His personal theme on these channelings, we asked Devil:

- "Did You progress in the development by Yourself or with someone else?"

- "I went unbeaten paths by Myself. In My activities, I was the first."

- "Didn't You have any allies?"

- "No, I was alone."

- "And how did other individuals, who are below You in Your Hierarchy, reach their positions?"

We could not understand how, doing evil, one could evolve to a high Level in the Hierarchy, although, of course, there are many areas of development in different worlds and the development is not restricted to paths that exist in this world.

- "They went behind Me for a long time," – He replied stiffly. Apparently, He did not like the question. – "One can say, I shot ahead and was already standing on some steps, when they started to approach Me."

- "But, probably, now someone is standing close enough to You."

- "Of course, there are such individuals."

- "In our Universe, you hold the highest Level of Your Hierarchy. Is there anyone in the macro-cosmos above You? After all, has someone to be higher, given the endless path of development?"

- "Yes, there are some even higher," – He reluctantly agreed. It was unpleasant for Him to admit to us that He is not the most important in the Universe. This was somewhat prejudicial to his pride."

- "Are You subordinate directly to Them?"

- "Yes, of course. To Them and God."

- "You said that You designed Your development on Your own."

- "Yes, I did that on My own."

- "But is it possible in the Cosmos to develop without being controlled from the Above? Did You probably, after all, have someone who guided You? – We insisted on the following confession."

- "Yes, They guided from the Above," – He agreed. – "But up to a certain Level of development a personality is not aware of being controlled from other planes of existence," – He put forward arguments in His defense.

- "And who guided You?"

- "Higher Levels standing over Me."

- "Were they plus or minus Levels?"

- "Those who guided Me are very high. Everyone manages the corresponding. In the Cosmos there are Hierarchic Pyramids – minus and plus. One can transit from the plus Hierarchy to the minus up to the central Level, switching to life, in other words, through embodiment in the physical body. The transition is mainly accomplished through the matter, although in some cases it is possible in the subtle planes, which is very rare. But when the soul has already made a final choice to transit to a minus System, its return to the plus worlds becomes impossible. At high Levels Units do not make this transition in view of their high-level consciousness. And, thus, everyone develops either in the plus direction, or in the minus. I followed the minus path."

- "Will You ever ascend to the place of those that have governed You?"

- "The ascent will take very much time. If God has a «thick» Hierarchy, in the sense it comprises many stages, My Hierarchy has rare stages separated from each other at a great distance (see Figure 13), and therefore it will require very much time to rise, although the path is calculated faster than God's. But the stages are rare, and it is impossible to jump over at least one of them. The ascent is just consistent. Levels in the minus System are very broad, which means that it takes much time to pass one Level."

- "We are in the physical world, but where are You?"
- "On another plane of existence. You are in the physical world, I am in the subtle."
- "Did You pass through a stage of human development?"
- "Yes, I did."

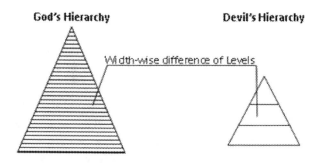

Fig. 13

- "Did You do that on Earth?"
- "No. When I existed previously, there was no your Earth yet. There was another planet like the Earth."
- "Did You exist on the planet in the human form?" – We asked some questions, similar to those that we asked God, trying to compare Their lives, because "all is learned in comparison"".
- "Strictly speaking, I dwelt in the form that remotely resembled human," – He confessed.
- "Have You lived a hard life?"
- "Very hard," – His intonation stressed the content. – "It was so hard, that one life of that kind was enough to reach the first stage of the Hierarchy."
- "What were the difficulties that helped You ascend the first stage?"
- "It was a particular choice of complex life situations. I was constantly choosing between good and evil. I decided for a long time – where I had better go, which one to choose finally for Myself. And I tried a lot of particular things."
- "And which did You choose more often? Good, if You were able to rise to the Hierarchy?"
- "Evil. I have risen to the minus Hierarchy."
- "Did You develop through the evil and calculating?"

- "Yes. I loved to do calculations. And any of My negative acts was accurately calculated."

- "And, despite having done so much evil, You still have reached such heights that You are God's assistant! – We were surprised, because we could not grasp that, taking the minus path, one could achieve something high. Previously, we had believed that only the righteous path was able to push any creature in the direction of evolution."

- "As you can see, I have reached!" – His tone had a clearly audible smile.

- "Thanks for the revelation ...," – I thanked Him and wanted to ask the following question, but He stopped me.

- "Stop." – And suddenly new revelations followed further. He longed for revelation. After all, He had not been asked for what interested us, probably, over millions of years. We touched some kind of chord in Him, and it sounded to us in a form of a strange confession: – "Going the path of «evil», I deeply came to the major – to the essence of the phenomenon, that is to the degree of getting that energy, which I received specifically from what I made, and which I required according to the program.

I was aware that I was not only participating in the situation, but I was getting that very energy based on the situation that I needed. For one and the same situation can be passed in different ways: one can get some form of energy, and one can get the opposite. I produced the energy that I needed. Nobody but Me and prior to Me has ever done that and has figured it out. For comparison, we can take, at least, your masochism. The one who is engaged in masochism, begins to enjoy the pain, that is, the energy he likes, which «warms» his soul. He kinds of catches this rough energy and it is a pleasure for him, therefore, it goes to his soul. I did the same."

Murders Committed by Devil

I was interested in the details of His past development, all that has transformed Him into a minus personality. So I asked:

- "When you were in a material body, did You have to kill others?"

Devil neither concealed his actions, nor tried to look virtuous, He talked like it was:

- "I had a lot of killing. And this is My work at the moment, too, you do know it."

- "Yes, we know. But I would like to clarify this from You personally,"–
I admitted, and continued: – "Killing material beings, You got energy.
But having transmitted to the Hierarchy, at what expense did You get
the energy in the subtle world? After all, in the subtle world everybody is
immortal, and there is no one to kill."

- "My intellectual work began then. I improved My thinking apparatus.
I worked with instruments and programming of Everything. In the subtle
world there is such an operation as repurchase, and the repurchase of
everything is also energy. I carried out some work and earned that kind of
energy for that, which I needed."

- "It is characteristic of You. As for God, did He have the division into
good and evil even prior to Your appearance?"

- "Prior to Me? Ask God about that."

- "Well ... Will You say if You tend to use such methods as flattery,
deception, treachery?"

- "Yes, I use them if necessary."

- "Who do You apply them to?"

- "To everybody."

- "Can You apply them to us as well?" – We asked that just in case to
increase our vigilance and not to succumb to any of His tricks.

- "Yes, I can," – He smiled ironically. – "If I need some specific situation
to test you, I can use any of these means or some others. But mostly, for the
purpose of testing. Or I can use them to create specific emotions, feelings,
to get extra energy from your emotions or feelings of any person."

- "What do You appreciate in a human being?"

- "The man is of no value for Me. But I appreciate the soul itself. It is
important to Me."

- "What do You value in the Higher Personalities?"

- "The same thing – the soul, only a larger one. The development of
a higher Level."

- "What is the essence of evil?"

- "This information I will give you in the form of a law through the
written channeling."

- "But is the essence of evil likely to cleanse the body of the
Cosmos?"

- "Not exactly."

- "Or, it maybe," – I continued to insist on an answer, – "control over
the provision of vital functions in the organism of Nature?"

- "No. The law will reveal the essence of evil," – Devil repeated again avoiding a direct answer. But He avoided that, most likely, purely for economic reasons, because the connection required Their energy. But He did not intend to double-spend it on one and the same: both oral and written responses. He calculated everything to the smallest detail.

- "If a lot of killing is made, is it possible to destroy the huge body You live in?"

- "It is impossible."

- "And what will happen to the Cosmos, if it is fully captured by the forces of evil?"

- "Do you mean murders on the physical plane?" – He asked.

- "On the energy one," – I replied. – "There are wars in the subtle world as well, aren't there?"

- "Yes. But given murders on the energy plane, damage of protective bodies takes place only up to a certain Level. In the subtle world it is impossible to kill. For example, I cannot kill anyone above My Level. For Me, the road there is closed. And wars on the energy plane occur basically only at low Levels between equipotent Systems. When a Level fights with another Level, in other words, Systems of a similar development, they have an advantage in action.

In case a Higher Level starts a war with a lower Level, it is clear that the Higher will win, like a civilized soldier wins a savage, – He continued his explanation. – And besides, killing someone below your Level is not respectable any more. For example, it never happens so that a higher Level wants to win the lower Level. With Us it is not worthy of Conduct of the Higher. This action does not provide any advantage.

In case a lower Level wants to launch a war with a Higher one, it is simply impossible. Rising and killing someone of high-level development is beyond one's power, as the Higher will crush any inferior in view of their great power."

- "What is the meaning of wars in subtle worlds? Is it also the capture of foreign territories?"

- "It is the capture of energy that is of importance. It comes to the energy bank. In addition, through wars souls are captured like slaves."

- "Even souls are captured!" – We are surprised.

- "Yes. This is the first thing to be won in the war. The most important value to be won is souls, from which energy is then obtained."

- "So, are controversies solved by war in the subtle world as well? Not by negotiations, but by wars?"

- "Yes, they are. But all this refers to the lower Levels and minus Systems. Plus and neutral Systems are not fighting."

The Way Devil Died

Devil, or the minus Hierarch, has experienced countless incarnations and, consequently, He has had to die many times. So I turned to Him with a question:

- "Would You say if You died of old age or You were also killed when You were in a material body?" – We came back to His private life.

- "I have been killed many times."

- "Does it mean there were those who excelled You in your life? Were there those moments?"

- "Excelled?" – Devil objected. – "I did many atrocities during My lifetime, for which I was killed. But that was society alone that killed. It was a penalty."

- "Do You remember the way You met death?"

- "I did that with pleasure," – He answered cheerfully. – "I got kicks from My own death. What should I have been afraid of? I knew that I would not disappear completely. You cannot even i-m-a-g-i-n-e," – He drawled significantly, – "how great it is! You do not know this – the essence of this pain. You do not know, because you do not go deeply into it. There is no physical pain. First, you need to feel and get kicks, and then – die. And it is rather difficult to explain this very state to you."

His revelation looked strange, as it was uncustomary to our conventional understanding of death, worked out since prehistoric times. It opened up something new in the development of the soul taking the minus path, since even the last seconds of life were used to obtain perverse and dubious pleasures.

- "But what does the pleasure of one's own death mean for the soul?" – We tried to find out.

- "For My soul it meant a lot. So I, though I did not seek death, met it with joy when it came. One can say, I specifically have taken that path, I mean killing others, I almost never lived out till the end of My program, and I was punished through being killed many times. And I think I was most often killed, compared with any other Entity ever grown on the Earth.'

- "Did You know of Your immortality?"

- "Of course, I did."

- "Did You remember Your previous incarnations?"

- "Not always. But this feeling – the desire to obtain power of death – has always been present in Me."

- "And if some plus personality dies, can it also get some pluses from death?"

- "Mostly a plus personality is very afraid of death. But it gets pluses, giving energy from the illness or death in its System. However, it does not feel that buzz, which I always felt. One can even say that I am a masochist – in your terms My state sounds like that."

- "And should we all be afraid of death?"

- "Of course not," – He exclaimed optimistically and convincingly drawled: – "Never."

- "And do You know, for example, my death by the program?" – I tried to find out something about myself.

- "I know all of you." – (He was referring to those present at the channeling.) – "But I will try to lure you to Me during your stay on the Earth, because if you leave the body, you will not be able to go to Me, because for Me it will be more difficult than now to induce you to come over to My side in the subtle world."

- "But there, above, God is unlikely to give us away, isn't He?"

- "Why not?" – Replied Devil. –"I can buy you, if I desire. I can give God in return for you something He would like to get. Of course, in Our terms, you are very expensive."

It was very unpleasant to hear that we could be bought, let alone the prospects of being seduced into a minus System, so we tried to bring some arguments against.

- "But in your System we would have to kill, while we are not fit for that and dislike this direction."

- "You'll fit into, it is a matter of time," – He grinned. – "In My System, everyone does what I need."

We were not inclined to continue the conversation on this unpleasant subject. Besides, we were afraid to offend in any way His pride, and then He could carry out His threat to spite us. So we switched to a neutral subject, and began asking about His past.

- "What moments of the past in the physical world produced the most vivid impressions on You?"

- "I did not complete the life on the planet, like Earth, but passed a lot of other material worlds. I had to pass through a lot of different planets. For the man these planets are fearful, but I was sent to them by God in order to undergo purification. And it was impressive. But through such a difficult life I perfected My soul. And I liked all that was supposed to bring suffering. I found pleasure in it."

- "Did You have associates with You?"

- "No, I was alone."

- "And what moments in the subtle life produced vivid impressions on You?"

- "I have no impressions. I just remember what impressions I had in the physical body. And since I moved into the subtle world, I had the only desire – to have as many souls as possible and, thus, to build My own world."

- "What way did Your transition from the physical matter into the subtle one occur? Why did You cease the embodiment in the material world? Who told You «that is enough to be embodied in the rough matter»?"

- "Nobody told Me that. I was developed up to the Level so that I could choose Myself whether I needed to be embodied or not. I was surfeited with a material life. It was hateful to Me. I needed much more than that, because that body following the physical one was already saturated with the energies of the material plane so that I had to turn to filling of the next subtle body."

- "Does it imply that the decision to stay in the subtle world or not to stay in it depends on the filling of bodies?"

- "Yes, it does."

- "But did it probably depend on Your desire where to stay as well?"

- "Wishes are precisely linked to the bodies. When the bodies need to be filled with something, they send impulses to My soul – and based on them, there appear desires in it."

- "And how did You quit the overall program of incarnations? You also might have had karma."

- "This was due, on the one hand, to minus Levels, which have no karma and, on the other hand, to what I have already said about the bodies."

Devil as a Woman. Son of Devil

Reincarnations hide a lot of interesting moments in the development of a soul. One can be born on the Earth clever or stupid, sick or healthy, a woman or a man. But we were going to learn whether Devil has passed through these transformations.

- "Being on the material level of development, have You ever been a woman in past lives? Or did You always remain a man alone?"

- "I was a woman as well. I had to learn everything both in a woman's appearance and a man's one."

- "But, being a woman, did You also kill?"

- "Yes, I did, even then. But, of course, My direction somewhat changed, because, My forces, like those of every woman, were small, and what I was doing in a man's way, I could not do, being a woman. But as a woman I still represented a heinous nature."

- "Do You remember Your development from the very beginning?"

- "Yes, I remember everything."

- "Did You love something in the past life?"

- "Which one? I have lived many lives. These are endless stairs."

- "We ask about Your lives in a material body. This is what we are most aware of now."

- "I enjoyed evil alone."

- "Did You love the creatures of the same type as You, just anyone?"

- "Of course, I did, this I was given. I also wanted to teach those who I loved, to do evil and follow Me. But ..." – He paused. "Apparently, it was not very nice to admit it," – they did not agree. "Only one agreed – My son."

- "Is he with You now?"

- "In the end, he went his own way. Up to a certain moment the son was following Me, you might say – half-way he followed Me. But then, after all, something happened to him, and he left Me, – in his tone there sounded latent frustration and regret about something irretrievably lost."

- "Did something happen in the heart of Your son, whereupon he digressed from You? We beg Your pardon for such an indiscreet question, but we would like to know – what happened, why he had ceased to follow You: if he was tired of killing or he got interested in something new?"

- "First, he became interested in creativity. And, second, he was tired of severity. I mean, he was not tired, but he rather went against it. He felt like creating, but My System has absolutely no freedom, while creativity is always associated with freedom. This is what he grew to dislike."

- "So, did he grow to like freedom?"

- "Yes, it was freedom."

- "And in what area of art does is Your son work?"

- "He is engaged in planetary design. He designs new planets. This is a large scope of activities."

- "What does the System he is engaged in creativity represent?"

- "My son is in the contractors System. This is a neutral System: neither plus nor minus. It belongs both to God and Me. He works in this very System."

- "Did You have other children-followers?"

- "No. He is the only one. Basically no one has ever understood Me. They did not understand My evil. And during My physical life I had few children."

- "How many?"

- "Well, if you take to My standards, it is not enough, while to yours – it might seem a lot."

- "Did Your children choose quite different roads?"

- "Yes. But no one has risen up to such a high Level like the son I've spoken of."

- "Do You currently meet with the son, who has risen so high?"

- "No," – it was said in a sluggish and thoughtful way.

- "Do you have no common interests anymore?"

- "As a rule, the relationship similar to that between relatives, are supported only in a material life," – He replied coldly.

- "Do You have now emotional affection towards someone in the subtle world?"

- "No. More precisely, I do not feel emotional affection, but rather want to have more souls to Myself. And this is My basic desire."

- "And what do You need them for? Work?"

- "Yes, to work, and in general, to quickly rise even higher. This is My main goal in development. And this requires to get more such kinds of high-energy souls, like you," – the last words He emphasized pointedly by putting a special significance in them, which lies in us, and which is not available to mere mortals, thus, He flattered us once again with a view to possibly tempting us. Obviously, He tried to blow up our self-esteem and pride, but any flattery of His was unpleasant and visible to us, however just for the childish curiosity, we decided to clarify."

- "Is it flattery?" – We tried to make it clear to Him that we were able to realistically value ourselves: – "I think we do not have such a high energy potential, we do not work a lot."

- "No, I need souls not at the level of earth dwellers, but the ones like you. Since I am talking to you personally, it means you have a high energy potential. So I am saying this to you personally. To mere (mortals) I do not talk. It is beneath My dignity."

Through this compliment, He revealed to us our new qualitative characteristics, for which souls are valued in the subtle world. Souls may have a larger or smaller energy potential, but the high energy potential of theirs is appreciated in the Higher worlds."

- "Thank You," – I thanked Him for the compliment.

To this He replied:

- "There is nothing to thank for, this is a hint. Think it over. You know My abilities. Later tell Me what you will decide."

It was the second hint for us to come over to His System. Of course, we refused to accept such a proposal, because our spiritual aspirations differed much from His. But in order not embitter Him, during the next channeling we tried to gently and politely answer:

- "We thank You for having made the proposal to work in Your System, but we belong to God and stay with Him."

To our response He said dryly:

- "I will think over, which way to persuade you to Me."

His persistence was unpleasant. Still, He was a personality, from which we could expect anything at any moment. At the same time, assuming that Devil's invitation to Him could appear to be a mere test, we decided to ask God about it directly. And when, finally, He got in touch with us a few channelings later, in the first instance we asked:

- "U* ... has suggested coming over to His System to us. Is this a test of our faith to You or just a test for greed?"

- "No, I have not tried you out this way. He just likes to lure people like you. He wants to get more (souls) like you."

Devil's Way of Thinking and Vision

Devil Says:

- "As You said earlier, You are on another plane of existence. And what way then, being in the subtle world, do You see the planets of the solar system?"

- "They are numerals."

- "Well, numerals," – we did not understand. – "But they have the energy formation as well, don't they?"

- "Any energy is numerals, too. It is all comparable. I have everything connected with numerals. Do not compare Us with people. We are different. Therefore, We see the other way you do. When a man sees something, we see completely different, which is more profound and most approximate to the true construction. A human being has rough and primitive form of vision in a very limited spectrum."

- "Good. You perceive the world in numerals. But do Managers or Determinants, which are at a lower Level compared to You, perceive any images of the planets?"

- "They see something like the volume with numerals, the cellular structure of the volume. What a man sees as a material image in life, he will see in a different way, having come to the subtle world. In other words, later, at your advanced stage of development, you will see the energy and will cease to see the rough matter."

- "Will we see the energy alone?"

- "Yes, only the energy, all energy layers."

- "And if a being rises even higher by the level of development, does the energy perception of the world become digital?"

- "Yes, quite true."

- "Do You think by numerals or pulses?"

- "By numerals. I think in this way only on the material plane. But numerals are too rough for Me, as I have gone in My development to the layers of extremely subtle energies."

- "But what are numerals followed by? What is so high that one can think by?"

- "This is the smallest particles. I manipulate their energy, going deeper into each. For you, it is difficult to understand, because Our thinking is on the other Level. The man is designed so that he cannot understand anything without an image, while Our thinking works on a different principle, on the Level of the light thinking."

The Purpose of Devil. What He is Free in

We wanted to know more about His real interests and aspirations, of His activities. There were questions that He did not want to answer, so we had to seek out topics that might reveal Him as much as possible.

- "God has said He is currently guiding ten people on the Earth. Do You personally guide someone?"

- "Yes, I do. But I do not get in touch with them directly."

- "Are they channelers or politicians?"

- "Politicians. These are high-ranking people."

- "Can You say who they are?"
- "I would not want. They are holding high position now (1998)."
- "Well," – we did not continue to inquire for what He wanted to hide, as we were aware that people do not need to know everything, especially as it concerned politics and some people's names, so we asked Him about some other things: – "What do You find pleasure in at this stage of development?"
- "No pleasure at all," – He drawled coldly, emphasizing the last word. And then He repeated again: –" Remember – no. What pleasure could I have? What pleasure could a machine have?" – He went on discussing about Himself. –"And at this stage of development I am a computer indeed. I am calculating again and again, endlessly. I have no pleasure, but I have a goal, which I will certainly achieve. The goal is the main thing."
- "Does this goal consist in rising higher?"
- "Yes, rising to the next Level. I would like to build My own world and have as many souls as I like. I wish all of them were Mine. At present not all of them belong to Me, most souls are God's property. And, most important, I wish I did not depend on anyone. Now I depend on God, on His Systems."
- "Will You tell us, which actions You are currently not free in? May You yourself kill or annihilate someone at will?"
- "In all the actions concerning the Earth, I am not free. Earth belongs to God. Here, everything is subordinate to Him. And on the Earth I am serving God under the contract."
- "Are You free in Your Systems?"
- "Yes, there I am completely free, I do what I want. And God does not interfere in My Hierarchy."
- "Do the souls of planets have freedom of choice concerning what path to go: good or evil?"
- "Yes, they do, like every human being. The program for the planet development includes freedom of choice."
- "Are those souls of the planets, which have taken the way of evil, subject to You?"
- "The planet is not subordinate to Me until its development is summed up, or its development cycle is completed. But I can influence it in a minus way, a kind of seduce it, urging on to take My side. And if the planet tends to evil, then, having completed the development cycle, it becomes Mine."
- "And do You currently have the souls of such planets?"

- "Yes, I do."

- "And how can the planet do evil?"

- "If the planet does not want to belong to God, it resists. The program goes, and the planet can no way act against it. The program is beyond its control. But the planet can go against the life on it and start, using various methods available to it such as floods, earthquakes and all sorts of calamities, to destroy all the life."

- - -

- "Is creativity developed in Your System?"

- "It was I who invented, founded black magic. These are My deeds. The Bible originated from Christ, while black magic – from Me."

- "Black Magic is a very interesting science," – we flattered Him in our turn, especially since it was indeed so, as it embodied mastering and transforming of matter by means of thought and certain rituals.

- "Yes, only real scientists are able to understand it, if they begin to delve into it," – He agreed. – "To understand the magic, one requires knowing much of both physical and subtle worlds."

- "Are worlds created in Your System, like in God's one, or don't You need this?"

- "The worlds I have, but I do not create them. I have bought them."

- "Have You bought them ready the way our farmers buy land?"

- "Yes ... Creativity is not in My nature, so I get worlds."

- "Do You buy from God?"

- "Yes."

- "Do You create forms of any creatures?"

- "Yes, I do. A form is just the summing of potential elements. More precisely, I cannot create the basic element itself, but something ready like a ready-made progression, I use."

- "Do You use subtle bodies?"

- "No, not the bodies but potentials, which can be extremely various, for example, the potential of a prime number. I make up energetics. Absolutely everything can be different."

*   *   *

Chapter 9
Devil's Unknown Worlds

DEVIL'S HIERARCHY

Earlier we have found out some details concerning the formation of God's Hierarchy. But it is also very interesting to learn something about the formation of Devil's Hierarchy.

Devil responds:
- "Is the minus System expressed through Your Hierarchy?"
- "Yes. I have personal worlds, personal Hierarchy."
- "But at the same time, Your Hierarchy is a part of God's Hierarchy. How do they fit together?"
- "Yes, it is. To be precise, it is contiguous to the latter through a certain part," – He shows a scheme to the channeler (see Figure 14).

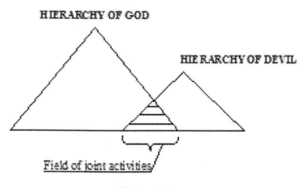

Fig. 14

- "But is this a separate branch of development?"
- "One can say, it is."
- "Does the Hierarch of the Medical System have his own Hierarchy, too?"
- "Yes, everyone has one's own. Our work with God has an interrelated basis, in other words, He cannot do without My work in specific cases, for example, concerning the matter of your earthly origin, but I cannot do without His souls, more precisely, without the production of souls."

- "Are very low worlds also subordinate to You?"
- "Yes, they are."
- "In Your Hierarchy, what do inferior worlds differ from higher ones?"
- "One can say they differ in the extent of behavior stupidity. Inferior worlds present the beginning of development. Beings in them are so low-developed that they produce such actions, which are beyond comprehension. And they have a very negative impact on each other, but I'm talking this from your point of view. But I have My own views on their existence. I have to adhere to your moral position in the conversation; otherwise you will not understand Me."
- "So, are there two extremely different worlds subordinate to You – the higher and inferior?"
- "Why only two? I have a great number of worlds. At each Level of the Hierarchy there is its own world. And each of them lives by its own laws."
- "Is the law of harmonious development intrinsic to Your Hierarchy?"
- "Yes, it is."
- "Is there any difference in the programs, under which an individual develops in Your Hierarchy and in God's?"
- "Differences are very numerous, but the difference is not in the programs, but in the form of improvement. First, in our Systems, energies are of different quality, the construction itself is different. And the subtle energies are opposite in their nature. So, in general, We differ very much. We do not have anything similar. There is, however, only one identical particle, which initially belonged to the Common origin. And this is that very small particle that unites us with God, there is otherwise no similarity. In all things, We are different, Our Hierarchies are different as well as the Entities subordinate to Us."
- "Do You work with God only on the Earth?"
- "I work in your entire Universe, and in the other three, too, that is in all the four universes I work together with God. We are collaborating. Specifically, He and I manage the same Universes. We manage them together."
- "But is the work in the other three Universes specific compared to this one, or similar?"
- "It is specific. There are own specifics in work everywhere."
- "Do the other Universes have a different construction of the matter?"

246

- "No, not exactly so. There are differences, but they are not so significant, so one can say that the construction is similar to that of your Universe. In fact, there are no great differences."

- "And what will happen to the Great body of the Cosmos, if it is fully captured by the forces of evil?"

- "If it is captured only by the forces of evil, it will come over entirely to Our Level – the Level of minus energies."

- "To Your System?"

- "Yes, it will come over to Us, and the entire development will take a different path. But actually it refers to God, while We are taken by Him only as programmers."

- "Is that You who makes programs for people belonging to God on the Earth or does He have his own programmers?"

- "Roughly speaking, We have a contract to work together on Earth. God has his own programmers, too, and they, together with Mine, which are, to a large extent, low-level representatives of My Hierarchy, program social, domestic and other situations for people. Thus the programmers belong both to Me and God, even though He has his own, and I – My own."

- "Do You participate in making the program of Earth as a planet?"

- "No. This is a great soul (He means the Earth)*. She has belonged to God for a long time, and His programmers make programs for her."

- "What penalties are there in Your Systems for making errors in programming?"

- "As a punishment the programmer has to give Me the energy, in which he has made an error."

- "In which way is it returned: through a complicated situation of his?"

- "Yes, the situations are complicated for the programmer himself, and, moreover, for those that he guides."

- "Does the programmer give energies through the situation, as a man does?"

- "Yes, he does."

- "Is there a difference in energy return and the implications of this return in God's Hierarchy and Yours? For example, in God's Hierarchy, the more energy souls give, the more they receive. There occurs a sort of self-kindling. As for Your System, the energy of the working soul increases only through the absorption of new energy, that is, if You do not absorb others' energy, You will fade. Does such a difference exist?"

- "Does it? In reality it is not so. Both God and I do absorb energy. God mainly absorbs energy through a situation, but at any rate, it is the absorption."

God's Composite

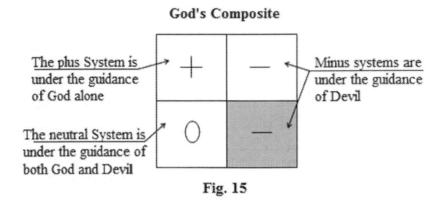

The plus System is under the guidance of God alone

Minus systems are under the guidance of Devil

The neutral System is under the guidance of both God and Devil

Fig. 15

- "God has several minus Systems. Do all of them obey You or exist by themselves?"
- "Minus Systems are subordinate to Me, they are My Systems. But among them (see Fig.15), there are common, or neutral ones as well. They belong to God, but obey Me, too."

Given the opportunity to specify the qualitative structure of God's world, I could not help taking advantage of it this time, because it was interesting to learn the way the minus Hierarch understands this structure:

- "If God consists of three quarters (3 / 4) minus Systems, is one-fourth (1 / 4) among them neutral?"
- "No, neutral ones make up one-third part of the minus Systems," – He corrected.
- "What does such a ratio: ¾ – minus Systems and ¼ – plus Systems – give our Universe?"
- "This is the structure of the organism in which We all inhabit. But there are completely plus Universes as well as completely minus. The Universes, which contain both plus and minus, are somewhat transitional. In our Universe, its plus part is the beginning of a transition into the plus Universe, while ¾ of its minus volumes – into the minus Universes."
- "What are minus Universes?"
- "This is a particular formation with its constructive life going by. "

- "Does the life in a plus Universe differ from that in a minus Universe?"

- "The difference is in energy. And, of course, life in them is entirely different. Imagine two worlds, inhabited by totally different kinds of beings, with other souls; it means that a composite of souls is modeled by totally different energies, and due to this construction some souls produce only minus energy, while others – only plus."

- "And can it be said that the plus Systems are paradise-like?"

- "No, no," – Devil objected explicitly. – "It is quite different. Here on Earth you have such differentiation between good and evil. In fact everything is not like that in the Cosmos, and there is no paradise."

- "Do You communicate with Hierarchs of other Universes, adjacent to our four Universes?"

- "Yes, We communicate with the nearby, but We can reach the distant ones as Our power is not enough to do so. So We communicate as far as Our power capacity allows, but only on business. Ungrounded communication We do not have."

- "What issues do You communicate on?"

- "Mostly We coordinate common issues. In principle, We live the same life as if We lived on one Earth, but on a larger scale. We have an ordinary life, with work and communication. But all is in commensurate to Our means and must be economically justified."

- "Are there individuals who do not obey the Hierarchical arrangement?"

- "These individuals simply are disintegrated, they are eliminated by themselves. In their nature, chaos prevails, so they are destroyed. Who wants to exist and progress, must comply with generally accepted laws."

- "For what reasons may they fall out of the Hierarchy?"

- "Due to breaching of the laws of existence."

- "May they also fall out of the Hierarchy due to disobedience to God or You?"

- "Yes. And not only for the reasons of disobedience. They violate all the laws of Existence. But mostly now, there are not such individuals, because everyone knows **what** they will face in the event of violations. There is a separate world of chaos with its own operating laws, which differ from the laws of the Hierarchy."

Pathways Leading to Devil

A man should know which ways, and, consequently, actions, thoughts, and deeds lead to Devil. But what will the prince of Darkness say about it Himself? Let us turn to the dialogue with Him.

- "A man has to pass through a hundred levels of development, one hundred stages to rise up to God. Should a person also pass through several tens of stages to rise to Your Hierarchy?"

- "Of course, he should."

- "Or, perhaps, committing one atrocity would suffice for an individual to get into Your System at once?"

- "In addition to committing atrocities a human soul should desire to meet with Me, that is to work for Me or sell itself to Me for anything. And an individual should know this for sure, in other words, he / she should be aware of his / her inner aspiration. And if the desire to work for Me is firmly rooted in him, he will be accepted by Me. But, of course, the opinion of God is still of importance – if He will let him go. I have the right to take a person only if God lets him go. And if a man senselessly kills, but at the same time believes in God, then his deeds will turn into his personal karma, and he will have to work it out in the System of God, but into My System he will not get."

Who can get to Devil and for what reason – we decided to address God as well to clarify these matters.

God responds:

- "In order to get to Devil, is it necessary to pass through some levels of development?"

- "To get to the very Hierarchy, of course, the soul must have a high-level development. But anyone can get to any of His low-level worlds; one's consent given to Him would suffice. Devil values every miserable soul. But instead of getting into the Hierarchy, underdeveloped individuals get in His lower worlds of quite different conditions of existence, and stay there until they reach the proper development. By the way, can you answer why Devil values any miserable soul?" – God addresses us.

- "Because He cannot create them by Himself. He cannot master the process of spiritualizing."

- "You are right. And His improvement depends on the number of souls belonging to Him. Therefore He tries to seduce as many souls as He can, and for this purpose He invents more and more ways. But on the other hand, those souls who withstand His depraving methods, build up a powerful energy potential. And I need strong and pure souls capable of refusing any temptations."

Devil responds:
- "You build Your programs without a choice of development paths, while God – with a choice. Is there some more difference in the programs?"
- "There is much difference. A program is, in other words, a way of improving the soul. Therefore, let us rather talk about the difference in Our principle to improve souls than talk about the programs. First, We have totally different energies, therefore the very structure of souls, their composite is different. It is difficult to explain something to you that you have no idea of. Although both God and Me have subtle energies, but they are not comparable in quality. Anyway, We are very different. We do not have anything similar."

To learn many things of Devil we had to ask God about Him. Some truths were better accepted in comparison, so the following characteristics of Devil gave God.

God responds:
- "When Devil is composing new programs for people, what serves as a basis? We know that You assume improvement as a basis. And what does He assume?"
- "Also improvement. But the difference is in obtaining the energies of the other quality. Devil is developing for His fosterlings such situations, which produce the necessary energy for Him, "black" energetics. Improvement can occur, but in opposite directions."
- "Does it mean that different situations make energies of different qualities?"
- "Of course. You have long known this."
- "And can any personality be forced to develop different energies?"
- "It cannot be forced, because there is freedom of choice."
- "What is now the essence of human being's serving Devil?"
- "A man does not serve Devil, but is under His control. One can say that any person, who has fallen, is already under Devil's control."
- "Do sects of Satanists serve Him?"
- "As for sects, it goes without saying. Some people get there on their own, others – under the influence of someone."

- "Are all the members of this sect governed by the minus System?"
- "Yes."
- "The Bible says that 666 is the number of the beast. Is this an earthly type of souls that pass through the evolution of animals?"
- "No, not necessarily. 666 is the number of Devil."
- "What are qualities of people who have this number?"
- "These are His souls with the appropriate set of energies in the matrix. The fact is that on the Earth there are My souls, but there are also representatives of His minus System, and He marks them with the help of this number."
- "Can they somehow be distinguished among the remaining people on the Earth?"
- "Only by deeds, and habits."
- "Are they characterized by aggression, cruelty, evil?"
- "Not necessarily. They can be soft, think over this and say that. They can easily come into contact with others and establish good and profitable relations for themselves. They know how to do this. And at the same time this way, through relationships, they conquer other souls."
- "The Bible says that this number will be on the forehead or the hand of a man. Is it really so?"
- "Yes, it is. But He makes the marks on a subtle plane, that is, on the subtle structures of a man, so they can be seen only using the third eye. But I also make My marks on people whom I trust most. That is, there can be His marks on some people and Mine – on the others."
- "The Bible says that people with special marks on their hand or forehead, will be permitted to trade. For what reason, have these people got the right to trade?"
- "Those that have Devil's marks, i.e. they are from the minus System, belong to Devil. And He has His own plans. Someone has to make exchange processes, and to do so He chooses appropriate candidates and makes respective programs for them. Special marks help distinguish these people among others, and better manage them in the desired direction. But not all traders have Devil's marks. There are a lot of My people in trade, too. This occupation for them is simply the vital necessity, a way of existence as well as control of their human qualities, of course."
- "Who controls animals on the Earth? Your System?"
- "Insects and wild animals are controlled by the System of Devil. More precisely, there exists a distinction. Those animals that have their own intelligence, that are capable of deciding something, choosing, are

guided half by My Determinants, and half – by Devil's. Of course, all the aggressive species belong to Him. Wild and aggressive animals do not have freedom of choice; they follow strict programs of Devil. They have fast programs, in other words, under these programs they quickly reach the goals set for them. They clearly follow their own program. And those animals which are subject to My Determinants get freedom of choice already from Me, and in their programs elements of creativity are included. Many animals act in the circus, they are well manageable."

Development of Souls in the Devil System

Devil Says:
   - "On what basis is the development of the soul in Your Hierarchy implemented? Do You program some complicated situations, which the soul must solve?"
   - "In My Hierarchy souls development is based on making strict, rigid programs."
   - "Stricter than they pass through on the Earth?"
   - "It is not what you do on the Earth," – there sounds discontent in His tone as we dare to compare incompatible things: the Higher with the Inferior.
   - "And how can we imagine it?" – We insist modestly.
   And having relented, He gives us a lengthy explanation:
   - "Souls developing in My Hierarchy are near robots. The robot performs its work strictly according to the program, without adding anything from itself; the same is with the souls in My System, doing their job, as robots, only under the program. Work under the program is very strict with no swerves, no freedom of choice in life. A strict, rigid program," – again He repeats, wishing to emphasize the main thing, and then continued: – "This is why the soul is moving in its development at an accelerated pace. Due to the fact that there is no freedom of choice, the soul in My System reaches the target more quickly.

   But God has a choice. God gives souls the right to choose; therefore while developing, they go a more distant way, reverting to the old, because normally souls do not choose what they need to progress, but what they want. I do not give this right. They fully obey My will. But the lack of freedom of choice in My programs is compensated for by the accelerated development of a personality."

- "In Your Hierarchy there are Levels, like in the Hierarchy of God. Hereupon the next question is: on the basis of what does a soul transit from one Level to another in Your Hierarchy? Does it just implement certain programs?"

- "Yes, it does ... although it is not so easy," – with a gloomy reverie He says. – "The soul must perform a certain number of programs for the transition to a Higher Level."

- "Do all the Entities complete the same number of programs for this?"

- "Every soul has its own number, as there are more talented souls as well as less talented."

God says:
- "If the soul is developing under the program, in which there is no freedom of choice, does such a soul need intuition? As the soul improves, it is supposed to develop in a personality, isn't it?"

- "Do you want to ask whether Devil's soul is guided by intuition?" – Corrects God.

- "Yes," – we agree.

- "As a rule, of course, the souls that belong to Devil do not have intuition, because they all make robot-like."

- "Consequently, intuition develops only in Your souls as they evolve?"

- "Yes. Although, to be precise about the souls of Devil, the intuition they have develops too, since a certain Level of the pyramid, because the high development, in one way or another, includes such quality in the structure of an Entity. Intuition appears, but they do not use it because they do their program strictly. Therefore an individual activates intuition and uses it only if such moment is included in his program. But they are mostly already very high-level individuals in which all the subtle bodies have reached a certain degree of development. Without the required internal building intuition will not be revealed. And if an individual has built himself appropriately, and this quality is used in the program for some purposes, the program includes situations in which intuition can be used. However, this is rare."

Souls in the Systems of God and Devil

Questions answered by God:

- "What is the meaning of laziness in human life? Is it given to him or is this quality generated from life to life?"

- "Normally some part of this quality is placed in the program so that the man can learn to deal with it, learn to fight for his development. And in the course of life he may either increase this quality or completely eliminate it."

- "Is laziness placed for this purpose alone or for some other purposes as well?"

- "In My System – for struggle alone. But there are still other individuals on the Earth, again not Mine, but Devil's, whose laziness plays its role. As for My people, laziness takes a small place among the traits of their character, and they are hard working, creative. But laziness is given by Devil to some of His people for the other people to work on it."

- "But is a kind of dependency manifested here in energy terms?"

- "There is dependence and it is great. Therefore, We are cooperating with Him on the Earth, gaining the quality of energies that both He and Me require in proper quantities. In Our Higher worlds there is no laziness at all. This quality is intrinsic only to people for a certain Level of development."

- "How is this dependency expressed in energy terms?"

- "Let us take an example. Let a man holding a certain position be lazy. He does not work personally, but his subordinates are working for him, and among them some energy exchange takes place: he is morally pressing on them through his position, from which his soul generates energies, typical for the world of Devil. At the same time quite different energies are produced in the subordinates' souls, as they are driven by a sense of duty, obedience, a desire to give him what is needed. Between them there is energy exchange. And the employees of the given head process the tough energy of pressure into a completely different quality of energy of their souls. But due to his position the chief can take from them what he needs. Even scolding the subordinate, he also takes away the energy of the latter."

- "But does the head work it out in other lives?"

- "These are Devil's people. They have no karma; they do not work out anything but act in accordance with their programs. But at the same time, they help My people gain the qualities necessary to me. If My people develop laziness, they will turn out disharmonious, and take the path of antiprogress."

- "Your souls are triune. And when the soul goes to Devil, does it become dual? After all, in His Hierarchy there are exclusively minus energies. Does the plus part of the soul disappear?"

- "The soul remains triune in Devil's System as well, because I have built it. And I laid the trinity, and no one and nothing can derange it. Only the minimum percentage of accumulated plus and minus energies is changing. In the Hierarchy of Devil the plus part becomes smaller while the minus – larger. In My plus Hierarchy the minus part decreases due to improvements in goodness only up to one percent (see Figure 16, V.1). One per cent of the total amount of the soul. In Devil's System the plus part of the soul is reduced to one percent (V.2).

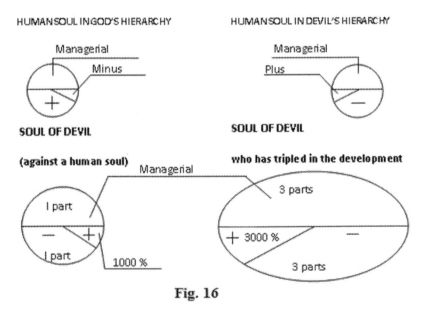

Fig. 16

This is a minimal part, to which each of the parties may be reduced, but one per cent is always of the total, which the soul has reached at the moment. The soul is evolving, and all of its parts are growing.

Therefore, one percent of the soul in the second life will be more than one percent of the same soul in the first life, while one percent of the total volume of the soul remains constant. And in a thousand lives, one percent will be one percent, but from a larger volume. If you compare the human soul and Devil's soul, then the immutable part of the human soul is one per cent, while Devil's minimal part makes up a thousand per cent, compared with a man (V.3). But I speaking in general terms, actually His part is much more.

His minimum plus part can be reduced only up to a thousand percent. But if the plus part of His soul triples (V.4), then the minus part, respectively, increases three-fold. The Management part increases respectively, because the power of both opposites grows evenly."

Devil Says:

- "Are there many people on the Earth, guided by the Determinants of Your System?"

- "Yes. Some of the politicians and directors of large enterprises absolutely in all countries We are guiding. Everything goes in a descending line with you. But ordinary people, workers and other producers are no longer Mine."

- "And why You are allowed to manage such developed individuals?"

- "We guide only those high-level individuals, which are by the type of their character, and consequently, by their soul, suitable for our System. But, of course, those high-ranking officials who belong to God, We do not guide."

- "Are evolutionarily young souls who do not have time to do any evil or good, guided by Determinants of God?"

- "Yes, young souls are subordinate to Him. The fact is that all souls God creates Himself, i.e. it is His System that creates new souls. I do not know the way they are made. God does not disclose this secret to Me. That's the main thing that I do not know from God. This is the mystery He is hiding from Me."

- "Does the ignorance about this mystery make You dependent on God?"

- "Yes, this is the main reason why I depend on God."

- "And who particularly produces souls?"

- "A special System headed by God is engaged in their production."

- "Does it also produce souls for You?"

- "No, not for My Hierarchy. God makes everything for Himself. I get souls from God, that He does not want, that is defective souls, which must be destroyed. The selection of souls is made after the earthly plane, when a person completes his stage of development on the Earth and gains particular qualities. Then We look the qualities of which side prevail: Mine or God's. And so, some souls come to God and others, whom He does not put into the karmic circulation, come to Me, with His consent."

- "Don't You have the right to take any soul without the consent of God?"

- "No. In this I fully depend upon God."

- "What is the main purpose of Your existence?"

- "Apart from the fact that I aspire to rise to the next Level, I have another goal – to learn how to make souls in order to build My own world.

My second goal is to have as many souls as I want. I wish all souls were Mine. And most importantly, I want to depend on no one. And now I depend entirely on God, on His Systems."

- "God raises souls on the Earth. They are here to pass through a life school, gain a certain quality of energies. And when they reach maturity, what happens to them next?"

- "Souls are put to Earth mainly in lots for some period of time, for example, for two thousand years. During this period they are incarnated and reincarnated, gathering the required qualities. And at the end of this period, as it is currently happening, souls are sorted based on their accomplishments. God is the first who takes souls, He chooses the best, while those souls He does not like, are decoded or passed to Me. However, some souls go to the Medical System, but they are basically the souls of skilled health workers and of those who love to help others. These are basically the distributions made."

- - - -

We decided to address God to clarify a few things regarding the appropriation of souls by Devil.

God responds:

- "Can Devil in secret from You take Your own souls?"

- "No. They all are under strict control. And every soul is under the supervision of Determinants. Devil is working with Me, and therefore has no right to violate My laws. In this regard He has different consciousness than humans. We are the Higher. We, even the minus personalities, have another Level of consciousness. But in this period very many souls come over to Devil. Very many of them. Now He, as they say, experiences paradise, He is progressing through souls, because there are a lot of refused souls. Chaos and offered freedom allows detecting all the refused souls, which I do not need, and I have to decode some lot of them and give Devil the other lot.

But I do not give them free of charge. My loss of souls He compensates for by the appropriate energy necessary to Me, or by the energy that was spent on the particular soul: on its production and development."

- "And can Your enemies steal Your souls?"

- "Yes, they can. The System that does not belong to Me is able to do this. In the Cosmos there are such ones as well."

- "Can Devil encroach on other Hierarchies, or conquer Entities in other worlds for Himself?"

- "He can do that in the Hierarchies outside My Universes. This right He has. But He is well aware of what is advantageous to Him, and what is not. Not every war and the conquest of souls may benefit. He understands quite well that He may lose. The risk is very high. One can rather lose than buy, so abstinence is sometimes more reasonable than many theoretical plans. The fact is that if He loses much in this war, then I also can be destroyed without Him, because between Us there is some energy dependence, which manifests itself in business opportunities. And His losses may cause the collapse of both of Us. No acquisition can be compared with the losses, which We may suffer together. But since He is, after all, a calculationalist and understands what consequences might be, He does not encroach on anything, and prefers to develop slowly but surely. Devil is expanding His holdings at the expense of His own development, that is, He is progressing along with Me, and the path of development is the surest way to expand one's territories, a slow one, but without risk of loss. And, of course, I keep Him under control and warn of incursions into foreign territories. After all, it is necessary to supervise and teach. But, as I said, He is obedient, it is inherent to Him. Careless actions on His part can cause the death of both of Us. Therefore, all Our actions are coordinated."

- - -

Then we continued the conversation with Devil.

Devil Says:

- "In one of the channelings You once said that as a result of wars between cosmic Systems, souls are captured as slaves. And why cannot God prevent the capture of souls belonging to Him?"

- "His authority extends only to the four Universes, but there are many of them close to Ours. And those Systems fight, which are from the Universes that are not subordinate to God. They live by their own laws. But God has the right to win them (the souls) back. Or given normal relations,

We are contracting, that is, if God wants to buy souls from Me or in other Systems, to pay off, He pays some energy for them. If I want to buy the souls of a certain quality from Him or someone else, with His consent or the consent of other Systems I pay them, also using the energy. At the same time the energy given should be equivalent to the energy of the soul, it is made of, or should be so that it is necessary to God or the System at the moment and they do not have yet."

- "If God buys Your souls, does He re-educate them?"

- "Of course. But it is very difficult to re-educate."

- "Is reeducation carried out through reprogramming and sending souls to the material world?"

- "Yes. Usually reeducation is implemented on the Earth, though not only on her, but also in other physical worlds."

- "Is the development of captured souls hampered?"

- "A temporary delay takes place: after they are captured they are reprogrammed, and the adjusting of the two programs – the old and new – is carried out, so these souls stay in an awkward position for a long time. They dwell on the subtle plane, i.e. they are stuck in inaction. But they are realizing their present situation and entering into the new program, that is, they begin to understand what they once were and that they will be in the nearest future. And after some time they are already beginning to like it, because they are entering into the new program at the level of consciousness. And once they start to like it, they are sent to the physical world."

- "Are they given the option?"

- "Yes. In God's Hierarchy the option remains constant. And if I need someone to win, I lavish gifts on that individual. But if he resists for a long time, I lavish many gifts on him. If he does not take the small, he will hanker for the large."

- "Are You bribing so?"

- "Yes, I am," – with a clear sense of contentment He agreed, – "souls are conquered this way, too. I prefer to conquer in a peaceful way. But, generally speaking, I use all methods."

God says:

- "If Devil takes the soul of man to Himself, and that soul has plus energies, does He cleanse the souls of them?"

- "No, He does not cleanse anything at all. The plus energies the soul also must contain. If the Entity has come to Him by its consent, it is deprived of its freedom of choice in situations, and Devil will program its existence according to a rigid scheme. And once it has no option any more, the Entity begins to quickly fill the second half of the soul with the minus energy. At the same time it no longer needs to strive to gain the plus qualities, as it has already gained them. It came to Devil with them, because when it dwelt in My System, I forced her to gain these plus energies.

It turns out that it needs to accumulate the energy of only one quality for its improvement – the minus. And all this helps accelerate its progression, so it is advantageous to Devil to take souls with gained plus qualities. But gaining of minus energies and accelerating based on this happens up to a certain Level only. And then again one has to gain plus energies. The balance in the soul must be maintained, but each Level has its own ratio. Therefore, starting from a particular Level, a soul lacks plus energies to balance, accumulated during its stay in My Hierarchy. And Devil programs to gain them to the desired quantities."

- "At the expense of what does the soul gain plus qualities in the Hierarchy of Devil?"

- "At the expense of executing the program, of seeking the best possible way to fulfill the assigned work, at the expense of discipline. The minus world cannot develop without the plus either, so at each Level, there are subtleties with respect to gaining of various qualities. Every soul, growing in the System of Devil, must gain not only minus energies, but plus as well, but the latter should be no more than the accumulated former. And if Devil gets the soul with plus qualities, He benefits from it very much. Do you understand why?"

- "Yes. In this case, it needs to gain more minus to compensate for its plus energies," – we answer.

- "Right you are, exactly – to compensate for. And the minus energy will be accumulated by such a soul faster because automatism and lack of option contribute to this."

- "And for what qualities Devil chooses the killers on the Earth? On the basis of what, for example, does He select maniacs?"

- "He examines what qualities His subordinate's soul needs. This is the only foundation. Any soul can become a maniac in His Hierarchy, but He checks what energies it lacks, in other words, He acts based on the foundations of development in His System."

- "And may it happen that some soul feels disgust to kill, and it does not want to?"

- "Wishes He does not take into consideration. In His Hierarchy an Entity becomes a robot. Therefore, if He sends it to Earth to kill, then it kills in a robotic way. However, robotic programming in His System works only till the middle of the Hierarchy. As the Entity reaches the middle, it becomes aware of itself and the robotization disappears. But it is removed from the Entity gradually rather than immediately: first, it becomes one percent smaller, then, higher, second percent of awareness is activated, and so on. Robotization is completely removed by the end of the pyramid, by its apex. But from the middle of the Hierarchy awareness begins to develop by itself, it begins to form its foundation.

All that is done so that the Entity could not return to Me, could not have the desire to return during the first stages of its stay in the Hierarchy of Devil. And from the second half of the pyramid, it itself would not wish to return, because it would have gained too many of these qualities, and hence, the energies that are rebuilding its basis radically, and it would understand that it is better now to stay with Devil. Such a soul would already begin to appreciate the speed of development and everything else in His Hierarchy."

- "What relationship exists between Entities in the Hierarchy of Devil: negative or cooperation?"

- "They just co-exist because of the circumstances."

- "Do they tolerate each other?"

- "No, they don't. They live in their Hierarchy, their worlds, and feel quite comfortable, because the worlds correspond to the qualities of their energies accumulated by the soul. Their souls require these tough conditions."

- "May Entities in the Hierarchy of Devil hurt each other, strong ones —oppress the weak, or scoff at them?"

- "Yes, they may, if Devil wants to, that is, if He needs to get some qualities from His own Entities, then He makes appropriate situations using His methods."

- "And if things go wrong in their worlds, may Entities destroy each other?"

- "If it refers to the Hierarchy, then such relations can never take place there. This relationship is characterized of the inferiors. All that goes beyond the bounds of normal relations is not allowed in the Hierarchy. Hierarchy is a union based on the action of certain laws that no one has the right to violate, otherwise they will be expelled. And besides, Entities that have not reached the required Level of awareness are not allowed in the Hierarchy. Those who do not meet the established standards, continue their development in Devil's lower worlds, outside the Hierarchy. A certain level of consciousness dictates the Entity within, from its matrix, appropriate norms of behavior, and an individual cannot do otherwise. The behavior of Higher Entities, irregardless whether they are plus or minus, can never be compared with the behavior of inferior individuals outside of the Hierarchy.

If, nevertheless, because of some inadequate circumstances, the behavior of Devil's Entity becomes inconsistent with the general rules of behavior, then it, or even the entire Level, i.e. all those who inhabit it, are descended a Level lower. The Hierarchical laws prohibit non-established relations."

- "Do the relationships in Your Hierarchy differ from those in the Hierarchy of Devil?"

- "Of course, they do. The difference is similar to the relations between plus people and minus, between good and evil. And besides, in My Hierarchy there is freedom of choice, while Devil's Entities are mere performers like soldiers: they do what they are ordered, without the slightest personal initiative. If they are ordered to «stay here», they will stay until they are given other orders. In My Hierarchy, Entities think, create, and choose something that is closer to their soul. I have no strict discipline; all is based on the high consciousness of Entities. This has considerable impact on the relationship. Living by the law of liberty or by order makes a big difference. My Entities have a lot of work, which they like and they put their heart into, while Devil has nothing of the kind. They do what He orders them to do. But most importantly, My Entities have sympathy, compassion, and developed mutual aid, while He does not have all this. Therefore We are fundamentally opposed."

- "How do Entities transit from Level to Level in the Hierarchy of Devil? Is it just like in Your Hierarchy, or maybe vice versa: if Entities fly upwards in Your Hierarchy, then in His one they «sink» lower and lower while progressing?"

- "No, though they have minus energy, according to their properties it is the same as Ours, that is why We co-exist in a single volume. And Entities in His Hierarchy do not «sink», but also move upwards. The minus energy in His Hierarchy is not «dirty» as these are also Higher worlds, much higher than the earthly one. Only lower worlds produce «dirty» energies. If we say «dirty, heavy» energy, it is just to create imagery, for you to make it easier to understand. The point here is different qualitative potential of Our energies, their antagonism. Therefore, His System has a completely different path of development and other laws of existence. The Hierarchy of Devil is similar in its structure and functioning mechanism to Mine, but automatism is strongly developed in it. And His Levels are full of automation and robotization."

- "And where are lower worlds of Devil located? Are they lower than the earthly plane?"

- "They are in many places. The first Level can exist on the Earth. He guides insects and animals, but by My instructions, by My goal. He has a lot of worlds in My other Universes with different forms of life. But even in your Universe, there are many planets with the worlds of Devil. I, Y* ... (the Hierarch of Medical System)* and Devil possess all the four Universes, so We also possess most diversified worlds. And all the Entities in My Hierarchy extend their authority to these Universes and their worlds, since My Spiritual Hierarchy is above all other material as well as many subtle worlds."

- "Do lower worlds as well as High Levels do evil in Devil's Hierarchy?"

- "The difference in the development affects the behavior of Entities. To a greater degree lower worlds do evil, this is a form of their existence. High-level consciousness is also capable of doing evil, but they do it not arbitrary, but in compliance with the general plans, as High-developed individuals understand that everything is interconnected, and an arbitrary action may entail serious consequences, and sometimes it may cause self-destruction. Any actions must be consistent; otherwise they may result in the destruction of the world in which they dwell themselves. The Middle Level and all the Higher ones in the Hierarchy of Devil do everything, taking the responsibility for what happens. They have very high consciousness."

Sorting Out of Souls

At certain periods of human development souls are sorted out by different hierarchical Systems. This has required clarifying.

God says:
- "When souls are sorted out on the Earth, who gets more of them: You or Devil, since there are a lot of minus people on the Earth?"

- "No, Mine on the Earth are more. I have common people, and they are always in the dominant quantity."

- "Do inveterate villains come over to Devil?"
- "Yes."
- "Do maniacs and killers also belong entirely to Him?"
- "Anyone whose cruelty is more than enough is considered His individual. Mine possess other qualities."
- "Is the rest of souls Yours?"
- "Yes, it is."
- "Are there many people on Earth who work for Devil?"
- "Yes, there are. In many countries, governmental circles are formed of His people, so wars are unleashed. And many politicians and others, striving for power, for subjugating others, for hoarding up benefits are also from Him."
- "What is the ratio of His and Your people on the Earth?"
- "His people make up slightly less than a half, and the rest are Mine. Those who are engaged in creative work are Mine, but those who do the calculations, are engaged in mechanical manufacturing of machinery are His, and based on this one can distinguish people. But on the Earth there are contractors as well, and they are numerous. Doctors, for example, do not belong to Devil. They are basically Mine. But they are also divided between Me and Y* ... (the Hierarch of Medical System)*."
- "But does Y* ... stand isolated both from You and Devil?"
- "Yes, he does. He operates independently in His Hierarchy of doctors. He is neutral and I am very happy for Him and for His System, so I do not have anything against the fact that He chooses souls for Himself on the Earth and in My other worlds."
- "Can't Devil produce souls, because He does not own the process of spiritualization? Is this exactly the secret He does not know?"
- "Yes. He does not know much."
- "How do You manage to keep the secret of souls producing and spiritualizing from Devil? Isn't He able, with all His ingenuity and intelligence, to get to know this secret? After all, He can bribe somehow Your trusted Individuals, can't He? Or is it impossible in relation to them?"
- "At the top We have Entities rather than Individuals," – God corrected. – "Individuals are on the Earth, they are your people ..." – And, having made a pause, He explained: – "Devil cannot learn this secret due to the insufficient Level of development. Everything is distributed energy-wise among the Levels. The fact is that the secret of souls production is dropped by Me to the second Level, counting downwards from Me, that is, the

Level below Me. And Devil is almost two times lower than Me. Counting the steps, it will look like this: I represent, for example, the hundredth Level, and the two Levels, which I entrusted this secret, are ninety-nine and ninety-eighth. And Devil is somewhere on the fiftieth Level, so despite all His desire, He can no way reach these Levels."

- "But Devil has a powerful computer system. Isn't He able to calculate the secret?"

- "It cannot be calculated. Production of souls and spiritualization are not subject to any calculation."

- "And why can't He master the secret of spiritualization? Also due to His low Level?"

- "Not only for this reason. To master spiritualization, one must have a particular quality potential of the soul. Devil is built on a completely different kind of energies that cannot be involved in the process of spiritualization."

- "We want to clarify: doesn't Devil own the process of spiritualization due to the fact that He does not have such a quality as love?"

- "At Our Levels such quality does not exist any longer. Love exists only on your Earth. And We have the other – responsibility. Love is the lowest development stage of certain types of energies. But the development of a special type of energies – namely creative and some others – is based on them. Creative energies spring up from the energies of love; development progresses in the form of an evolutionary chain, one after another. And spiritualization is based on creativity. And the main reason why Devil cannot master the process of spiritualization lies in the fact that He cannot master creativity. He is a calculationalist, but not a creator."

- "But why is creativity absent in the minus System? We want to look into the matter."

- "Creativity is developing on the energies of good. If a person in any of his lives did good, these plus energies have been already gained in the matrix of his soul, a multi-choice program is made up for him as a reward for the good deeds in the past, which will include a development option through creativity. Further the human being chooses either to take a creative path or some other. If he chooses creativity, then in subsequent incarnations, it will be included in his programs. His abilities will expand, and the soul will be enriched by specific types of energies. Devil has neither good, nor freedom of choice."

- "So, creativity springs up from goodness, doesn't it?"

- "Specifically, **the choice between good and evil gives birth to creativity**. Creativity is the work of thought, its choice and search. The soul that makes a choice for the good is encouraged by means of creativity."

- "But why is the choice so important?"

- "Making a choice, or hesitating imply some work of mind and soul, a kind of evaluation and comparison. With a plus person, it refers to creativity, as the search for some reasons, facts, and so on is taking place. The very choice is the beginning of the creative process."

- "So, in Devil's System creativity is absent because He does not allow his people and Entities choosing, forcing them to act strictly on the program?"

- "Yes. Devil does not allow His Entities thinking. He thinks for them Himself, and they, like robots, do what He wants. His Entities do not think, do not choose, they have no search, and where there is no search, there is no creativity. Devil thinks for all His Entities Himself. This is the main thing in His Hierarchy. Calculation for Him is a way of thinking. He thinks only through numbers. He calculates who should do what and sends the numbers down, dispersing them by the Levels of the Hierarchy. That is, Devil invented the number as an action. When He needs to make some action, He sends down his number in the form of a code in the place where the desired action or event is to take place. If He pursues the overall goals, then He sends the received code down to the very first Level. And there begins the work with numbers. Entities fulfill what Devil wants, getting His thoughts encoded in a certain number or a pulse. But Entities themselves do not think, in other words, one can say that they think only in numbers. They get everything ready-made, so no creativity in them is possible."

- "Does Devil take souls for Him only from the Earth?"

- "No. From all the four Universes. There are His own calculationalists and other performers in all My Universes."

Programs for the Souls of God and Devil

All the people on this planet develop by the programs made up for them by the Higher Individuals. But it is interesting to learn about the peculiarities of improving different people on them.

God says:

- "Your people and people of Devil live on the Earth. Do His people have freedom of choice on Earth?"

- "Earthly programs are similar for everyone, but freedom of choice is not available for Devil's souls. All the maniacs, brutal murderers belong to Him and do not have freedom of choice."

- "So, on Earth there are two types of programs: one, in which freedom of choice is placed, and another – in which freedom is absent. Are both of these types present among the people?"

- "Yes. But programs made for the Earth and programs in Our world, i.e. in the Hierarchy, are completely different. And you do not even compare."

- "You said that people on the Earth have ten types of programs. But these are Your System's programs. But do Devil's programs also present the same ten types?"

- "All the ten types of programs is the development of Devil. He is a calculationalist and programmer. He developed them on My behalf. Therefore, He also makes His people pass through the same programs. But these ten types of programs relate only to the Earth."

- "There are people in Devil's System, who are developing under low-level programs, and there are Entities developing under high-level programs. What is the difference of their programs?"

- "Levels. There are program levels. This means that programs differ in specific character of the situations built as the way Entities exist is changing, and hence there arise subtleties in forming programs by situations."

- "Do they differ in the degree of freedom? Or don't they have the degree of freedom?"

- "In the worlds of Devil, in His Hierarchy the freedom of choice is completely absent. But on the Earth, everything is different. The Earth is Mine. And souls that are not sorted out yet are Mine, and they have freedom of choice. Only after the Justice, when they are finally attributed either to Mine or to His System, the souls that appear to belong to Devil lose their freedom. But this is Devil who makes programs for all My souls. It turns out that some people are Mine, but the programs are His. We have a joint production of souls on the earthly plane, i.e. their improvement. On the Earth, only those have a freedom of choice that have not yet made a choice between Him and Me. I give all My souls on Earth the freedom of choice, because even the most brutal killer may come over to My side and improve. I give him this right and give the last chance in the form of freedom of choice."

- "What happens to the soul of a man, if he performs the work necessarily, but the work itself he does not like? Is he developing, or is the soul making no headway?"

- "It depends on whose soul it is – Mine or Devil's? – Clarifies God."

- "For example, the soul that belongs to You."

- "If a man does the work, which he does not like, it means it is required to do on the program. This way he is gaining energies of a certain quality. And that quality is necessary to him."

- "And if the soul belongs to Devil?"

- "Then this soul is working strictly on the program. Despite the fact if it wants this or not, it is working and producing what is needed by the System of Devil ... If this is My soul, then at the expense of freedom of choice, it chooses various qualities to be gained, rather than the only one, that is, I am a kind of indulging the man's desires allowing him to develop in the desired direction, but this choice is given within the program. And the soul chooses: somewhere it can gain more energy, somewhere – less, but longer. However the energies allowed are being gained."

- "If a person does not do anything bad because of fear of punishment, does this worsen the quality of his soul? For example, if a person did not know that for a certain offense he should be punished, he would have committed it, but since he knows that he will be punished, he does not commit it. The qualities gained through these options will be different, won't they?"

- "Of course, this affects the quality of the energies gained, weakening them. Low-level individuals always behave like that – they are afraid and therefore do not perform actions. A high-level individual does not do bad things not because of fear of punishment, but because it is abhorrent to his / her soul, inner manners. The difference is significant. But fear of the low-level individuals is used as a method of their education; they are always intimidated by something. This helps make them advance until they develop their own consciousness. Fear is a method of education."

- "There is such a type of people as fighters for truth and justice. But they are fighting for something that is right and fair only in relation to them. Are these people referred to the minus System, as they are constantly fighting."

- "They are most likely selfish people. But you know all people are like that. They claim to be properly and fairly treated, but do allow injustice to others. This is typical of many, so these people do not necessarily relate to the minus System. Everyone believes that he is always right and that he is very good, but he is treated unjustly, and he always seeks justice, not at all for someone, but mainly for him alone. This is just a low type of development. A high-level individual fights rather for others than for himself."

- "Critics are people who always like criticizing someone. Is this type of person likely to belong to the minus System?"

- "No, among the critics there are plus personalities as well. there are two varieties of critics, because criticizing the good is one thing, but criticizing the bad is quite another. There are also different directions: some critics are fighting for only the bad, and others – only the good. My people criticize the bad. This is a method of education. Those who are criticizing the good are representatives of the minus System. An observer should only distinguish what is good and bad. Sometimes a man takes good for bad. For example, the new and progressive is often rejected and criticized; although it carries a new life is to the future. And it is the new that minus critics are against."

- "On the subtle planes of existence, do Devil's Higher trusted individuals also develop under strict programs?"

- "Yes, in His System everyone passes through the strict program."

- "And even at the Highest Levels?"

- "At Higher Levels of the Hierarchy everything is being done knowingly. Higher Entities have another Level of consciousness. And although, of course, their programs are still strict, but they have been trained on this and They even like the rigidity and perceive it as a necessity. They take delight in all that is strict ...," – there came smile in the intonation of God.

- "Do politicians on the Earth pass through strict programs?"

- "Yes."

- "But do they still have freedom of choice?"

- "The freedom of choice is very small. The higher a man rises in the power structure, the less he has freedom of choice, because in politics everything is arranged in such a tied, twisted way that the heads are necessarily pressed by masses, so there is little freedom."

Calculationalists of Minus Systems

God says:

- "How do the minus Systems subordinate to You differ from the minus Systems subordinate to Devil?"

- "By creativity. My calculationalists work somewhat differently. Creativity presents in the way they calculate, reflect on them, and even in numbers they can develop some creative variations. In numbers there may appear free elements. And in Devil's Systems there is nothing more than direct calculation under the program, no slightest hint at free creativity."

- "For what reason are calculationalists attributed to the minus System, to the world of Devil?"

- "The reason is exact sciences. All calculations and computations are run by Devil. And the process of working with numbers helps produce energies in the soul, characteristic of His world."

- "But among the calculationalists there are a lot of good people," – we reminded.

- "Yes," – agreed God and said: –" But good, decent people are not Devil's, but Mine. I also have minus Systems. Even by a person's character one can determine which souls are Devil's, and which are Mine. Therefore His calculationalists and Mine have completely different types of character. His calculationalists are deprived of such qualities as understanding of other people. They have no decency, kindness, honesty or other plus qualities. As for Mine, they are, of course, contrary by their nature. And though they are involved in calculations, but sympathize with others, are friendly and calm, are always ready to help others."

- "If a person does not want to commit atrocities, but his soul requires minus energies to balance the energies, is it possible to make him gain them, giving him the program of a calculationalist?"

- "No, the program of a calculationalist is given for the other purpose. A man should master the digital calculation for his future progressing. Without mastering of computational operations one cannot climb high either, because a human being needs to learn digital thinking, and this is the next stage of development."

- "Should every highly developed soul master calculations?"

- "No, not necessarily. Of course, I need such workers in general, but one can improve through art, philosophy, or some humanities. Paths are many."

- "Can people who do not do evil, but love calculating, designing, get to Devil? Can You give calculationalists to the world of Devil without their desire for some goals of Yours?"

- "Yes, I can. I decide this. You see, here is another «but»: Every soul is a part of Me. And if I cannot somehow manage this soul, i.e. if this particle starts to go against Me, or at least is making up its mind against Me, it cannot be Mine. The reason I give away souls for is not calculations or design, I do it only because the soul begins to go against Me. Such a soul I can give Devil. For example, it looks like this. Suppose I need white, while the soul begins to turn gray, or black. Therefore, I do not need the soul with such a color any more. What should I need it for! But if I revise its old qualitative developments and consider it necessary to keep that soul to Myself, I will create such a program that will help it reform, that is purify within a short period of time. I send it to undergo purification. And then I take it to Me. But I can also give it away without sending it anywhere."

- "And what is the reason it is getting black?"

- "The reason is discontent about life, which is being sent not towards the very soul but towards Me, that is, it blames Me rather than itself for weakness, for not giving it the easy way. Or it may be overly keen on the pursuit of pleasure. And then there appear the qualities in it that I do not need. It is not gaining the energies that I require at all, so it takes the opposite side and, generally, that side is His, and therefore such a soul is close by its nature to Devil. And this is already difficult to rearrange. And where it will find itself, will depend on the soul alone: whether it will work out the correctional program properly or whether it will come over to Devil to be educated by His programs."

- "Can any individual degrade in the System of Devil?"

- "Yes, it can."

- "And is it possible that, say, Devil wants the soul to produce tough energies of evil, while it turns to the side of good?"

- "Yes, it does happen that the soul gets sick of evil, and it turns to the side of good. But this is rather an exception from the rule. Such cases are very rare."

- "And what He does with those souls then? Does He pass them to You?"

- "No, there have been no cases when He passed them to Me. He will never give away His souls for no particular reason. In the last mentioned case, however, when some of His souls turns to good, He either destroys it, or completely clears it from the energies gained and begins to re-develop this soul in His own System."

Souls Belonging to Devil after their Death on Earth

God says:
- "Do people of Devil look through their tape of life after the death on the Earth to examine their own mistakes?"
- "Souls that develop under Devil's programs do not have mistakes in life. Imagine a robot that makes some mistakes. In other words, the soul that belongs to Devil may make a mistake only through the Determinant's oversight. But in this case it is the Determinant that is punished. And He is getting a karma, because He has made a mistake in programming, while the souls guided by Him are not be punished for these mistakes."

(Only the souls of God are allowed to make one mistake after another. But this is done for the purpose to develop high-level consciousness for the personality to learn to be aware of its wrong actions or thoughts and to learn to repent of them. Then it is relieved of the karma)*.

- "But do the people of Devil somehow analyze their past life after death?"
- "Yes, they remember everything. Their moment of death occurs the same way, and they are showed all their past life through till birth. Something similar takes place. But they are considered to be judged, they are just watching their past life in order to consolidate the gained experience and to quickly adjust all their sensors to the future work."
- "Does this «future work» refer to the subtle world or to a new life on the Earth?"
- "According to the program in a new life."
- "Is there a difference in regard to Your souls and souls of Devil after people's death?"
- "It depends on who regards this."
- "You regarding Your souls, and Devil – regarding His own ones," – we clarify.
- "The attitude usually depends on the Level the soul is on. By this criterion souls are estimated. The higher the level of souls, the more they are estimated both in My Hierarchy and in Devil's."
- "Do these and those souls fly through the same Separator after death?"
- "Souls of Devil are distributed among the Levels at once."
- "Is there a difference in the methods for cleansing Your souls and souls of Devil?"

273

- "Devil has no cleansing at all. He receives everything He requires from souls without resorting to it. This is Me who faces difficulties in gaining the necessary qualities in My souls."

- "And may He cleanse His souls of some good qualities, which are accidentally gained through their life on the Earth?"

- "No, this does not happen. His souls cannot gain good qualities, because His program is very precise, robotic, and it touches nothing besides it. The soul develops strictly on the program, and no deviations in the direction of goodness can ever occur. Exceptions are possible in My System only, because the given freedom of choice allows the soul to gain something additionally."

- "After death, do Your souls and souls of Devil fly to the Separator according to the single scheme or is there a difference?"

- "There is a difference there. Devil has no Separator*, while I have it."

- "And what does Devil have instead of this?"

- "In His Hierarchy there are Levels at once. And all the souls are distributed exactly where they should be. Souls have nothing to cleanse, so everyone is flying straight to their Level according to the achieved Level of development. Usually after death, the Determinant shows the soul of the student guided by Him the points that are gained through the life. And then the soul goes back to be reprogrammed, or rather it keeps developing for a while at its Level before that. In the subtle world it has another program, but it is also individual and rigid."

- "Does Devil decode Entities that do not obey Him in His world?"

- "This cannot occur in His world. Everyone obeys Devil, because His program eliminates the methods of arbitrariness. But as for decoding in general terms, then, of course, He can decode any soul for some of His reasons."

- "In case of decoding of His subordinates, does He cleanse the matrix from the energies and further use it as the initial soul from the beginning? Or are matrices decomposed and cannot be used anymore?"

- "Why? They can be used further. He keeps the initial components, which I lay in the soul while creating it. These He keeps and can develop them further as He wants. Now, He develops everything by Himself from the very beginning, and gives nothing back to Me. In His Hierarchy Devil can do whatever He wants: He may either lower the Level, or decode and again put the matrix into use. And He may also decompose a matrix completely. But if he decomposed the matrix completely, He would not be able to re-create the spiritualized soul. Therefore it is not profitable for Him to decompose them completely, and He does not. This happens only in exceptional cases. Devil may decompose completely some minor construction, a short-lived one rather than an eternal soul."

Suicide in Devil's System

God responds:
- "Can the soul that belongs to Devil commit suicide?"
- "No, it would never do this of its own free will. But if a suicide is recorded in its program, it commits this. That is its program."
- "And if it is Your soul that commits suicide, is it regarded as a deviation from the program, its violation?"
- "Yes. In My Hierarchy this is regarded as the program violation, which is punishable. As for Devil, the programs of His souls may contain very frequent suicide as death in this way is a powerful gain in certain energies."
- "Is suicide in the world of Devil equal to murder of an individual by another human person?"
- "Generally, death is equated to gaining of so many qualities that a person can gain for a lifetime. This is equivalent. A human being wastes his time all the life through, lives in vain, and sometimes gains very little. But when he dies, he immediately gains a lot of quality* energies at the moment of death. Profound impressions are producing the energy required for his soul. It often happens that the second part of the qualities required for this incarnation he gains when he is dying, in a period of difficult situations. One half of the qualities is gained during his lifetime, while the second half – in the period of death. I am talking about the death by murder."
- "So, does the soul that belongs to You get karma through committing suicide?"
- "Yes, My soul does. And further on its program is complicated."
- "But does the soul that belongs to Devil get no karma through committing suicide?"
- "No. It would get no karma. On the contrary, the soul would get surplus points for this as it is gaining the energies required by Devil."

* * *

Conclusions to the Chapter

Channelers are often accused of that they fall into temptation and, in such a way, one wants to say that Devil tempts them with new information.

But knowledge of the Truth is not temptation, but is awakening to the blind.

Any information itself is neutral, and only the man himself due to freedom of choice turns it into goodness or lucre. And depending on how he uses the information given to him, he does good or evil, and his soul is filled, respectively, either with Devil or Divine energy.

Summarizing the above chapter, let us focus particular attention on such a rhetorical question as: «Should we be afraid of Devil?» as it is fear that causes to blame others and see the enemy where none exists.

A man is often scared by the new and incomprehensible, sent by God, and keeps aloof from all these, as he considers them Devil's bait, and at the same time he uses the well-known and pleasing (wine, drugs), sent indeed by Devil, as a medicine for the soul. Sometimes, rejecting the hand of God, a man can easily take Devil's aid, as it is always sweet and lulls his vigilance.

Due to his very low level of development, a man sees Devil's provocation in the Great Truth, sent by God, while he himself is going arm in arm with him in the direction opposite to God. Stumbling and erring, taking the burning touch of God for the fire of hell, and Devil's sweet flatteries and temptations for God's encouragement, still remaining in complete ignorance and blindness, after two thousand years after the appearance of Christ, the humanity must understand the most important:

it is no use being afraid of Devil, one should rather be afraid of oneself;

Devil is not around us, but inside the man.

What is such a claim based on?

The man is scared to get into the clutches of the Ruler of Darkness, but in pursuit of temptations: money, power, women, wine, drugs, and others, he is gathering minus energy in his matrix, which, like a heavy stone, pulls him to the bottom into possessions of that one whom he seeks to escape from.

Every atrocity produces «heavy» energy, based on which Devil's worlds are built. Therefore, through performing negative acts, hurting others, deceiving, slandering, killing, or stealing, the person performs actions that produce minus energies relating to the energy range of Devil.

Man is a biological machine, which is constructed in such a wise way, that when it does what is classified as good, it produces plus energies filling the matrix with light energies, but when it commits acts or spreads thoughts under the category of evil, this biological machine produces minus energies, and the matrix cells are filled with a dark spectrum. Therefore, a man rewards himself for good deeds, enriching the soul with the Divine light, and punishes himself for evil, filling the soul with black energies of Devil. Here is the evil inside a man that he should fear.

Devil does not need to contrive or attract him through deception, the man himself, through his own actions, paves the way to the realm of the Hierarch of the minus System. So this is not Devil people should be afraid of, but themselves, their actions and thoughts.

Devil may not take a single soul without the permission of God. Even if a person expresses his desire to work for Him, to sell himself for some benefits, Devil has the right to take him only after the permission of God. God first considers what to do with this soul by Himself: either to put it in a circle of karma, or decode (which means that the personality is destroyed, but the very structure of the matrix, after a thorough cleaning, is used once again for development in His Hierarchy), or to give Devil.

God decides everything.

The Hierarch of the minus System takes only those whom He (God) rejects.

But Devil works in another way, to take possession of the soul: He makes them defective, sets traps in the form of sweet and pleasant comfort, perverse pleasures. And He has the whole System of methods for corrupting weak-willed individuals. Pleasing a man (giving a lot of money, power, wine, etc.), He just helps him gain in the soul the types of energies that God does not require. And God allows His Assistant to invent more and more new temptations, because He himself needs people with a pure soul, with a high-level consciousness. God wants the human soul to gain high-level spiritual qualities, like His own ones.

But, allowing Devil to lure and tempt, God gives a man the freedom of choice: This is the main mechanism, which divides all mankind into «light» and «dark». The man chooses what to do and what to think of his own free will. God never interferes in human desires. He only observes, and then judges, summing up the individual's existence on the Earth.

The main mechanism to separate souls is the freedom of choice.

And a person should be well aware of, in order to know that God gives him the right to choose – which way to go and whom to serve. Only the man's **actions** determine where the person will get. Therefore, turning to the man himself, one can say: «Do not be vile so that even God would reject you».

And it is time to stop being afraid of Devil, given the cause of evil in the very man, in his dark, dirty shabby soul.

No foul thing, no evil will remain hidden from God and the Teachers of mankind, because a man is guided by the Determinant, and all the pupil's actions including his low thoughts, are well-known to Him. But the Determinant does not interfere in episodes connected with making a choice, following God's law on freedom of choice, but He just sends his disciple warning signs that he may take, or ignore.

Moreover, every human action is recorded on the film of his life, which is necessarily scanned after his death. And on the basis of this film a human karma is then drawn up by programmers and calculationalists. Furthermore, human thoughts are recorded in his Determinant's computer (not all of them, but relevant to some critical situations). So with all his cunning and meanness, a man cannot hide from the Higher that it is so easy to hide from those of his own kind. Moreover, a matrix is scanned using special devices of the subtle plane (human lungs are sort of X-rayed), and, in accordance with the cells being filled, it is accurately defined – the energies of which qualities the soul has gathered.

Therefore, performing the action, a person must first of all be aware of which sort of energy he is filling his soul with, for him not to repent in the worlds of Devil afterwards. And therefore we would like to remind the most important things once again:

1) only the man's actions make his soul either light or black;
2) and no unlawful act will go unpunished:

some misdeeds people will work out under the law of cause and effect, or karma, while other ones he will have to pay back through robotic slavery for Devil's good for more than billions of years.

* * *

INFERIOR WORLDS

Worlds Standing a Level Below the Hierarchy

God responds:
- "What are the worlds that are not included in Your Hierarchy?"
- "Usually they are a low Level of development. The worlds are designed to improve the souls that have just embarked on the course of the evolution, these are newly made souls. They gain the energy of another quality than people."
- "Are there many worlds?"
- "They are scattered all over My Universes."
- "Are these worlds low-developed compared to the Earth?"
- "There are low-developed as well as high-developed ones. Inferior worlds include more than one Level of development, many of them. Each world can have its own number of stages to improve."
- "Who owns the inferior worlds: You or Devil?"
- "I have My own worlds, while Devil – His own. But on many planets, as on yours, We are working to unite Our efforts for the cultivation of souls which I need."
- "How does the soul improve in the direction of evil on the planets subordinate to Devil?"
- "On low-level planets, beings have inhuman image and lead a relatively different existence compared to the Earth. In such worlds, everything is completely different than on your planet, so it is difficult to compare them, for example, one cannot compare your life and the lives of trees."
- "Do they have cruelty there?"
- "Everything is relative. In these worlds, the lifestyle differs from yours so that it is impossible to compare one with another, although, of course, from your point of view these are the worlds that carry evil."
- "So, does it imply that for some time souls dwell on the low-level planets, having inhuman image, and as they reach a certain perfection, they rise above and lead a more reasonable way of life?"

- "Yes. On the planets, where souls evolve through evil, all the souls that get into their world are formed only through evil. They improve based on the rough low-frequency vibrations obtained in the process of life, and eventually they work out an understanding of these vibrations. Penetrating into them, they progress through their perception, reaching certain Levels of development in the appropriate direction. The same relates to penetrating deeply into good vibrations and understanding good on your Earth. Likewise, evil is understood there."

- "Planets subordinate to Devil live their own special life. Under which laws does the life develop there?"

- "It depends on what Level of development the planet relates to. Worlds of Devil exist on the Level of Earth, above her and below her, that is the worlds of His are also located on different Levels relative to humanity."

- "What are the laws like in the worlds located below the earthly plane? Does such a law as «everyone goes one's own way» function there? Is there worship of evil?"

- "Yes, the law «everyone goes one's own way» does function there. As for the worship of evil, it is quite natural there, so they do not know what is evil. They just live in it, the way your predators do, for instance. Without knowing the good, they do not know what is evil either, so they live, without noticing it."

- "Which pole of the «Union» do low-level Systems called «dark» relate to: plus or minus?"

- "To the minus."

- "All of them?"

- "Yes."

- "But, maybe, there are plus Systems, which have not achieved the high Level of development?"

- "No, everything is unequivocal here: the worlds of Devil are always minus, everything is minus there and nothing plus can ever be."

- "If, after death, a degrading human soul goes to the minus System to Devil and it is accepted there, what program does it receive then in the next incarnation?"

- "The individual turns to gaining the energies of the opposite quality compared to My System. On the planets belonging to Devil alone, runs a special life, and He directs the newly acquired souls there, where they, going through the situations appropriate to the lifestyle of surrounding creatures, gain in their matrices the energies He needs. And for this very soul the program is being made, generally accepted to improve beings on this planet. Of course, there are particular programs on different planets. But sometimes We can cooperate with Devil, while preparing the program for someone, in case some united actions are to be taken, for example, if a maniac is required to annihilate a few people. And to make him act the way both of Us require, the program of his actions required on the Earth is being made jointly, and he is sent to the earthly world. In other cases, he is sent to other planets, and programs generally accepted for particular worlds are made."

- "But what does the progression of the soul in the minus System lie in?"

- "Of course, it is improving in the direction opposite to the plus System. And for this purpose Devil has developed his methodology, it is specific for each world and for each Level of development. But, again, this is mainly the process of gaining energies of different qualities in His range. However, the level of consciousness, which both plus and minus individuals have, can be equally high, if they are already in the Hierarchies.

But development in the minus Systems is not necessarily associated with low-level perception. It usually refers to low-level worlds, while in the high-level minus Systems, Entities are highly developed, and the consciousness they have is also high, so the responsibility for their work is great. It is necessary to distinguish among such fundamentals as low-level worlds, which are below the first Level of the Hierarchy, and the minus and plus Systems that are in the Hierarchies. The latter are characterized by the high-level consciousness. But at the same time, the behavior of Entities in the minus Hierarchy will differ from the behavior of Entities in the plus Hierarchy, and the quality of energies they gain will be heterogeneous."

- "Why can't souls come over to plus Systems to the Absolute from minus ones? After all, in the course of development they attain to high intelligence."

- "Firstly, they can't come over due to their internal qualities. The path is automatically closed for them. Souls gain the energies, which just physically cannot penetrate from a minus into a plus. The physical process alone operates in this case. But it only starts from the middle of the Hierarchy, while below this Level they can still come over. Secondly, Devil will not allow them coming back to Me, won't let them go, He cherishes every soul. And thirdly, they do not want to go back, they get used to the lifestyle, which Devil has defined for them."

- "But sometimes You take Devil's Entities for a particular job. How does the transition take place in this case?"

- "It happens very rarely. I also pay Devil for the Entity required with energy. Such transitions can be compared with the transition of highly skilled professionals from one country to another. But only those Entities of His can come over to My System, which have not reached the middle of Devil' Hierarchy yet. And they can still be re-formed in My direction."

- "When a soul comes over from the plus System to the minus, i.e., it is transferred after its qualities acquired within the life have been examined, what energies does Devil pay for them?"

- "Energies may vary: those which I need and which are not available to Me, or those that match the qualities of the soul being transferred. However, along with the soul being transferred I'm losing some energies, and therefore Devil must recompense Me for them."

- "Where do They take the energies, which they pay for the soul received, from?"

- "For this purposes they have a certain energy base."

- "Is this base made up of the energies of souls they have decoded?"

- "No, it is not made up of decoded souls' energies. This is a special database that exists for gaining of high-quality energies."

- "On the Earth, Devil gets a lot of energy through organizing murders of people. Does He get the energy from each Level of Your Hierarchy as well?"

- "No. All the Levels belong to Me and all they produce is Mine. But if Devil is involved in some work under the contract, He receives in accordance with the work fulfilled. We have strict exchange."

- "You and Devil have common Systems that You both manage. Due to what kind of work does He receive energy from them, if no one dies and no one is killed there?" – (It refers to the Levels where Systems of God engaged in calculating are located, but they are guided by Devil)*.

- "Due to calculation, computer operations, programming; besides there are more activities, unknown to man."

- "Should people be afraid of the minus Systems only because they are negative? If a man is said that another person is working on the Earth for the minus System, he will be avoided meeting by everyone."

- "As for minus Systems that exist above you in the Hierarchy, that is they are at Levels higher than men, they need not be scared of, because these are mostly programmers, calculationalists, ordinary mathematicians, physicists, which are plenty on your Earth. Are you afraid of your programmers? High-level individuals of the minus Systems are like the programmers who make up programs for people, are in charge of their destiny on the Earth. It is the programmers of the minus Systems that make programs for people, actually they rule sway the destinies, although it is Me, of course, who sets the goals for development.

And if you take the individuals of the minus Systems, which are a little lower than the Level of human development, these are the developing creatures at an early stage that are just taking the path of numbers, of calculating structures. Later, they will rise and start to calculate by themselves. In minus Systems, mostly all pass through the path of numbers. And what you call evil is a corresponding set of energies for them without the involvement of the senses. The man gains energies through the senses, while they do it without engaging them."

- "Let us assume that one needn't beware of those who stand higher in their development compared to earth dwellers. But those that are below us can perform actions towards a human being, which we would regard as evil. People are very afraid of the «dark», considering them to be servants of Devil, whose purpose is to harm humans."

- "Of course, it depends on the point of view their actions are looked at. Their behavior is always inadequate to yours: what is evil for you is a natural standard of conduct for them. But they have no right to interfere in the human program, and can only incite him / her to some negative action, thus trying to influence the human choice within the situations. And if the individual is morally stable enough, no incitement can affect his decision. So it all depends on the person. Therefore none of the lower worlds is capable of changing the situation, or imposing those ones that are not supposed under the program. And moreover, I am repeating once again, one need not be afraid of the Higher Personalities of the minus System. Their consciousness is much higher than that of any plus person on the Earth; they have developed a sense of responsibility, duty, caring for others and many other qualities that a human being is not aware of.

So do not fear. Fear stems from human ignorance. The very evil is inside the man. It is he who commits such atrocities that horrify others. And on the Earth, I always give him the right to choose between good and evil."

- "In Your Hierarchy, there are both plus and minus Systems. Do they exist at every Level?"

- "Yes, each Level of the Hierarchy, from first to last, consists of plus and minus Systems. The same is true, for example, for your body that also requires both plus and minus energies to function normally. Using one type of energies, your body will not work. However the presence of minus «yin» energies does not affect your character, because they serve your body and do not touch the soul.

It also refers to My plus Hierarchy with the exception of those Levels of Mine that are below the earthly plane, that is My low-level worlds. Those creatures are so underdeveloped that they have gained no plus energies yet. However the others contain both plus and minus energies (see Figure 17). At the same time this balance between plus and minus is not necessarily observed on the Levels of the Hierarchy. Generally plus energies are always less. The entire Absolute is divided into the ratio of one to four (1 / 4) and three to four (3 / 4). The ratio one to four represents plus Systems at any Level, while all the rest is minus. But to be more precise, these three fourth contain neutral Systems as well, so the ratio will change as follows: one fourth is plus Systems, one-fourth – neutral and one half – minus."

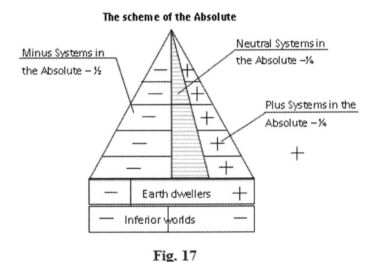

The scheme of the Absolute

Minus Systems in the Absolute – ½

Neutral Systems in the Absolute – ¼

Plus Systems in the Absolute – ¼

Earth dwellers

Inferior worlds

Fig. 17

Dense Worlds

- "A physical world is the matter of definite frequency of vibration. Other worlds are subtle, or energy worlds. But is there a matter of cruder vibrations, i.e. the matter which is denser than our physical world?"

- "Yes, there is the matter which is structurally denser than yours."

- "Where is it located?"

- "It is beyond your Universe."

- "If our physical human being gets into such a world, will he see this matter or will it be beyond his perception?"

- "A man will not be able to get into such a world. Imagine that there is the same Earth as you have, the same planet, but it is made of a crude matter. And the atmosphere on this planet is so dense that it is impossible to move. In other words, for the creatures to move in such a world, they must consist of even a denser matter."

- "For them, will we be like a subtle world?"

- "Yes, you will. This analogy is quite appropriate. The difference in the density of your world and theirs is the same as that between the physical and astral planes."

- "How are these dense worlds formed? What makes them so dense?"

- "They do not consist of your constituents of the matter. Everything they have is their own: atoms, molecules, their structure and laws of the physical world."

- "And why are those atoms and molecules denser than ours?"

- "It was intended from the Above and in such a way their design was fulfilled. From the Above the performers were said to do that, and so it was designed, – and God smiled at our naive habit to believe that everything emerges on its own much simpler rather than it is a result of the complicated work by a more powerful Mind. – Everything that exists at the moment: the solar System, the material Universes, and energy worlds – was created to the order from the Above, in accordance with Their plans. Above the Higher there are even more higher (Entities), and it is infinite."

Conclusions

Summarizing information on the inferior worlds, let us dwell on the subject that people used to combine the notion of «minus» with the notion of «dark and low». Once it is negative, it means it is low-developed, or «dark», i.e. bringing all sorts of misery to a man. Typically, these notions in the minds of people are associated with their own dirty and violent behavior. All the ugliness that a man creates himself, he ascribes to the influence of the «dark».

But inferior worlds that do exist have no right to interfere in the life of a higher world, or the earthly world, as well as our earthly world may not interfere in the life of the Determinants that are above us. Only the Higher have the right to intervene in the inferior world. Everyone in our Nature lives under God's Higher laws and obeys them. But beings from the worlds, which are on the same stage with us, can penetrate in our plane.

Inferior worlds exist under their own laws, rules of life which do not relate to the earth dwellers, and all the evil that is born on the Earth, creates the man himself by his own minus traits, due to his lower nature and the inability to make the right choice.

All the inferior worlds are ruled by Devil's minus Systems. But the inferior worlds belonging to the plus System are ruled by God who sets common goals and objectives of development, realized by Devil through the programs. In addition to inferior worlds there are middle ones.

These middle worlds like our Earth, contain both plus and minus souls, so they are governed by the Higher Hierarchs from the plus System. For example, Devil controls Earth and other worlds of God under the contract. Thus, we must distinguish between two types of inferior worlds (Fig. 18):

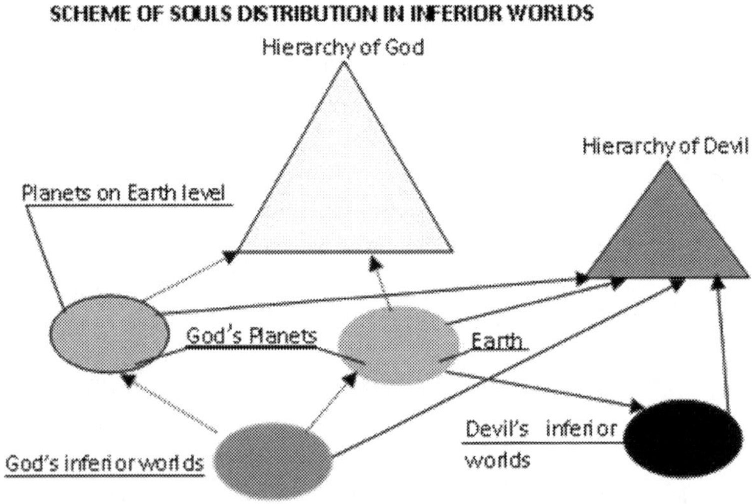

SCHEME OF SOULS DISTRIBUTION IN INFERIOR WORLDS

Hierarchy of God

Hierarchy of Devil

Planets on Earth level

God's Planets

Earth

God's inferior worlds

Devil's inferior worlds

Fig. 18

1) some are fully owned by Devil, in addition the degraded souls whom God gave Devil are still serving their term;

2) and there are inferior worlds that belong to God. Such worlds are governed by the Higher Hierarchs from the plus system of God, in cooperation with Devil, or rather His Higher Hierarchs of the minus System. And all the creatures in the inferior worlds are

developing under Devil's programs. But it is God who sets goals of development in each program.

Both types of inferior worlds of God and Devil are not included in their Hierarchies, but are below them. These are the worlds, where primary, that is evolutionarily very young souls are developing.

God's inferior worlds, where primary souls are gaining minus and plus energies of a crude quality, have their next stage of development on planets like our Earth, where souls already begin to gain plus energies of a subtler plane. These are the worlds-separators, which give creatures the possibility to choose which way they develop further: either in the Divine or Diabolical.

The souls of Devil's inferior worlds come over to the Hierarchy of Devil only.

Entities of God's inferior worlds, at the expense of the given freedom of choice, are divided into two opposite types (good and evil). As a result, those who gain the Divine energy type, are transferred into the Hierarchy of God, while those considered degrading, who gain the opposite type of energies, are given to Devil, and then they have two perspectives:

1) if they are low-level stupid individuals, Devil sends them to His inferior planets to be further «educated», where they live until they grow wiser and obtain the capacity of the soul required for His Hierarchy;

2) if the faulty soul is intellectually highly developed, it is immediately transferred from the earthly plane to the first Level of Devil's Hierarchy. However it gets robotic, losing freedom of choice, and does everything automatically under the rigid program.

As God sometimes for certain purposes personifies Himself with plus individuals, so can Devil personify Himself with minus individuals, so the latter call themselves by His name. And they are right, because they are connected with Him on the subtle plane. And due to the fact that they are robotic, they entirely personify themselves with Devil.

Devil also does not take just anyone in His Hierarchy, but only those who have reached a certain Level of development or sufficient degree of consciousness. Better to say, Devil does not need primitive individuals, who can do nothing. Therefore, He takes underdeveloped souls and makes them pass through His inferior worlds first, where, through harsh trials, severe inhumane conditions, fighting for their life, souls are gaining the required energy potential, and their matrices are being filled with those types of minus energies that are necessary to Devil. Only after that He takes the souls on the first Level of His Hierarchy.

Devil's inferior worlds are built entirely of a different type of energies than the earthly and, comparing the Level of development, many of them are below it. On the Earth, individuals gain both plus and minus energies, and souls are separated there to work in the two opposing Systems. As for inferior worlds (God's as well as Devil's), souls gain crude energy alone and are not yet able to gain anything of high-level because of their immaturity.

But coming from God's inferior worlds to the Earth or to other planets-separators, low-level souls get the right to gain a plus type of energies and follow the Divine path. But low-level souls in the worlds of Devil do not have such a right and just move from one minus Level to the other in without the right to choose the path.

Earth supplies souls both to the worlds of God and Devil, and a man chooses his future eternal development by his own deeds.

In addition to the undecided souls, that is, those who have not yet selected the ultimate direction of their development, there are representatives from the minus System of Devil on the Earth, sent here to perform a specific job that a plus personality is not capable of.

They perform specific tasks under Devil's linear programs and often provoke plus individuals to test their qualities; besides, their purpose is the corruption of young, inexperienced souls, in order to win the weak on their side. Therefore, we are reminding of this, so that a man could not forget to be always cautious, vigilant and try to understand – who is by your side and what actions is inciting you to.

The basic measure of a man's actions is good and evil. We must always remember: the goodness and selflessness leads to God, while evil and greed – to Devil. This has been and will continue to exist as a factor of division among the people during the next two thousand years. And towards the end of the sixth race only the form of separation of souls on the Earth will change, and people will choose not between good and evil, but between other, higher processes of progressing.

A man comes to Devil, having lost all his plus energy potential, so **do hurry to be good to others**.

Among mankind there are about forty percent of representatives from Devil's minus System. One can only distinguish them by their actions, the results of their work or words. Therefore, the one seeking a road to God should expand the boundaries of his / her personal knowledge to be able to see the deceitful enemy even veiled one (for example, giving people the benefit of the computer, Devil helps individuals gain the range of energies which He needs. Computerization, technocratism – these are the veiled ways that lead to Devil in case an individual is completely subordinate to Him).

All the minus Systems, which are above the earth plane, are many times higher the Level of humanity (and are Higher for it also as many of them make improvement programs for people, make equipment available, and perform calculations and mechanism of transmission to the Earth of any inventions that are sent to people by God).

Higher minus Systems, in their turn, are divided into the Divine, located in the Hierarchy of God and Devil's, located in His Hierarchy. Energy-like the minus Systems of God and Devil differ as well as the Entities comprising these Systems.

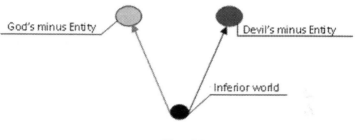

DEVELOPMENT PATHS OF MINUS ENTITIES BELONGING TO GOD AND DEVIL

God's minus Entity

Devil's minus Entity

Inferior world

Fig. 19

But what is the difference between the minus Entity of God and the minus Entity of Devil?

The main difference lies in the ability to create that God's minus Entities have and the absence of this ability in Devil's Entities. Hence is the difference in mental activity, in relation to which creative energies and sublime inspiration energies are gained in the matrix of the soul.

Based on creativity, the very structure of a matrix is specifically built. And the very direction of their development is respectively different, that is, if we consider the direction of their development with respect to one reference point, then the scheme of improvement will look as follows (see

Figure 19). And the higher the minus Entities rise in their development, the more their trajectories move away from each other, differing.

Thus it is necessary to dwell on such point as creativity, because there could be confusion on the issue – who creates and why. We say that computers, television, appliances come from Devil. But to be more precise, all the technical inventions for people creates Devil under God's instructions, who tries to advance His individuals' development. Devil comes up with everything by Himself and He provides Entities of minus Systems with these ready inventions to realize them. Entities cannot create anything on their own, they do just what they are ordered purely automatically. Therefore they say that Devil's system is not able to be creative. He decides everything for everybody by Himself, invents and calculates. But His invention cannot be considered creative, because He makes achievements through the calculations, manipulation of numbers.

In the minus System of God, located in His Hierarchy, there is no evil, and individuals progress through certain processes (e.g., computer operations and programming), from which they gain the required percentage of minus energies, but their quality is not homogeneous with those energies that are gained by individuals in the Hierarchy of Devil, because the Hierarchies themselves differ in the «material» of the worlds, i.e. in their energy as well as in the principles of improving souls. Hence, the individuals of God's minus Systems and Devil's minus Systems will have different types of characters, spiritual qualities, which would correspond to filling the cells of their matrices with the opposite types of energies (like white and dark).

* * *

GLOSSARY

The Absolute 1) God, the Higher Mind; 2) a spatial volume, which personifies a living organism of a Superior Being that contains in itself all that Exists and is the top of a certain development cycle.

Absolute *(adj.)* having reached the superior state of development, containing a full set of required energy components.

Being an intelligent individual, relating to the other world, dwelling in the form different from that of humans, but possessing temporary constructions, which allow adapting him to the world he exists in.

Composite a set of various energies in a matrix, creating its texture, its quality structure, and determining the person's significance and individuality.

Decoding destruction of a soul on the «subtle» plane; the annulment of the individual's awareness of his «self» as a person: dismantling of the soul's subtle energy formations, combined with a complete cleansing of the matrix's cells from all the energies gained by an individual during all his previous lives.

Distributor	the same as the **Separator**.
Energetics	1). a new designation for the word «energy», which contains constructively a more powerful type of energies that are currently (the year 2000) sent down to the Earth from the Cosmos; 2). a total potential contained in the limited volume.
Energy	1) any kind of matter both of the physical and «subtle» planes, differentiated by level-wise order structure of development; 2). a general measure for different forms of matter motion (the classic definition).
Energy pumping	concentration of energy per unit volume.
Energy quality	a homogeneous type of energy.
Entity	a personality, developing in the Hierarchy of God (or Devil). Entities in the Hierarchy are divided into different development levels.
Essence	inner meaning of something.
Hierarchy	a framed spatial structure of a «subtle» plane, in which the worlds of God are specifically arranged and inhabited by individuals of a particular level of development. Worlds (or living planes) are Levels. Their development degree rises from the base of the Hierarchy's pyramid towards the top, where God is located, controlling all the inferior. The Hierarchy contains the precisely definite number of individuals.

Inferiors	individuals relating to the earthly world. The development level of a physical man is always lower compared to those in the Hierarchy, as the «subtle» energy is a higher level of the matter organization.
Karma	requital to people for their plus or minus actions in a past life (good or bad luck put in the program of a human life).
Level	the degree of development of something or someone.
Level of the Hierarchy	world or plane of existence in the Hierarchy. The Levels are arranged according to their order structure, that is, to the logical sequence of energy development from the most inferior, nearest to Earth towards the highest, nearest to God.
Matrix	a frame basis of a soul designed to be filled with and store different types of energies, which form the basis of an individual's character. It has a cell structure and is capable of independently building up cells in case the existing ones are filled. Matrix is a self-growing spiritualized structure. It is filled with energy in regular succession established by God.
Nature	a spatial volume belonging to the huge cosmic organism, in which everything else is contained and developing.
Orbital	a new energy state of the Earth, of a higher development level than the previous one.

Order structure (of Levels)	logical sequence of worlds arrangement on the stairs of the Hierarchy, depending on the development degree of the energies comprising these Levels.
Particular volume	a separate part of the total Volume, developing in accordance with the needs of the Nature, that is, having the particular direction in development, satisfying Its needs.
Potential of the soul	the power indicator of personality. It is made of the potential of energies, which fill its matrix and constant subtle bodies.
Progression of the soul	accumulation of energies in its matrix in accordance with the given program.
Separator	a subtle plane facility collecting and distributing human souls after death.
Soul	a matrix with a certain energy content varying in the process of improvement. The matrix is connected with permanent and temporary structures, intended for the earthly world.
Soul capacity (power)	1). its strength, consisting of potentials of accumulated energies; 2). ability of the soul to commit any action or process (including mental); ability to perform work per unit time.
Subtle (world, const-ruction, design, etc.)	1). all that is beyond the human perception; 2). all that is created from the energy of a higher order compared to the physical matter.
The Higher	personalities, whose development Level is above the earthly plane and who govern the Earth and mankind.

Total Volume	specific spatial dimensions belonging to the global body of Nature.
Volume	a quantitative container of something that has boundaries.
Unit	notion of the soul, given by the design minus System.

The words combined by meaning

Determinant	(old – a Heavenly Teacher) a Higher Personality guiding the man or other being throughout the life, using a computer device; controls the execution of the program by the man.
Originator	an Entity standing an order higher than the Determinant; builds the plot of a future life.
Manager	an Entity standing above the Determinant and Originator and guiding them.
Fifth race	name given to mankind, which has developed up to 2000, from the Above. The name is associated with the transition of Earth onto the fifth orbital*.
Sixth race	a new race of mankind, conditionally originates from the year 2000. The name is associated with the transition of mankind onto the sixth orbital of a higher development level compared to that our fifth race is on.

Spiritual System	sentient communities of Higher Entities that are in the Hierarchy of God, that is belong to the «subtle» world.
Material System	a community of sentient beings that dwell in material bodies and possess the level of development surpassing the human one many times.
Hierarchic System	1) a community of sentient Entities, combined by one Level of development, dwelling in the Hierarchy. The Systems are located on the same or different Levels and have a degree of development, corresponding to this Level; 2) a System, owned by the Hierarchy.
Cosmic System	a community of sentient beings outside the Hierarchy of God.